PEOPLE, MARKETS, GOODS:
ECONOMIES AND SOCIETIES IN HISTORY

Volume 1

Landlords and Tenants in Britain, 1440–1660

T0340625

PEOPLE, MARKETS, GOODS:
ECONOMIES AND SOCIETIES IN HISTORY

ISSN: 2051-7467

Series editors
Nigel R. Goose – University of Hertfordshire
Steve Hindle – The Huntington Library
Jane Humphries – University of Oxford
Kevin O'Rourke – University of Oxford

The interactions of economy and society, people and goods, transactions and actions are at the root of most human behaviours. Economic and social historians are participants in the same conversation about how markets have developed historically and how they have been constituted by economic actors and agencies in various social, institutional and geographical contexts. New debates now underpin much research in economic and social, cultural, demographic, urban and political history. Their themes have enduring resonance – financial stability and instability, the costs of health and welfare, the implications of poverty and riches, flows of trade and the centrality of communications. This new paperback series aims to attract historians interested in economics and economists with an interest in history by publishing high-quality, cutting-edge academic research in the broad field of economic and social history from the late medieval/early modern period to the present day. It encourages the interaction of qualitative and quantitative methods through both excellent monographs and collections offering path-breaking overviews of key research concerns. Taking as its benchmark international relevance and excellence it is open to scholars and subjects of any geographical areas from the case study to the multi-nation comparison.

Landlords and Tenants in Britain, 1440–1660

Tawney's *Agrarian Problem* Revisited

Edited by

Jane Whittle

THE BOYDELL PRESS

© Contributors 2013
All Rights Reserved. Except as permitted under current legislation
no part of this work may be photocopied, stored in a retrieval system,
published, performed in public, adapted, broadcast,
transmitted, recorded or reproduced in any form or by any means,
without the prior permission of the copyright owner

First published 2013
The Boydell Press, Woodbridge

ISBN 978 1 84383 850 0

The Boydell Press is an imprint of Boydell & Brewer Ltd
PO Box 9, Woodbridge, Suffolk IP12 3DF, UK
and of Boydell & Brewer Inc.
668 Mount Hope Ave, Rochester, NY 14620-2731, USA
website: www.boydellandbrewer.com

A catalogue record for this book is available
from the British Library

The publisher has no responsibility for the continued existence or accuracy of URLs for
external or third-party internet websites referred to in this book, and does not guarantee
that any content on such websites is, or will remain, accurate or appropriate.

Papers used by Boydell & Brewer Ltd are natural, recyclable products
made from wood grown in sustainable forests

Printed and bound in Great Britain by CPI Group (UK) Ltd, Croydon, CR0 4YY

Contents

List of Figures

List of Tables

Abbreviations

BL	British Library
DCD	Dean and Chapter of Durham
DP	Durham Probate
HEHL	Henry E. Huntington Library, San Marino, Calif.
HHC	Hornby Castle estates, uncatalogued archives
HUL	Hull University Library
LA	Lancashire Archives
LRO	Lichfield Record Office
NRO	Norfolk Record Office
ODNB	*Oxford Dictionary of National Biography*
RPS	*Records of the Parliaments of Scotland, to 1707*
SA	Sheffield Archives
TNA	The National Archives
TRHS	*Transactions of the Royal Historical Society*
VCH	Victoria County Histories

List of Contributors

Professor Christopher Brooks, Professor of History at Durham University, is the author of numerous books and articles on the social history of early modern law including, most recently, *Law, Politics and Society in Early Modern England* (Cambridge, 2008). His interest in agrarian history was inspired by attending Joan Thirsk's postgraduate seminars in Oxford in the 1970s.

Professor Chris Dyer, Emeritus Professor of local history at the University of Leicester, has written on various aspects of agrarian, landscape and rural history, mainly in the later Middle Ages. His most recent book, published by Oxford University Press in 2012, is called *A Country Merchant: Trading and Farming at the End of the Middle Ages*.

Dr Heather Falvey completed her PhD on 'Custom, Resistance and Politics: Local Experiences of Improvement in Early Modern England', supervised by Professor Steve Hindle, at the University of Warwick in 2007. She is currently the editorial assistant for the *Economic History Review* and has published a number of articles including 'Voices and Faces in the Rioting Crowd: Identifying Seventeenth-Century Enclosure Rioters', *The Local Historian*, 39:2 (May 2009), pp. 137–151 and 'Searching for the Population in an Early-Modern Forest', *Local Population Studies*, 81 (2008), pp. 37–57.

Professor Harold Garrett-Goodyear, Professor Emeritus of History, Mount Holyoke College, South Hadley, Massachusetts, has long focused his research on manorial courts, lords and their customary tenants, and common law jurisdiction in the early sixteenth century. He co-edited with Carolyn Collette *The Later Middle Ages: A Sourcebook* (Basingstoke, 2010) and published an early foray into 'private' jurisdictions and royal justice in late medieval England as 'The Tudor Revival of *Quo Warranto* and Local Contributions to State Building', in *On the Laws and Customs of England*, ed. Morris S. Arnold et al. (Chapel Hill, North Carolina, 1981), 231–295.

Dr Julian Goodare, Reader in History at the University of Edinburgh, is author of *State and Society in Early Modern Scotland* (Oxford, 1999) and *The Government of Scotland, 1560–1625* (Oxford, 2004). He has edited and co-edited numerous books.

Dr Elizabeth Griffiths is a Research Fellow at Exeter University. She is the author with Mark Overton of *Farming to Halves: The Hidden History of Sharefarming in England from Medieval to Modern Times* (Basingstoke, 2009) and with Jane Whittle of *Consumption and Gender in the Early Seventeenth-Century Household: the World of Alice Le Strange* (Oxford, 2012).

Jennifer Holt is a social and economic historian with a particular interest in the north-west of England. Her edition of the *Diary of Thomas Fenwick of Burrow Hall (1729–1794)* was published by the List and Index Society in four volumes in 2011 and 2012. Earlier work includes volumes 172 and 176 for the Lancashire Parish Register Society. She is editor of a forthcoming volume for the Chetham Society based upon documents relating to the Hornby Castle estates, as well as being coordinator for the Lancashire Place Name Survey.

Dr Briony McDonagh is a Leverhulme Early Career Fellow, in the School of Geography at the University of Nottingham. She is the author of articles including 'Subverting the Ground: Private Property and Public Protest in the Sixteenth-Century Yorkshire Wolds', *Agricultural History Review*, 57(2) (2009), 191–206 and 'Women, Enclosure and Estate Improvement in Eighteenth-Century Northamptonshire', *Rural History*, 20(2) (2009), 143–162.

Dr Jean Morrin is Honorary Research Fellow in History at the University of Winchester and coordinator and researcher for the *Victoria County History of Hampshire*. Her work on the Durham Cathedral estates is drawn from her PhD.

Professor David Ormrod is Professor of Economic and Cultural History at the University of Kent. He is the author of *The Rise of Commercial Empires: England and the Netherlands in the Age of Mercantilism, 1650–1770* (Cambridge, 2003) and 'R.H. Tawney and the Origins of Capitalism', *History Workshop Journal* 18 (1984), 138–59, among many other publications.

Dr William D. Shannon is Honorary Researcher in History at the University of Lancaster. His PhD on 'Approvement and Improvement in Early-Modern England: Enclosure in the Lowland Wastes of Lancashire c.1500–1700', supervised by Dr Angus Winchester, was awarded in 2009. Publications include 'Approvement and Improvement in the Lowland Wastes of Early-Modern Lancashire' in R. W. Hoyle (ed.), *Custom, Improvement and Landscape in Early Modern Britain* (Farnham, 2011); 'The Survival of True Intercommoning in the Early-Modern Period', *Agricultural History*, 86:4 (2012); and 'Adversarial Map-Making in pre-Reformation Lancashire', *Northern History*, 47:2 (2010).

Professor Jane Whittle is Professor of Rural History at Exeter University. She is the author of publications including *The Development of Agrarian Capitalism: Land and Labour in Norfolk* (Oxford 2000), 'Lords and Tenants in Kett's Rebellion 1549', *Past and Present* 207 (2010), and, with Elizabeth Griffiths, *Consumption and Gender in the Early Seventeenth-Century Household: the World of Alice Le Strange* (Oxford, 2012).

Professor Andy Wood is Professor of Social History at Durham University. He is the author of *The 1549 Rebellions and the Making of Early Modern England* (Cambridge, 2007) and *The Politics of Social Conflict: The Peak Country, 1520–1770* (Cambridge, 1999) among numerous other publications.

Professor Keith Wrightson is the Randolph W. Townsend Jr. Professor of History at Yale University. He is the author of several books including *Poverty and Piety in an English Village: Terling, 1525–1700* (New York, 1979: co-authored with David Levine) and *Earthly Necessities. Economic Lives in Early Modern Britain* (New Haven, 2000).

Acknowledgements

The chapters for this book were discussed and developed at Exeter University in 2011. Thanks are owed to all those who took part in this meeting, especially Joe Barker, John Broad, Henry French, Juliet Gayton, Steve Hipkin, Richard Hoyle, Jonas Lindstrom, Miriam Muller, Leigh Shaw-Taylor, Nicola Whyte and Margaret Yates, and to the British Agricultural History Society, the Economic History Society and the Royal Historical Society for providing financial support. Alwyn Harrison provided valuable last-minute editorial assistance at the start of a busy academic year.

Jane Whittle
University of Exeter, October 2012

Foreword

KEITH WRIGHTSON

Early in my undergraduate career, my Cambridge supervisor in Economic History set two of us an essay on the agrarian problem of the sixteenth century: 'was it less a problem of enclosures than of rents?' (a good question). In trying to answer it we were not required to read Tawney's great book. We read *about* Tawney; not Tawney himself. That did not matter, because we were advised that Tawney was 'an old sentimentalist' who had failed to recognise that England was already a ruthless and competitive contract society in the sixteenth century, a society of which our supervisor clearly approved. Much later, I learned from another Cambridge economic historian that the trouble with Tawney was that, along with other 'reformist' economic historians, he suffered from 'middle-class guilt'. Worse, he wrote 'Mandarin' prose.[1]

When I actually read Tawney's *Agrarian Problem* for myself, shamefully late, I expected to find it a work with which I would have some sympathy, but which would inevitably be dated in both content and style. What a surprise, then, to find that Tawney's tone was predominantly cool, authoritative, and not at all sentimental; I thought him rather tough-minded. His purplish passages were justified in context and seemed to spring from indignation rather than guilt. His dominant manner was a sustained effort to explain, in a multi-faceted and at times distinctly distanced way, a set of profound and complex changes. If his sympathies were clearly with the losers in that process, he did not wallow in the celebration of victimhood. As for *content*, I was startled to discover how much that I had previously taken to be the findings of more recent agrarian historians he already knew, or at least intuited (and sometimes presented in a more lucid manner than his successors). I felt, as with so many other 'classic' works that are more read about than actually read, that it would be better to get

---

1   D. C. Coleman, *History and the Economic Past: An Account of the Rise and Decline of Economic History in Britain* (Oxford, 1987), pp. 65, 71. In fairness, one should note that, while critical of Tawney's interpretative perspective, Coleman recognised the rigour of his scholarship, and thought his prose 'redeemed by a strength and vigour drawn from the English of the Authorized version'.'

students to read key passages of Tawney's argument than the often garbled accounts of those whose expository purpose was to diminish it.

The attractive common feature of the papers in this collection is that their authors have actually read Tawney and sought to engage with him constructively. Inevitably, such a revisiting of *The Agrarian Problem* is likely to highlight those things that Tawney, writing more than a century ago, got wrong, or out of proportion; the issues he didn't pursue; the revisionist implications of placing things in a fuller context that was simply not available to him. Fair enough. One would expect his account of things to be modified and challenged. These essays bring out the importance of a larger understanding of the late medieval context; how tenant resistance could be remarkably successful; how tenants could benefit from enclosure by agreement (if they could bear the costs and risks); how lord–tenant disputes involved far more complex coalitions of interest than the adversarial court pleadings reveal; how tenants themselves could be relatively privileged, aggressive, excluding, entrepreneurial and exploitative; how forms of tenure might be less important indicators of the advance of agrarian capitalism than farm size, grain markets, occupational structures or rent regimes. We might agree that the emergence of agrarian capitalism was a longer, slower, messier business than Tawney imagined; that he exaggerated the impact of the Interregnum and misunderstood the common law attitude to copyhold; and also that in comparison to Scottish tenants, their English counterparts were fortunate in having rights at all.

All this was to be expected. Yet these essays also acknowledge how much Tawney got essentially right. If there is much that he did not, and could not, know in 1912, one remains impressed by what he either did know, or intuited, or suggested. He was prescient in mapping the contours of the 'agrarian problem'. He lacked our knowledge of population dynamics, but grasped the significance of the 'price rise' before it was ever quantified. His views on enclosure were far more nuanced than his critics allow. He lacked our detailed grasp of the process of 'engrossing', but he understood the role of ambitious tenants and the importance of the late-medieval differentiation of holding size. He may have known less about the politics of agrarian change, but he certainly appreciated that the outcome of the processes he addressed depended on cultural and political as well as economic factors. And he knew very well that custom shaped the political struggle between landlords and tenants. One could go on. Above all perhaps, he knew that all parties were struggling to sustain their interests in a complex and demanding field of demographic and economic forces. He quoted, but never endorsed, the simple story of the complaint literature of the age, and he transcended it.

Does this mean that this collection just works out the implications of a century-old reconnaissance that was pretty good? No. That would be to compare an early estate map to the Ordnance Survey. The details matter. Tawney set an agenda that remains relevant. Yet it is in the detail, amassed partly in response to his inspiration, partly in the effort to prove him wrong, that we encounter the full complexities, ambiguities and ironies of a massive process of change, and its varying chronology and outcomes in particular places. It is also in the detail that we confront, and reassess, the issues of causation and motivation to which he directed attention.

This collection also points, with respect, but without deference, to how we might get closer than Tawney could to one if his central concerns. In his preface he said that the 'supreme interest of economic history' lay in 'the clue which it offers to the development of those dimly conceived pre-suppositions as to social expediency' that most influence peoples actions (often unconsciously).[2] This was his way of expressing his conviction that economic change also involves cultural and political change. He was very much aware that what he called 'social readjustments to meet the new situation', or the 'regrouping of social forces', involved change in the 'living body of assumptions as to the right conduct of human affairs', even 'great change in men's conception of social expediency'.[3]

Great change in conceptions of social expediency: that is a formulation that would bear fuller investigation. For while many historians of this period have touched upon it, the extent to which economic change involved forms of normative adjustment remain inadequately explored and as yet unresolved. It deserves attention, for it is a matter of importance in our own time. That we live with changing conceptions of social expediency is one more reason to understand how people coped with them in 'Tawney's century'.

---

2   R. H. Tawney, *The Agrarian Problem in the Sixteenth Century* (London, 1912; repr. New York, 1967), p. xxiii. All references in this book are to the 1967 edition, unless otherwise noted.

3   Ibid., quoting, in order, pp. 179, 231, 347, 184.

Introduction

Tawney's *Agrarian Problem* Revisited

JANE WHITTLE

One hundred years ago, in 1912, R. H. Tawney published his first book, *The Agrarian Problem in the Sixteenth Century*. Tawney became famous as a socialist thinker and campaigner; his reputation as a historian rests largely on his best-known book, *Religion and the Rise of Capitalism* (1926), and his later contribution to the debate on the causes of the English Civil War.[1] Yet *The Agrarian Problem* has been deeply influential in the economic history of late medieval and early modern England and is still a regular feature on undergraduate reading lists. It remains readable, lively and relevant. Its importance stretches well beyond the history of rural England in the sixteenth century. From at least Marx's *Capital* onwards, changes in the property rights and class relations of rural England between 1440 and 1660 – particularly the enclosure of land and increased land-lessness – have been highlighted as a turning point in the development of capitalism, crucial in explaining why England became the 'first industrial nation'. To quote Marx,

> The prelude of the revolution that laid the foundation of the capitalist mode of production, was played out in the last third of the 15th, and the first decade of the 16th century . . . the great feudal lords created an incomparably larger proletariat by the forcible driving of the peasantry from the land.[2]

Tawney was not a Marxist and did not cite Marx in *The Agrarian Problem*. But the topic he chose to focus on was exactly that highlighted by Marx:

---

1 T. S. Ashton, 'Richard Henry Tawney', *Proceedings of the British Academy* 48 (1962), 460–82; Ross Terrill, *R. H. Tawney and His Times: Socialism as Fellowship* (Cambridge Mass., 1973); J. M. Winter, ed., *History and Society: Essays by R. H. Tawney* (London, 1978); David Ormrod, 'R. H. Tawney and the Origins of Capitalism', *History Workshop* 18 (1984), 138–59; Anthony Wright, *R. H. Tawney* (Manchester, 1987); Norman Dennis and A. H. Halsey, *English Ethical Socialism: Thomas More to R. H. Tawney* (Oxford, 1988).

2 Karl Marx, *Capital*, 1 (Moscow, 1954), chapters 26 and 27.

the loss of land by much of the English population during the sixteenth century. Part I of *The Agrarian Problem* offers a subtle and masterful overview of the relatively prosperous circumstances of the English peasantry in the fifteenth and early sixteenth century. Part II provides a much more controversial argument about the growth of capitalist agriculture causing enclosure, the transfer of land to leasehold, and evictions of customary tenants. Part III ties these changes to the popular protests and legislation of the Tudor period. The book provides an account that not only encompasses the whole of England, but also integrates the economic, social, legal and political changes of the time. The present volume revisits Tawney's *Agrarian Problem* on the occasion of its centenary: the chapters that follow reassess many of the issues that Tawney highlighted. This introduction offers a history of the book itself. It first examines how and why Tawney wrote *The Agrarian Problem*; secondly it looks at how *The Agrarian Problem* has been regarded by historians; and thirdly offers an assessment of what was right and wrong in the arguments Tawney presented. We hope this volume will encourage historians, from undergraduates to experienced researchers, to look again at the vivid history of rural England that *The Agrarian Problem* presents.

I

Tawney wrote *The Agrarian Problem in the Sixteenth Century* in a relatively short period of time between 1908 and April 1912.[3] This was a remarkable achievement given the book is over four hundred pages long, and analyses a large selection of manuscripts and printed literature from the period 1440–1660. It is all the more remarkable given that Tawney had no formal training as an economic historian. He had studied History and Classics at Oxford at a time when economic history was not on the syllabus, graduating in 1903. The only Oxford academic who offered a link with the history of rural England was Professor Paul Vinogradoff, whose encouragement he later noted.[4] After graduating, Tawney spent a period living in East London at Toynbee Hall organising holidays for working class children, but he returned to academia in 1906–8, as an assistant economics lecturer at Glasgow University, before becoming involved in the Workers' Educational Association (WEA).

The WEA commissioned a book from Tawney in 1909 having noted 'the lack of textbooks suitable' for their classes. He was to be paid a salary not

---

3   Winter, 'Introduction', in *History and Society*, p. 5. LSE archives: Tawney/II/31/2: a letter from the book's printers, 23 April 1912.
4   Terrill, *Tawney and His Times*, p. 25.

only for teaching WEA classes but also for writing the book.[5] The experience of teaching adult, working-class students for the WEA undoubtedly shaped *The Agrarian Problem*. In the preface Tawney noted 'two debts which are beyond acknowledgement'. The first was to his wife, and the second 'to the members of the Tutorial classes . . . with whom for the last four years it has been my privilege to be a fellow-worker. The friendly smitings of weavers, potters, miners and engineers, have taught me much about the problems of political and economic science which cannot easily be learned in books.'[6]

Much of the speed and skill with which Tawney prepared the book must certainly be put down to his intellectual ability and enthusiasm. However, Tawney also had a network of intellectual friends working in related fields, most with Oxford or Manchester connections.[7] In the preface to *The Agrarian Problem* Tawney thanked Reginald Lennard and Henry Clay for reading the whole book in draft and offering him 'numberless criticisms and improvements'.[8] Both were fellow WEA tutors. Lennard graduated from Oxford in 1907 and became a historian of English medieval and early modern agrarian history, later a reader in economic history at Oxford.[9] Clay wrote a WEA textbook on economics, and was subsequently Professor of Economics at Manchester.[10] Tawney's correspondence in the year leading up to *The Agrarian Problem*'s publication reveals that George Unwin, Vinogradoff and Gerard Collier also read and commented on significant portions of the book.[11] Unwin was Professor of History at Manchester University from 1910 and an expert on sixteenth- and seventeenth-century industry.[12] Gerard Collier lectured in history at Birmingham University before moving to Cornwall in 1917,[13] and was author of *Economic Justice: A Textbook of Political Economy from a Christian Point of View* (1924). It was Collier who consulted the estate maps in Oxford college archives for Tawney.[14] Others Tawney credited with helping him included Professor F. M. Powicke at Oxford; Lucy Toulmin-Smith, a literary scholar and librarian at Manchester College Oxford and editor of *The Itinerary of John Leland* (1906–10), who lent him a series of court rolls; Lieutenant-Colonel Henry Fishwick, a Lancashire antiquarian who sent documents; and Dr

5 Winter, 'Introduction', p. 5.
6 Tawney, *Agrarian Problem*, p. xxv.
7 Tawney lived in Manchester while employed by the WEA.
8 Tawney, *Agrarian Problem*, p. xxv.
9 *Who Was Who 1961–1970* (London, 1972), p. 667; see also his numerous publications.
10 'Clay, Sir Henry (1883–1954)', *ODNB* online.
11 LSE archives: Tawney/II/31/2. On the influence of Unwin and Vinogradoff on Tawney, see Winter, 'Introduction', pp. 6–9.
12 'Unwin, George (1870–1925)', *ODNB* online.
13 Philip C. Hills, 'Father Bernard Walke and Gerard Collier', August 2007 (walkecolliercornwallpeace.weebly.com/index.html).
14 LSE archives: Tawney/II/31/2.

George Herbert Fowler, a zoologist, historian and pioneering county archivist.[15]

Nor did Tawney claim that all the archival research was his own. He credited two female assistants – Miss Niemeyer and Miss L. Drucker – in his preface, who 'transcribed for me a large number of surveys and rentals', as well as his wife 'who has collaborated with me throughout, and without whose constant assistance this book could not have been completed'.[16] Manorial surveys and rentals provide the backbone of *The Agrarian Problem*. Both Niemeyer and Drucker were published authors. Nannie Niemeyer was the sister of Otto Niemeyer, a contemporary of Tawney's at Balliol.[17] She was a lecturer in history at the Normal College, a teacher training college in Bangor, and published a series of popular history books from 1917 into the 1930s.[18] Niemeyer wrote to Tawney in October 1911 regarding her attempts to find another suitable researcher: 'At last I have found somebody for the Record Office. The people I tried first were County History people, because I know that they had some knowledge of history. But I can't find anyone who is not full up.' Instead she identified a 'record agent': Miss Drucker.[19] Lucy Drucker had been a member of the LSE medieval palaeography group supervised by Hubert Hall in 1902–3, a group which included the historians F. G. Davenport and E. M. Leonard, and produced an edition of the Winchester Pipe Rolls. Drucker charged Tawney £3 1s 6d for twenty-seven hours' work 'making lists of tenants etc.' after spending November and December 1911 transcribing manorial surveys from Northamptonshire and Leicestershire.[20] Nor should we overlook the contribution of Tawney's wife. Tawney married Jeannette Beveridge in 1909 just as he began work on the book.[21] Jeannette had taken French at Somerville College, Oxford and was the sister of Tawney's close friend William Beveridge.[22] Tawney's biographers have been dismissive and occasionally insulting about Jeannette.[23]

---

15   Tawney, *Agrarian Problem*, pp. xxv, 126; all are listed in the preface. See 'Powicke, Sir (Frederick) Maurice (1879–1963)' and 'Smith, Lucy Toulmin (1838–1911)' *ODNB* online; 'Fishwick, Lieut-Col Henry', *Who Was Who 1897–1916* (London, 1935), p. 246; 'Fowler, George Herbert', *Who Was Who 1929–1940* (London, 1947), p. 471.

16   Tawney, *Agrarian Problem*, p. xxv.

17   'Niemeyer, Sir Otto Ernst (1883–1971)', *ODNB* online.

18   (A. F.) Nannie Niemeyer, *Stories for the History Hour from Augustus to Rolf* (New York, 1917); *Stories from History: Henry III to Edward IV* (London, Toronto, 1921); *Piers Plowman Social and Economic Histories*, 7 vols (London, 1921 onwards); *Tales from History* (Collins, 1932).

19   LSE archives: Tawney/II/31/2: Letter from N. Niemeyer to Tawney, 13 October.

20   LSE archives: Tawney/II/31/2: Letters from Lucy Drucker to Tawney, 15 November 1911; 17 November 1911; 22 December 1911.

21   Jose Harris, *William Beveridge: A Biography* (Oxford, 1977), pp. 69–70.

22   Harris, *William Beveridge*, p. 68.

23   Terrill describes her as 'somewhat pathetic' and 'a trial to Tawney', and criticises Jeannette for keeping an untidy house and her 'stunning extravagance' with money:

Yet she was an intelligent woman, the daughter of a pioneer in women's education.[24] Jeannette took a serious interest in early modern history, publishing an edition of Richard Baxter's *Christian Directory* in 1925, and was co-author with Tawney of an article on 'An Occupational Census of the Seventeenth Century' in the *Economic History Review* of 1934.

The Agrarian Problem offered the first overarching account of changes in the relationship between landlord and tenants from the mid-fifteenth to mid-seventeenth century. But Tawney was not working in a void.[25] Much historical research had already been published. He built on the work of Maitland, Vinogradoff, Davenport and T. W. Page on the medieval manor and serfdom; Savine and Hibbert on the dissolution of the monasteries; Leonard on poor relief; Thorold Rogers on prices; Russell, Powell and Oman on popular rebellion; and Hasbach and the Hammonds on agricultural labourers: all these books are cited in *The Agrarian Problem*.[26] Enclosures and the security of copyhold tenures were already topics of discussion. I. S. Leadam's initial research on enclosures was followed by important articles by Edwin Gay and Leonard. Tawney corresponded with Gilbert Slater, and cited Gonner's book *Common Land and Inclosure* which also appeared in 1912.[27] Leadam, Gay and Alexander Savine had debated the security of copyhold tenures.[28]

Tawney and His Times, pp. 108, 110. Ralf Dahrendorf is kinder in his assessment, but dwells on the same issues: *LSE: A History of the London School of Economics and Political Science, 1895–1995* (Oxford, 1995), p. 239.

24 See *ODNB* entry for her mother, 'Beveridge [née Akroyd], Annette Susannah (1842–1929)'.

25 Winter, 'Introduction', pp. 10–13.

26 F. W. Maitland, *The Domesday Book and Beyond: Three Essays in the Early History of England* (Cambridge, 1897) and 'The History of a Cambridgeshire Manor', *English Historical Review* 9:35 (1894), 517–34; Paul Vinogradoff, *Villainage in England* (Oxford, 1892) and *The Growth of the Manor* (New York, 1905); F. G. Davenport, *The Economic Development of a Norfolk Manor, 1086–1565* (London, 1906); T. W. Page, *The End of Villeinage in England* (New York, 1900); Alexander Savine, *English Monasteries on the Eve of the Dissolution* (Oxford, 1909); F. A. Hibbert, *The Dissolution of the Monasteries* (London, 1910); E. M. Leonard, *The Early History of English Poor Relief* (Cambridge, 1900); J. E. Thorold Rogers, *A History of Agriculture and Prices in England* (Oxford, 1866–87); F. W. Russell, *Kett's Rebellion in Norfolk* (London, 1859); E. Powell, *The Rising in East Anglia 1381* (Cambridge, 1896); Charles Oman, *The Great Revolt of 1381* (Oxford, 1906); W. Hasbach, *A History of the English Agricultural Labourer* (London, 1908); J. L. and Barbara Hammond, *The Village Labourer, 1760–1832* (London, 1911).

27 I. S. Leadam, 'The Inquisitions of 1517: Enclosure and Evictions', *Transactions of the Royal Historical Society (TRHS)* 6 (1892), 167–314; Edwin Gay, 'Inclosures in England in the Sixteenth Century', *Quarterly Journal of Economics* 17 (1903), 576–97; E. M. Leonard, 'Inclosure of Common Fields in the Seventeenth Century', *TRHS* 19 (1905); Gilbert Slater, *The English Peasantry and the Enclosure of Common Fields* (London, 1907); E. C. K. Gonner, *Common Land and Inclosure* (London, 1912) cited in Tawney, *Agrarian Problem*, p. 8.

28 I. S. Leadam, 'The Security of Copyholders in the Fifteenth and Sixteenth

At the heart of *The Agrarian Problem* is a large collection of manorial documents. Tawney achieved wide geographical coverage with a carefully directed approach. Writing before the establishment of county record offices, he relied predominantly on the manuscript collections of 'the Record Office', later the Public Record Office, now the National Archives. These were supplemented with a wide range of documents already in print as a result of the activities of local historians, record and antiquarian societies, and the Victoria County Histories. He did not go rifling through the attics of country houses, the only other way of gaining access to manorial documents in this period, although he did thank the Oxford colleges of All Souls and Merton, the Earl of Leicester and the clerk of the peace for Warwickshire for allowing him access to manuscripts.[29] The manorial documents he used were overwhelmingly surveys, although he did make use of some court rolls.[30] These were supplemented with an impressively wide range of literature from the sixteenth century.

The circumstances in which Tawney wrote *The Agrarian Problem* have many parallels in early twenty-first-century academic life. He wrote to a tight deadline using research assistants to collect much of his primary data. The book was delivered late and over-length to the publishers and shows some signs of hurried production: the footnote references to secondary works are wonderfully inconsistent, and in the appendix Tawney notes data from a manor 'of which I have mislaid the name'.[31] Yet the use which Tawney made of the materials available to him was exceptionally thorough. These were synthesised into a readable, clear and perceptive account of agrarian change.

II

The reputation of *The Agrarian Problem* as a work of historical research has waxed and waned over time. The immediate reception was very positive, with favourable reviews by leading historians. Its low point was the 1960s, after Tawney's death in 1962, when his reputation as a historian was

Centuries', *English Historical Review* 8:32 (1893), 684–96; Edwin Gay, 'The Inquisitions of Depopulation in 1517 and the "Domesday of Inclosures"', *TRHS* 14 (1900), 231–303; Alexander Savine, 'Copyhold Cases in Early Chancery Proceedings', *English Historical Review* 17:66 (1902), 296–303 and 'English Customary Tenure in the Tudor Period', *Quarterly Journal of Economics* 19 (1905), 33–80.

29 Tawney, *Agrarian Problem*, p. xxv. The Earl of Leicester gave him access to the Norfolk manors in the Holkham manuscripts.

30 Tawney, *Agrarian Problem*, p. 299.

31 Tawney, *Agrarian Problem*, p. 424; LSE archives: Tawney/II/31/2: letters from Longman's to Tawney dated 2 December 1911 and 6 March 1912.

attacked by Geoffrey Elton and Eric Kerridge. Yet the tide turned back in favour of *The Agrarian Problem*. Robert Brenner revamped Tawney's main arguments and placed them at the centre of a new debate over the causes of England's long-term economic development. Textbooks of the economic and social history of the sixteenth century, from Hoskins, Youings and Clay, to Overton and Wrightson, continued to cite *The Agrarian Problem* as essential reading.[32]

The Agrarian Problem was quickly reviewed in the major history and economics journals of the time. In the *English Historical Review* of 1913, economic historian J. H. Clapham was enthusiastic, noting Tawney's 'solid contribution from the documents', and that he was 'always alive to the complexity of the agrarian and legal problems in hand'. He found Tawney's judgement to be 'balanced; though he sometimes sneers, and in the section on the poor laws there is an excess of invective'.[33] Another economic historian, W. J. Ashley of Birmingham University, offered fulsome praise in the *Economic Journal*, describing it as 'a substantial, most useful, and altogether notable book' as well as 'balanced and fair-minded . . . We feel that now we really know the agricultural life of the sixteenth century in its fullness and complexity.' Ashley's criticisms were all on minor points of interpretation.[34] S. F. Bemis, an American diplomatic historian, stressed the book's 'deep insight into English history, afforded by the discussion of the social revolution brought about by the agrarian changes and their reaction on the state', although he doubted Tawney's figures on the extent of enclosure.[35] Conyers Read, a Tudor historian at the University of Chicago, wrote a long and detailed review agreeing with all *The Agrarian Problem*'s main arguments. He noted Tawney's careful reading of existing research as well as his 'painstaking and profitable labor in the sources', and considered that, unlike most economic historians, Tawney had actually made the material 'at once convincing and delightful'. Read did, however, note that Tawney could have given more consideration to the positive economic impact of landlords' actions on farming techniques.[36]

The most critical review came from a historian of rural England, H. L. Gray at Harvard, who must have been in the finishing stages of writing his

---

32 W. G. Hoskins, *The Age of Plunder: The England of Henry VIII, 1500–1547* (London, 1976); Joyce Youings, *Sixteenth-Century England* (London, 1984); Christopher G. A. Clay, *Economic Expansion and Social Change: England 1500–1700*, 2 vols (Cambridge, 1984); Mark Overton, *Agricultural Revolution in England: The Transformation of the Agrarian Economy, 1500–1850* (Cambridge, 1996); Keith Wrightson, *Earthly Necessities: Economic Lives in Early Modern Britain* (New Haven, Conn., 2000).

33 J. H. Clapham, review, *English Historical Review* 28:111 (1913), 567–9.

34 W. J. Ashley, review, *Economic Journal* 23:89 (1913), 85–89.

35 S. F. Bemis, review, *American Historical Review* 18:4 (1913), 794–95.

36 Conyers Read, review, *Journal of Political Economy* 21:4 (1913), 363–67, quotation from p. 367.

book on field systems, published in 1915.[37] He noted that *The Agrarian Problem* was the best of a group of books, such as those by Slater, Johnson and Gonner, which summarised and popularised English agrarian history but contrasted the 'scanty nature of the evidence upon which many of the generalizations are based' in Tawney's book with the 'extensive research' by Savine on copyholds, and Gay on enclosures. Gray noted the geographical bias of Tawney's selection of manors, and that they 'very inadequately represent the thousands' for which records existed, also pointing out the wealth of information in manorial court rolls which Tawney had largely ignored. However, even Gray concluded that it was an 'eminently sane and readable book'.[38]

There was little further criticism of *The Agrarian Problem* during Tawney's lifetime. Beresford's *The Lost Villages of England* (1954) substantially revised a major part of Tawney's arguments, demonstrating that more villages were depopulated, and that depopulation occurred earlier than Tawney had thought. But Beresford held Tawney in great respect, and gently rebuked him rather than attempting to dismantle any of his wider arguments.[39] Rather, *The Agrarian Problem* seems to have slipped gradually from popularity, epitomised by the volume of essays presented to Tawney on his eightieth birthday, which contains not a single footnote reference to the book.[40] Tawney himself was partly responsible for this: realising its shortcomings, he refused to allow *The Agrarian Problem* to be reissued until he had made revisions, which unfortunately he never did.[41]

Tawney's death in 1962 unleashed a barrage of sharp criticisms of his historical work. Those who had the most substantial criticisms to make were kindest in their approach. Reginald Lennard, an old friend and colleague, included Tawney amongst those who had succumbed to the 'pitfalls' lying in wait for agrarian historians. He stressed the implications of Beresford's research for *The Agrarian Problem*'s key conclusions and noted the large-scale sheep farming of the medieval period.[42] Lawrence Stone, another Tawney supporter, wrote the introduction to the new edition of *The Agrarian Problem* in 1967 and highlighted the degree to which knowledge of population change now undermined other

37   H. L. Gray, *English Field Systems* (Cambridge, Mass., 1915).

38   H. L. Gray, review, *American Economic Review* 3:4 (1913), 904–7.

39   Maurice W. Beresford, *The Lost Villages of England* (London, 1954), especially p. 150.

40   F. J. Fisher, ed., *Essays in the Economic and Social History of Tudor and Stuart England in Honour of R. H. Tawney* (Cambridge, 1961).

41   Ashton, 'Richard Henry Tawney', 464.

42   Reginald Lennard, 'Agrarian History: Some Vistas and Pitfalls', *Agricultural History Review* 12:2 (1964), 85–7.

elements of the book's argument.[43] Yet neither was entirely comple-
mentary about Tawney. Lennard portrays *The Agrarian Problem* as the
work of a naïve young man overly influenced by his moral and religious
views; while Stone begins his introduction by implying that Tawney's
Christian socialism and 'aristocratic distaste' for 'the rise of a new and
vulgar monied class' coloured his opinions.[44] These comments are put
in the shade by Geoffrey Elton's declaration in his inaugural lecture that
'there is not a single work which Tawney wrote that can be trusted' because 'everything he wrote was written to a propaganda purpose', and
'his history was not good, not sound, not right, and not true'.[45] This
was followed by Tawney's former student, Eric Kerridge, writing in the
introduction to his book *Agrarian Problems in the Sixteenth Century
and After* (1969), which was published in a series edited by Elton, that
'Tawney the politician barred the way to Tawney the scholar' and that
'he tended to see the whole world past and present in terms of socialist
dogma', which led him to 'his wholly untrue picture of early capitalism
as cruel and greedy'. Tawney had 'led whole generations of history students into grievous error'.[46]

We will return to the substantive historical arguments in section III, but
these attacks were not just about the historical arguments made in *The
Agrarian Problem*. Rather, they were about styles of history and political differences. Tawney's approach to history had fallen from fashion: instead of painting vivid pictures of everyday life in the past and employing
empathy, history was flirting with pretentions to be 'scientific'. The great
debate over the scientific nature of history was carried out in the 1960s
between E. H. Carr, who argued against, and Elton who argued for its
scientific and objective nature.[47] Stone reveals the common assumptions of
the time when he wrote in his introduction that 'the problems of economic
history' were now being 'tackled in a more objective and more statistical
manner'.[48] This trend crossed the political divide: the new, and at that time

---

43   Lawrence Stone, 'Introduction to the Torchbook Edition', in Tawney, *Agrarian
Problem*, p. xi.
44   Lennard, 'Agrarian History', 85; Stone 'Introduction', pp. vii–viii.
45   Geoffrey R. Elton, *The Future of the Past: An Inaugural Lecture* (Cambridge, 1968),
pp. 15–17; see also William Lamont, 'R. H. Tawney: "Who Did Not Write a Single Work
Which Can be Trusted"?' in *Historical Controversies and Historians*, ed. William Lamont
(London, 1998), pp. 107–17.
46   Eric Kerridge, *Agrarian Problems in the Sixteenth Century and After* (London, 1969),
p. 15.
47   E. H. Carr, *What Is History?* (London, 1961); Geoffrey R. Elton, *The Practice of
History* (London, 1967). See also John Tosh, *The Pursuit of History* (Harlow, 2002),
pp. 164–203 for a longer view.
48   Stone, 'Introduction', p. xi. See also Coleman, *History and the Economic Past*,
pp. 63–92.

Marxist, journal *Past & Present* had as its subtitle from 1952–58 'a journal of scientific history'.[49] But it is important to concede that the differences were not only about style or method. Also evident were a strong distaste for Tawney's socialist views, and the way these influenced his vision of the past, particularly his sympathy with the experience of the ordinary peasants and labourers and his contempt for wealthy landowners and capitalist farmers.

Tawney made no attempt to hide his political morals when he wrote history, and it is this that offended Elton and Kerridge so much. Against the backdrop of the Cold War, the rise of Marxist history in Britain in the 1940s and 1950s – with the formation of the Communist Party Historians' Group, the publication of Maurice Dobb's *Studies in the Development of Capitalism* and the founding of *Past & Present* – had sharpened the political divide amongst historians.[50] Tawney had chosen to focus on those issues which Marx had highlighted as crucial in the development of capitalism in England: he corresponded with Dobb and reviewed his book favourably.[51] Yet Tawney, although not naïve in his approach to history,[52] made no direct references to Marx, and was too under-theorised in this respect for the Marxists to hail him as a pioneer or hero.[53]

Tawney the historian was gradually rehabilitated during the 1970s.[54] For *The Agrarian Problem* the crucial step was Robert Brenner's work on the transition from feudalism to capitalism, which accepted almost wholesale Tawney's description of social and economic change in agrarian England from 1440 to 1660 and placed it in a stimulating comparative perspective at the heart of a Marxist explanation of long-term economic change.[55] This sparked a lively debate which highlighted the importance of Tawney's key concerns: class conflict, security of tenure and the emergence of capitalist farming.[56] History in the early twenty-first century is now largely

49   Raphael Samuel, 'British Marxist Historians, 1880–1980: Part One', *New Left Review* 120 (1980), 84–5.
50   Maurice Dobb, *Studies in the Development of Capitalism* (London, 1946). The resulting debate is printed in R. H. Hilton, ed., *The Transition from Feudalism to Capitalism* (London, 1976; repr. London, 1978). See also Harvey J. Kaye, *The British Marxist Historians* (Basingstoke, 1995).
51   Review printed in Winter, ed., *History and Society*, pp. 202–14.
52   See R. H. Tawney, 'The Study of Economic History (1933)', in *History and Society*, ed. Winter, pp. 54–64; Dennis and Halsey, *English Ethical Socialism*, esp. chapter 9 'Tawney's Social Theory', pp. 184–98.
53   Ormrod, 'R. H. Tawney and the Origins of Capitalism', 139.
54   J. D. Chambers, 'The Tawney Tradition', *Economic History Review* 24:3 (1971), 355–69; J. M. Winter and D. M. Joslin, eds, *R. H. Tawney's Commonplace Book* (Cambridge, 1972); Winter, ed., *History and Society*.
55   Robert Brenner, 'Agrarian Class Structure and Economic Development in Pre-industrial Europe', *Past & Present* 70 (1976), 30–75.
56   T. H. Aston and C. H. E. Philpin, eds, *The Brenner Debate: Agrarian Class Structure*

both post-Marxist, in the sense of abandoning attempts to prove Marx's schemes of historical development, and post-modern, in the sense of abandoning any pretence that history can be wholly scientific or objective.[57] As a consequence, Tawney's work should be back in fashion: the chapters below show the extent to which it already is.

III

It is possible to greatly admire and value a work of history without agreeing with all its conclusions. Tawney's *Agrarian Problem* got many things right, in the sense that what he wrote has been reinforced or reiterated by more recent research, but he also got many things wrong, in the sense that some of his ideas have been disproved or widely disputed. The following section looks first at the strengths of *The Agrarian Problem* before dwelling at greater length on its weaknesses. This uneven approach does not imply that Tawney got more wrong than he did right: it is intended to provide readers with a guide to the current state of research with which to compare Tawney's ideas.

The great strength of *The Agrarian Problem* lies in the rich and vivid picture it paints of rural England in the period 1460–1660. Often present-day researchers battle their way through piles (or rolls) of original and largely unstudied evidence in manorial documents to produce some original insight into sixteenth-century rural society, only to find Tawney had the idea first.[58] The description of rural society in Part I of *The Agrarian Problem* is particularly strong, as is the discussion of 'the agrarian problem and the state' in Part III. Part II is more patchy but still contains much of value. Certainly we cannot say that Tawney's 'history was not good, not sound, not right, and not true'.

Tawney had a good awareness of important variations within English rural society. *The Agrarian Problem* discusses and illustrates regional variations in the extent of enclosures and types of tenure,[59] and stresses the importance of variations between manors in manorial custom.[60] He was aware of the wide range in landholding sizes among customary tenants, the role of the tenant land market in creating this situation, and that tenants

---

and Economic Development in Pre-industrial Europe (Cambridge, 1985).

57   See for instance Ludmilla Jordanova, *History in Practice* (London, 2000), pp. 91–112; Ulinka Rublack, 'The Status of Historical Knowledge', in *A Concise Companion to History*, ed. Ulinka Rublack (Oxford, 2011), pp. 57–78.

58   This is my own experience: see Jane Whittle, *The Development of Agrarian Capitalism: Land and Labour in Norfolk 1440–1580* (Oxford, 2000). See also Dyer's comments below.

59   Tawney, *Agrarian Problem*, pp. 8–9, 24–6, 47–54.

60   Ibid., pp. 21–4, 125–31, 172.

engrossed and enclosed land themselves.[61] The book explains how 'enclosure' could mean a variety of processes in the sixteenth century, and that many types of enclosure took place.[62] Tawney was right that large leasehold farms existed most often on demesne land, and that the importance of pastoral farming had increased since the fourteenth century.[63] He was also right about the pressures caused by monetary inflation in the sixteenth century, and landlords' desire to 'tap the surplus' in land values that was accruing to their tenants.[64] The importance of common rights to small landholders is sensitively explained.[65] Tawney understood the power of manorial custom in protecting the tenants' interests, and the support provided by central courts,[66] but correctly identified the two most significant weaknesses in this regime for tenants' rights: the limited duration of copyholds for lives, and the variable rates of some entry fines.[67] He notes the government's motivations for protecting the interests of the small tenant,[68] and the range of agrarian issues raised by sixteenth-century popular rebellions.[69] Given the complexities of all these issues, this is an impressive list. His approach repeatedly reinforces the statement on page one that the agrarian problem of the sixteenth century was 'at once economic, legal and political'.

There are also statements and arguments in *The Agrarian Problem* which are inaccurate or just plain wrong. Sometimes this is because of the limits of historical knowledge at the time, but sometimes it is because Tawney chose to overlook evidence, occasionally evidence that he himself cites elsewhere in the book. For instance, Tawney described an evolutionary scheme for the development of the English landscape in which there was a transition from less commercialised open-field agriculture to more commercialised enclosed agriculture. Thus he saw counties that were very largely enclosed such as Devon, Cornwall, Essex and Kent as having once been open, and as more commercialised than open-field areas.[70] Yet many of these counties were old-enclosed: they had never been farmed in open fields.[71] There is no evidence that old-enclosed farms were more market-orientated than those in open fields. Tawney showed little awareness of different agricultural systems, dividing agriculture simply into arable and

61   Ibid., pp. 60–82.
62   Ibid., pp. 9–10, 87–8, 149–50, 178–83.
63   Ibid., pp. 91–3, 202–3, 209–10.
64   Ibid., pp. 198–9, 304–5.
65   Ibid., pp. 238–41.
66   Ibid., pp. 125–31, 292, 357–61.
67   Ibid., pp. 280–302.
68   Ibid., pp. 317, 343–7.
69   Ibid., pp. 317–39.
70   Ibid., pp. 153–4, 167, 172, 363, 405.
71   W. G. Hoskins, *The Making of the English Landscape* (London, 1955); Joan Thirsk, *England's Agricultural Regions and Agrarian History, 1500–1750* (Basingstoke, 1987).

pasture. He was unaware that large-scale sheep farming was integral to successful arable agriculture in regions of light soils and did not necessarily entail enclosure. The foldcourse system of Norfolk and Suffolk, and sheep-corn husbandry of the chalk downlands of central southern England, allowed thousands of sheep to be kept without enclosing land, although this caused other problems for tenants.[72]

Perhaps most significantly, Tawney did not consider demographic change as a factor.[73] Despite noting the impact of the Black Death in the fourteenth century, he imagined that England was less populated in the medieval period than in the sixteenth century.[74] Awareness of demographic change has had a profound impact on how historians view the rural economy of the fifteenth and sixteenth centuries. By current estimates the population of England reached a high level in the early fourteenth century of 4.5–6.0 million. The Black Death of 1348–49 reduced it by more than a third, and population levels continued to fall until the mid-fifteenth century when they were around 2 million.[75] They did not increase significantly until the early sixteenth century, but then increased rapidly to reach 4.1 million by 1600 and 5 million by 1670.[76] In a society of small farmers, population change had a strong effect on the demand for land: high population levels pushed up rents and other payments; when population levels were low, land lay vacant and payments from tenants to lords fell. Pastoral farming requires less labour than arable, and thus the rise in the proportion of pasture on demesnes in the fifteenth century was a response to low population levels and high wages. However, population change cannot explain everything. Brenner's important contribution to the understanding of change over time was to point out that population change caused opposite effects in different circumstances.[77] For instance, population growth lay behind the fragmentation of peasant farms into smaller units in the period 1250–1348, and the engrossment of larger farms in the sixteenth century. These differences cannot be explained without stressing the increased commercialisation of the rural economy, as Tawney did,[78] although starting at an earlier date.

72 K. J. Allison, 'The Sheep-corn Husbandry of Norfolk in the Sixteenth and Seventeenth Centuries', *Agricultural History Review* 5:1 (1957), 12–30; Eric Kerridge, *The Agricultural Revolution* (London, 1967) and *The Common Fields of England* (Manchester, 1992).

73 Stone, 'Introduction', p. xi.

74 Tawney, *Agrarian Problem*, pp. 3, 88–9.

75 John Hatcher, *Plague, Population and the English Economy: 1348–1530* (London, 1977); Bruce Campbell, 'England: Land and People', in *A Companion to Britain in the Later Middle Ages*, ed. S. H. Rigby (Oxford, 2003).

76 E. A. Wrigley and R. S. Schofield, *The Population History of England 1541–1871: A Reconstruction* (Cambridge, 1981).

77 Brenner, 'Agrarian Class Structure'.

78 e.g. Tawney, *Agrarian Problem*, p. 404.

Beresford has shown conclusively that large numbers of parishes that contained villages in the early fourteenth century were later depopulated and put down to pasture for sheep. However, this trend reached its height earlier than Tawney argued: in the fifteenth rather than the sixteenth century.[79] Instead of seeing this as the result of evictions, many historians now argue that tenants mostly moved away out of choice, gravitating towards communities which offered more freedom and sociability, better-quality or cheaper land, and wider commercial opportunities.[80] Evictions and depopulation were rare in the sixteenth century. Nonetheless, Allen has shown how villages which were deserted, or partly deserted, and enclosed in the fifteenth century were not repopulated in the sixteenth and seventeenth centuries, increasing the demand for land elsewhere.[81]

So Tawney was mistaken in seeing depopulating enclosures peaking in the period 1547–58, and perhaps more fundamentally, he was mistaken in believing enclosure led to widespread evictions of tenants, and that such people made up the ranks of vagrants and the poor in sixteenth-century England.[82] At the heart of this mistake was the assumption that the majority of customary tenures were insecure, and a tendency to take literally the legal pleadings that customary tenants were 'very simple and ignorant of their estates' and 'cannot make the matter plain to lawyers',[83] despite evidence noted to the contrary. This allowed Tawney to generalise about the conflict between gentry landlords and wealthy leaseholders on the one hand and vulnerable customary tenants on the other, despite noting the large size of some customary landholdings, the fact that customary tenants often held land by lease, and that gentlemen purchased customary land.[84]

Tawney was right that types of tenure determined how far lords could increase payments and exercise control over their tenants' activities. Copyhold for lives was a finite tenure which offered lords far more scope than copyhold of inheritance, and while customary rents were fixed, entry fines could be fixed or variable. Missing from this picture is a third type of customary tenure which was the dominant form across much of northern England: 'tenant right', discussed by Morrin and Holt in chapters 7 and 8.[85] As Tawney noted, some lords did transfer copyhold for lives

---

79   Beresford, *Lost Villages of England*, esp. p. 150.

80   Christopher Dyer, *Making a Living in the Middle Ages* (New Haven, 2002), pp. 349–52.

81   Robert C. Allen, *Enclosure and the Yeoman: The Agricultural Development of the South Midlands 1450–1850* (Oxford, 1992), pp. 37–55.

82   Tawney, *Agrarian Problem*, pp. 260–75.

83   Ibid., pp. 149, 302.

84   Ibid., pp. 56, 61, 91.

85   Tawney's chapter on 'tenant right' discusses the rights of tenants rather than tenant right tenure.

into leaseholds in the sixteenth century, but he failed to realise that many sixteenth-century leaseholds were 'beneficial leases' which differed little from customary tenures.[86] While entry fines might be raised where custom allowed, there is no evidence that lords managed to recoup the whole of rising land values as Tawney argued: Holt's study in Chapter 8 shows that this was extremely unlikely.[87] Tawney thought copyholds for lives predominated: Richard Hoyle's recent research suggests that in fact the much more secure copyhold of inheritance was more common.[88]

The generally secure and profitable nature of customary tenures is demonstrated by the fact that these holdings were acquired by gentry and townspeople from the fifteenth century onwards.[89] Nor were customary tenants ignorant of their rights or unable to defend themselves via litigation. From the medieval period onwards tenants grouped together to challenge their lords, and took cases to the London courts to defend their rights.[90] Tawney thought that customary tenants had 'for centuries no dealings with the state at all', but recent research shows that village elites were involved in assessing taxes, organising the militia and sitting on county-level juries.[91] Legal cases and popular rebellions show many customary tenants to have been intelligent, well-informed and politically aware.[92] They were a force to be reckoned with, and the behaviour of both lords and governments acknowledges this. Those who really lost out in sixteenth-century society were those who lacked customary tenures. Insecurity, short-term leases and rack rents characterised the relationship between customary tenants and their subtenants. Tawney acknowledged

86   Christopher G. A. Clay, 'Lifeleasehold in the Western Counties of England 1650–1750', *Agricultural History Review* 29 (1981), 83–96; Jane Whittle, 'Leasehold Tenure in England c.1300–c.1600: Its Form and Incidence', in *The Development of Leasehold in North-Western Europe, c.1200–1600*, ed. B. J. P. van Bavel and P. R. Schofield (Turnhout, 2008), pp. 147–50.

87   Tawney, *Agrarian Problem*, pp. 305, 309.

88   Ibid., pp. 300–1, 407; R. W. Hoyle, *Landlords and Tenants in Tawney's Century: Tenurial Change in England 1540–1640* (forthcoming).

89   Whittle, *Development of Agrarian Capitalism*, pp. 188–9, 200–3.

90   R. H. Hilton, 'Peasant Movements in England before 1381', *Economic History Review* 2 (1949), 117–36.

91   Tawney, *Agrarian Problem*, p. 123; Christopher Dyer, 'Taxation and Communities in Late Medieval England', *Progress and Problems in Medieval England*, ed. Richard Britnell and John Hatcher (Cambridge, 1996), pp. 168–90; R. B. Goheen, 'Peasant Politics? Village Community and the Crown in Fifteenth-Century England', *American Historical Review* 96 (1991), 42–62; Montgomery Bohna, 'Armed Force and Civic Legitimacy in Jack Cade's Revolt, 1450', *English Historical Review*, 118:477 (2003), 563–82.

92   Andy Wood, *Riot, Rebellion and Popular Politics in Early Modern England* (Basingstoke, 2002) and *The 1549 Rebellions and the Making of Early Modern England* (Cambridge, 2007); Jane Whittle, 'Lords and Tenants in Kett's Rebellion, 1549', *Past & Present* 207 (2010), 3–52.

the presence of subtenants but was not aware of their large and growing numbers after 1550.[93]

How did a large class of subtenants and smallholders emerge? Tawney stressed eviction and insecurity of tenure,[94] but I would stress a more gradual process of dispossession, in which security of tenure has less relevance than wealth. Copyhold of inheritance was very secure, allowing it to be bought and sold between tenants for the going price, with only a small fine paid to the lord. After the disappearance of serfdom this land became an attractive investment for non-peasants, pushing up the price of land. Population growth fuelled this rise further. The sale price of land increased particularly rapidly in the mid-sixteenth century: the period when Tawney thought evictions were at their height.[95] The price of land meant those who did not inherit a family holding were increasingly unable to acquire land of their own. Overton shows how bad harvests affect small and large farmers differently: large farmers profit from bad harvests by selling a reduced surplus at very high prices, but small farmers lose their surplus altogether and are forced into debt. As peasant farms became more commercially orientated, this drove many to sell their land.[96] The dispossessed did not flood into towns or become rootless vagrants as Tawney thought, but became subtenants, craftsmen, specialist workers and labourers in a diversified rural economy.[97]

IV

The chapters in this volume have been chosen to showcase the latest research on the issues discussed by Tawney in *The Agrarian Problem* centring on the relationship between lords and tenants. Some are overviews. In Chapter 1, Christopher Dyer focuses on the early part of the period: despite the book's title, Tawney wrote a great deal of *The Agrarian Problem* about the fifteenth century. Here Dyer stresses the importance of understanding demographic change alongside the moves towards commercialisation before 1520. Harold Garrett-Goodyear (Chapter 2) and Christopher Brooks (Chapter 11) examine the legal security of copyhold tenures at the beginning and end of the period using the records of

---

93   Tawney, *Agrarian Problem*, pp. 80–1.; C. J. Harrison, 'Elizabethan Village Surveys: A Comment', *Agricultural History Review* 27:2 (1979), 82–9; Whittle, 'Leasehold Tenure', pp. 144–7.
94   Tawney, *Agrarian Problem*, p. 377.
95   Ibid., p. 316; Whittle, *Development of Agrarian Capitalism*, pp. 110–19.
96   Overton, *Agricultural Revolution*, pp. 20–22.
97   Tawney, *Agrarian Problem*, pp. 268–75; E. A. Wrigley, *People, Cities and Wealth* (Oxford, 1987), pp. 169–71; Whittle, *Development of Agrarian Capitalism*, p. 236.

the central courts. Although Tawney discussed the protection of tenures by the state, he had only a few printed cases and published state papers to work with: these two chapters demonstrate how this area of research has advanced. Garrett-Goodyear shows that the protection of customary tenures by the common law courts was driven by manorial lords rather than tenants, while Brooks demonstrates how secure copyhold tenure had become by the mid-seventeenth century. Julian Goodare (Chapter 6) compares tenurial changes in sixteenth-century England with those in Scotland. While the names of tenures and the system of law courts were different in the two countries, many of the economic and demographic pressures were the same. Yet in Scotland, by the early seventeenth century, the central law courts had undermined tenants' rights of inheritance and thus their security of tenure. David Ormrod (Chapter 12) examines Tawney's idea of capitalism and provides a historiographical account of the debates over the development of capitalism since *The Agrarian Problem*'s publication. He relates this to research on the level of rents, arguing these can be used to pinpoint the moment when agrarian capitalism emerged.

The remaining chapters are case studies. Detailed local studies allow the complexities of change in early modern rural England to be unravelled. Although the focus of these chapters is local, the implications are much wider. Briony McDonagh, Heather Falvey and Andy Wood (chapters 3, 4 and 5) examine enclosure disputes. They show the range of the different interest groups involved and the care needed when interpreting often contradictory evidence from long-running legal cases. McDonagh demonstrates the variety of types of enclosure that could occur even within a single community, and Falvey the importance of understanding local forms of agriculture and tenure. Both reveal that enclosure disputes were not necessarily straightforward lord–tenant conflicts. Wood examines an urban dispute over rights to common land, showing the power of custom and memory in shaping a long-running conflict between the privileged and the poor. Chapters 7 and 8, by Jean Morrin and Jennifer S. Holt, look at landlords' attempts to modernise customary tenures in different parts of northern England. In both case studies, lords faced stout resistance, and any victories over the tenants were partial or short-lived. William D. Shannon and Elizabeth Griffiths (chapters 9 and 10) provide the lords' perspective. Shannon examines how lords drew profits from the enclosure of wasteland, but left the risk to tenants. Griffiths shows how Norfolk lords, although keen to raise incomes by creating large leasehold farms just as Tawney argued, left copyhold tenures alone.

Research into lords and tenants in Britain has moved on since Tawney wrote *The Agrarian Problem* in 1912, but Tawney's book remains a crucial reference point: it contains much to inform and inspire the twenty-first-century historian seeking to understand the changes that took place in rural England between 1440 and 1660. As Stone wrote in his 1967 introduction: '*The Agrarian Problem* remains a great book.'[98]

98 Stone, 'Introduction', p. xviii.

The Agrarian Problem, 1440–1520

CHRISTOPHER DYER

R. H. Tawney's *Agrarian Problem* was an extraordinary achievement: it dealt with so many dimensions of the subject, identifying the key issues and presenting them with clarity and vigour. It is hard to appreciate that a hundred years have passed since its publication, and there are few books which retain their value after such a long passage of time. We tend to read a work of this period in the expectation that it will seem quaint and naïve. Instead, Tawney's treatment of his subject is not so different from our own. Often in planning and writing this chapter, I supposed that he would have omitted some part of our analysis of the period which I imagined to be relatively new, only to find that the thought had already occurred to him. The 'modernity' of his research and presentation is apparent in his awareness of regional differences, for example. He practised empathy, imagining how countrymen of the sixteenth century saw the changes of their own lifetime.[1] He grasped points intuitively, as when he said that there was no great general advance in agricultural productivity between the later Middle Ages and the seventeenth century, which has been confirmed after painstaking archival research. He used a wide range of sources, which included not just the manorial and state records, and pamphlets and sermons, but also estate maps which mark an early venture into 'landscape history' before that term was invented. This should not be a matter of surprise as Tawney, a young progressive of the post-Victorian years, was a contemporary of Stravinsky, Picasso, T. S. Eliot, Einstein and Henry Ford: he belonged to a modern movement that still influences the way we live and think in all spheres of human activity.

For Tawney the 'problem' lay in the conflicts arising from the commercialisation of the sixteenth century, which allowed the new holders of enclosed farms to undermine the cohesive and relatively egalitarian peasant communities of the Middle Ages. This was a trend in agrarian society perceived by modern historians observing the changes in the distribution and management of land, but above all it was the problem witnessed by

---

1 Tawney, *Agrarian Problem* (1912 edn), p. 59.

the 'commonwealth' writers of the sixteenth century, from Thomas More onwards, who saw enclosures as a social evil, arising from the covetous aims of the minority of farmers, graziers and landlords. The period, in Tawney's memorable phrase, saw 'a struggle between custom and competition'. It might be added, as he himself noticed, that although much of the commentary on social trends belongs to the middle of the sixteenth century, the first complaint about rural depopulation, attributing the displacement of villagers to human greed, was made by John Rous of Warwick who petitioned Parliament in 1459 and provided detailed evidence in the 1480s.[2]

The main point of this chapter is to show how the subject has changed, and in particular how conjunctural matters – trends in prices, population, production, wages and rents – have preoccupied historians and allowed them to see the period in a rather different light. These trends were all matters for concern for Tawney, but they have increased in prominence in the last thirty years. There is no better indication of the shift in emphasis in research than the range of sources used in 1912 and those which have been exploited in recent decades. Tawney made effective use of estate surveys and rentals to reveal the size and tenure of landholdings, and he also cited a wide range of literary works and state papers.[3] Now historians search for long series of documents which allow the compilation of systematic statistical data, such as manorial court rolls with evidence for the land market, entry fines and mortality.

Twenty-first-century researchers tend to identify as a 'problem' the lack of growth in population and production in the period after the Black Death, and in particular in the decades between the depths of the mid-fifteenth-century recession in 1440 and the eve of the price revolution in 1520. This chapter focuses on those eighty years, which coincide with the early part of the period covered by Tawney. The issues can be broken down conveniently into three themes: population and resources; markets; and peasant society.

I

Tawney knew that the population before 1500 had reached a low level. He regarded the Black Death of 1348–49 as a great influence on the whole period, and referred to the 'empty holdings' in fifteenth-century manorial records, and to the cheapness of land. In a long footnote he attributed the slow rate of recovery in population in 1377–1500 to late marriage, which

2   Ibid., p. 12.
3   Ibid., pp. 4–9.

was reversed in the sixteenth century when a growing number of wage labourers married at a young age and contributed to a rising birth rate.[4] We
now believe that the English population had arrived at a low level in c.1500,
at about 2.2 million, which is comparable with the numbers in the eleventh
century.[5] In parts of continental Europe, where losses from epidemics in
the fourteenth century were similar to those suffered by England, populations had been climbing back to their pre-plague levels during the fifteenth
century, but in England the occasional hints of recovery after 1470 made
little headway, and sustained growth came only after 1520.[6] Generally high
levels of mortality combined with epidemics have been identified as the decisive factors in preventing any rise in numbers of people, and the evidence
from monastic houses suggests that the expectation of life at the age of
twenty-five was falling in the late fifteenth century, and rising after about
1500. Inmates of institutions, which included schools as well as monasteries, were peculiarly vulnerable to the spread of infection, even among a
privileged population who were well fed and well housed.[7] Epidemics are
recorded in the general population, notably twice in the 1470s, at the end
of the fifteenth century and in 1512–13, and evidence for expectation of
life for tenants in chief of the Crown and small samples of Essex peasants
suggest that while the monks experienced a rather extreme mortality, the
story of high death rates in the late fifteenth century may be applied to the
population as a whole. It cannot be said, however, that mortality at the end
of the fifteenth century is reflected in sudden falls in land values or a jump
to higher wages.[8]

The problem lies, of course, in the existence of plentiful evidence for
deaths, but not for the age of marriage or fertility. Recent demographic
analysts would agree with Tawney's emphasis on the age of marriage as
a key variable, but they would link this to earnings rather than to pro-
letarianisation. The period should have been one of frequent and early

---

4   Ibid., pp. 104–6.
5   R. M. Smith, 'Plague and Peoples: The Long Demographic Cycle, 1250–1670', in
The Peopling of Britain: The Shaping of a Human Landscape, ed. P. Slack and R. Ward
(Oxford, 2002), p. 181.
6   S. R. Epstein, *An Island for Itself: Economic Development and Social Change in Late
Medieval Sicily* (Cambridge, 1992), pp. 60–74.
7   e.g. B. F. Harvey, *Living and Dying in England, 1100–1540: The Monastic Experience*
(Oxford, 1993), pp. 112–45; P. Nightingale, 'Some New Evidence of Crises and Trends of
Mortality in Late Medieval England', *Past & Present* 187 (2005), 33–68; J. Hatcher, A. Piper
and D. Stone, 'Monastic Mortality: Durham Priory, 1395–1529', *Economic History Review*
59 (2006), 667–87. I have benefited from conversations on this point with Rebecca Oakes.
8   L. R. Poos, J. E. Oeppen and R. M. Smith, 'Re-Assessing Josiah Russell's Measurements
of Late Medieval Mortality Using the Inquisitions *Post Mortem*', in *The Fifteenth-Century
Inquisitions Post Mortem*, ed. M. Hicks (Woodbridge, 2012), pp. 155–67; L. R. Poos, *A
Rural Society after the Black Death: Essex 1350–1525* (Cambridge, 1991), pp. 115–20.

marriage, as it presented young people with opportunities for employment in agriculture and industry, and holdings of land were relatively easily available. Fertility should have been high, with good prospects for the survival of children, as food was cheap, housing gained in quality, and the countryside in particular was far from overcrowded. Tawney thought that because the civil wars of 1455–85 had threatened the security of the peasantry, the economic climate might have changed with the restoration of peace.[9] We now disregard the economic impact of the Wars of the Roses, as they cannot be shown to have caused much local destruction. Perhaps they damaged confidence because they created a climate of anxiety and uncertainty? If this was the case, those problems continued until 1497, as Henry VII faced a series of challenges and uprisings: there is, however, little specific evidence to support the idea.

For Tawney there had been a turning point in 1489, the year of the first national legislation directed at curtailing depopulation and enclosure, but in terms of the conjunctural changes in population and other economic and social variables, the year 1489 has little significance, and the change in direction fell in the years around 1520. There are, however, some puzzling fluctuations and discrepancies, not all of which can be readily explained. Grain prices hovered around the level of the 1450s, with occasional short-term rises caused by poor harvests (as in 1481–82) until 1516, when a long-term upward trend began.[10] The long period of stability must have been related to the low level of demand from a relatively small population of consumers. The prices of sheep, cattle and wool picked up in the 1480s, then fell back, but again were rising in the late teens of the sixteenth century. Animals and animal products increased in price a few years before those of grain, and they tended to move more rapidly upwards.

Tawney regarded the increasing size of the wage labour force as an important trend in the sixteenth century, and he used the word 'proletariat' in a way that we would now avoid, because so many wage earners were either smallholders or servants, and not lifelong property-less workers who were entirely dependent on earnings. The daily wages of building workers reached a plateau during the fifteenth century, which persisted until about 1520, of 6d per day for a skilled craftsman and 4d for a labourer (in southern England). These rates of pay were not very sensitive to short-term changes and for some employers had taken on a stability suggestive of a well-established custom.[11] The remuneration was potentially benefi-

---

9   Tawney, *Agrarian Problem* (1912 edn), p. 37.

10   P. Bowden, 'Agricultural Prices, Farm Profits and Rents', in *The Agrarian History of England and Wales, 4: 1500–1640*, ed. Joan Thirsk (Cambridge, 1967), pp. 593–695, 814–70.

11   E. H. Phelps Brown and S. V. Hopkins, *A Perspective of Wages* (London, 1981), pp. 13–59; D. Woodward, *Men at Work: Labourers and Building Craftsmen in the Towns of Northern England, 1450–1750* (Cambridge, 1995), pp. 169–72.

cial to workers because of the low and steady prices of foodstuffs, though the purchasing power of their wages began to slip in the years immediately preceding 1520 as the prices of grain, meat and other foods began to increase.

Contemporaries were highly critical of those who refused employment, or expected to receive high wages. Restrictions on rates of pay were renewed in the legislation of 1495. Would-be employers connected the shortage of labour and its high cost with the large numbers of beggars and vagrants, who they believed were capable of work but preferred idleness. In particular they prohibited the time-wasting and potentially disorderly games played by the lower orders. They resented the tendency of those dispensing alms to relieve the poverty of those who did not deserve charity.[12]

The agrarian problem for Tawney, reflecting the views of More, Latimer, Starkey and other contemporary 'commonwealth men', lay in the plight of the husbandman, whose livelihood was threatened by the erosion of his rewards from farming by enclosure. 'Husbandmen' was the contemporary term; we might identify them as middling or better-off peasants. From the conjunctural perspective, the husbandman had troubles which can be attributed to low prices and high costs. It is now acceptable, in a way which Tawney would have found too speculative, to make some estimate of a husbandman's budget. In 1500 a customary yardlander who was cropping twenty acres each year in an open-field system could hope to produce twenty-eight quarters of grain. The peasant household was consuming ten quarters of grain as food and drink, reserving eight quarters for seed, and could have been feeding two quarters to animals. The eight quarters of surplus grain would have sold for about 32s. Hiring a moderate amount of labour, say for thirty days to cover hay making, harvest and other peaks, could incur a cost of 10s. If 15s was needed to pay rents and taxes, 7s would be left for clothing, shoes, household goods and foodstuffs such as fish which could not be produced on the holding. How would any of the succession of occasional extra expenses be afforded? A sum of 20s would be needed to carry out extensive repairs to a barn, and the same amount would pay for a new cart with iron tyres to enable produce to be taken to market. Replacing an old or sick ox would cost 10s, and a daughter's marriage would involve an outlay of 40s. The pastoral side of the holding's activities was important as a source of cash: if the yardlander kept 30 sheep, their wool could have been sold for about 10s, and profits from 2 cows and a sow could have brought the annual revenue from animal husbandry near to 20s. Any threat to the common pasture from enclosure or overburdening

---

12 P. Cavill, 'The Problem of Labour and the Parliament of 1495', in *The Fifteenth Century, 5: 'Of Mice and Men': Image, Belief and Regulation in Late Medieval England*, ed. L. Clark (Woodbridge, 2005), p. 143–55.

by a profit-hungry farmer would have made these occasional outlays difficult to afford, and would have been very damaging to the husbandman's fragile productive and domestic economy.

Tawney's perception of the agrarian problem, with its emphasis on the appropriation of resources by the lords, farmers and graziers, and the problem that is apparent from the conjunctural approach, come together in the reconstruction of the economy of a yardland holding, as the availability of pasture emerges as a vital contribution to the peasant's welfare. A further variable in both approaches was the level of rent. Were rents rising significantly, or were they mainly stagnant at this period? And was their behaviour determined by market demand, or by the politics inherent in the lord–tenant relationship? Much rent that was paid per annum by both free and customary tenants, assize rent, was fixed by law or by custom, so a high proportion of the annual payments to lords did not change. There were significant differences, however, in the efficiency with which the rents were collected, as on some estates – like those of the dukes of Buckingham which had been notorious for the build-up of arrears in the mid-fifteenth century – rents were still being paid slowly or incompletely in 1500–20. Arrears also continued to pose a problem after 1500 on manors of the bishops of Durham. On other estates, such as that of the bishops of Worcester, although rents were pegged at the same level, the officials made sure that they were paid promptly and in full, or if a rent was impossible to collect they removed it from the records rather than maintaining the fiction that it would eventually be levied.[13]

Entry fines on customary land could be fixed at a moderate level, such as the 13s 4d per yardland in west Berkshire around 1500. More often they fluctuated without a marked trend, as at Great Horwood (Buckinghamshire) where they varied between 8s and 13s per yardland in the period 1500–30. At Broadway (Worcestershire) they formed a clear pattern of growth, from around 2s–6s per yardland in the 1490s to 13s 4d–20s in 1500–20. They increased decisively on the estates of the Percys, earls of Northumberland, from a figure corresponding to 50 per cent of a year's rent, at most, in the late fifteenth century to a full year's rent in the early 1520s. Really high fines, comparable with those levied before the Black Death, are found on the manors of Wick Episcopi and Whitstones near Worcester, where they stood at about £1 to £3 per yardland before 1500, and rose in some decades in 1500–40 to £4 or £5. In south Gloucestershire, on a number of manors clustered around Bristol, at Henbury, Rockhampton, Stoke Bishop

13   B. J. Harris, *Edward Stafford: Third Duke of Buckingham, 1478–1521* (Stanford, Calif., 1986), pp. 116–19; C. Newman, *Late Medieval Northallerton: A Small Market Town and Its Hinterland, c.1470–1540* (Stamford, 1999), pp. 89–90; Christopher Dyer, *Lords and Peasants in a Changing Society: The Estates of the Bishopric of Worcester 680–1540* (Cambridge, 1980), pp. 189–90.

and Stoke Giffard, fines above £4 are recorded in the late fifteenth century, and they tended to rise to attain levels as high as £7 and £8 between 1480 and 1540.[14]

Leasehold rents were in theory renegotiable when the term ended, but often they remained at the same level in the late fifteenth and early sixteenth centuries. A striking example of increases comes from the Duchy of Lancaster estates in Derbyshire, which reflects the rising value of pasture around 1500, but also the robust management policy practised by the estate. They could push up a rent by 50 per cent, for example the 'new herbage of Crook Hill' which rose from just under £32 to more than £48, mostly in the period 1485–1520.[15] Enclosure of a pasture could make a dramatic difference to its rent: a large area of grazing at Westcote in Tysoe (Warwickshire) increased in annual value from £4 in 1444 to £13 6s 8d in the 1490s.[16] In Kent, Surrey and Sussex in the early years of the sixteenth century, tenants were willing to pay substantial sums to acquire a leasehold, and sitting tenants were assigning unexpired years on the term of a lease to new tenant, again for a considerable payment. Estate officials carefully surveyed assets, noting that higher rents could be extracted from specific pieces of land.[17] The large increases in rents for pastures tended to be paid by lessees (farmers) and entrepreneurs, whereas the peasants or husbandmen were more often customary tenants of one, two or three yardlands for which the entry fine could change, but not the annual rent.

These disparate examples do not resolve the dilemma of measuring the burden of rent, but the overall impression is that while rents changed dramatically only when there was some major reform of the management of the estate, or when investment improved the productive capacity of the land, land values were tending either to remain stable or to move upwards during this period, especially after about 1480. Support for the idea that land was becoming more desirable comes from the evidence that towards the end of the fifteenth century, and in the first decades of the sixteenth, customary holdings were being acquired by heirs more often than had

14   M. Yates, *Town and Countryside in Western Berkshire, c.1327–c.1600: Social and Economic Change* (Woodbridge, 2007), p. 145; M. Tompkins, 'Peasant Society in a Midlands Manor, Great Horwood 1400–1600' (unpublished PhD thesis, 2006), pp. 160–5; TNA PRO SC2 210/32, 33; J. M. W. Bean, *The Estates of the Percy Family 1416–1537* (Oxford, 1958), pp. 51–67, 138–40; C. Dyer, *Lords and Peasants*, pp. 287–91; Gloucestershire Archives Badminton Muniments, MJ9/1–3; MJ11/1/2–5. The Gloucestershire and Worcestershire examples are median figures calculated for each decade.
15   I. S. W. Blanchard, ed., *The Duchy of Lancaster's Estates in Derbyshire 1485–1540* (Derbyshire Archaeological Society Record Series, 3, 1971), p. 3.
16   Christopher Dyer, 'Deserted Medieval Villages in the West Midlands', in *Everyday Life in Medieval England*, ed. Christopher Dyer (London, 1994), p. 41.
17   M. Mate, *Trade and Economic Development, 1450–1550: The Experience of Kent, Surrey and Sussex* (Woodbridge, 2006), pp. 223–31.

been the case in the mid-fifteenth century. The sons of tenants in Norfolk and in the west midlands were finding it less easy in the period 1470–1520 to pick up land on the market, and were attracted back to their family holding where they had a hereditary claim.[18]

This upward trend in the demand for land, however patchy and inconsistent, is worth contrasting with the situation in the period 1380–1450, when manorial accounts are full of decayed rents, with records that a holding once yielding 10s per annum is now being let for 7s, and court rolls tell us of land lying in the lord's hands, or being rented out informally to gain some revenue. How can this turnabout be explained? Prices of grain did not rise, wages remained much the same, the profits of livestock farming were higher than arable, but this had been the case for many decades. The pathway to a significant increase in profit lay in a complete restructuring of a large piece of land, with enclosure, conversion to pasture, and a drastic reduction in the labour force, but this was not possible in the many husbandmen's yardlands cultivated in an open-field village. Nonetheless after 1480 or 1500 higher entry fines were being paid for these traditional holdings, and their annual rents, though not increased, were being paid more promptly.

II

Tawney did not say much about towns, industry and trade, not because he was unaware of them, but because he chose to concentrate on agrarian themes. Our understanding of the size of the urban sector allows us to reappraise his idea that commerce impacted on the countryside with new force in the sixteenth century. All of the research and academic energy invested in late medieval towns in response to the 'urban decline' controversy allows us to say that the population of most towns was reduced in the period 1320–1520, and that large numbers of markets which had been founded in the thirteenth and early fourteenth centuries had fallen out of use.[19]

This did not mean, however, that the commercialisation process of the pre-Black Death era had been forced into retreat. A network of markets still survived, most of them located in towns large and small. Most of the rural population still lived within 7 miles (11 km) of a weekly urban market, or a place which held an annual fair, and had many alternative

18   Whittle, *Development of Agrarian Capitalism*, pp. 119–77.
19   A. Dyer, *Decline and Growth in English Towns, 1400–1640* (Basingstoke, 1991) and '"Urban Decline" in England, 1377–1525', in *Towns in Decline AD 100–1600*, ed. T. R. Slater (Aldershot, 2000), pp. 266–88.

opportunities for selling and buying through informal trading centres, inns and farm-gate negotiations.[20] The towns themselves, though cumulatively smaller in their built-up area, and in their population, still accounted for near to a fifth of the total population.[21] A few towns had ceased to exist, and they had always shown signs of fragility, but a few new ones had grown up, such as the cloth centre of Stroud, or fishing towns like Brixham. In the clothing districts a few towns which had already existed before 1350, like Cullompton, had increased in size, and many rural settlements had expanded because of the burgeoning cloth industry with its many jobs for spinners, weavers, fullers, dyers and shearmen. London lost population, but its expanding suburbs of Southwark and Westminster ought to be taken into account.[22]

We do not have figures for the output of the cloth makers, as the amount sold within England is not recorded, but the export figures climbed from 40,000 cloths in 1400 to 60,000 in the 1490s and almost 100,000 in 1519–20. The decline in wool exports to below 10,000 sacks per annum in 1500–20 – a third of the mid-fourteenth-century figure – reflects commercial growth, because an ever-growing proportion of the wool was being sold to clothiers for manufacture in England.[23] Other industries based in the countryside were also doing well in the decades 1500–20, especially tin mining in Cornwall and Devon, and coal in the north-east.[24] Technical innovation is represented by the arrival of the first blast furnace in Sussex, and the first paper mill in Hertfordshire, both in the 1490s.[25] The industrial sector, which in the context of the early sixteenth century means an important part of the rural labour force, working often for entrepreneurs based in the country, showed every sign of health in terms of the volume of production and a willingness to invest in new methods.

A surplus of agricultural production was needed to feed the urban population. Some town dwellers grew at least some of their own food in gardens, and in fields sometimes attached to towns, but the substantial numbers of rural industrial workers must have taken the section of the

20   Christopher Dyer, 'The Hidden Trade of the Middle Ages: Evidence from the West Midlands', in *Everyday Life*, ed. Dyer, pp. 283–303.
21   S. H. Rigby, 'Urban Population in Late Medieval England: The Evidence of the Lay Subsidies', *Economic History Review* 63 (2010), 393–417.
22   D. Palliser, ed., *The Cambridge Urban History of Britain 1: 600–1540* (Cambridge, 2000), pp. 396–403, 605, 607, 638, 762.
23   E. M. Carus-Wilson and O. Coleman, *England's Export Trade 1275–1547* (Oxford, 1963), pp. 48–72, 75–115.
24   J. Hatcher, *English Tin Production and Trade before 1550* (Oxford, 1973), pp. 152–63 and *The History of the British Coal Industry 1* (Oxford, 1993), pp. 486–7.
25   H. Cleere and D. Crossley, *The Iron Industry of the Weald*, 2nd edn (Cardiff, 1995), pp. 111–17; A. Sutton, *A Merchant Family of Coventry, London and Calais: The Tates, c.1450–1575* (London, 1998), pp. 22–5.

population who depended on others for food to about a third of the population, unevenly scattered over the country.[26]

Industrial performance can be linked with a modest growth in consumerism, as the households of peasants, artisans and labourers could afford to spend more on clothing, housing and domestic utensils than their predecessors had done. An increased acquisition of material goods is apparent before 1520, anticipating the changes often attributed to the late sixteenth century, as peasant wills and inventories often include some pewter vessels, and a few silver spoons became an affordable status symbol. Yeomen and their wives might wear imported textiles, and in the last phase of occupation at Wharram Percy in Yorkshire, around 1500, at least one house was fitted with a glass window, and the inhabitants were drinking from imported German stoneware cups.[27] The expanding industries were concentrated in the clothing or mining districts, but scattered over the whole country were the artisans and traders who in market towns satisfied the demand among customers below the ranks of the gentry for consumer goods. We find spicers selling pepper, and mercers and drapers providing a range of textiles. Tailors cut and stitched clothing, and a part of the small-town goldsmiths' trade lay in making silver spoons. Building workers lived in both town and country, and they were responsible for an increasing number of two-storey rural houses, including superior structures with tiled or slated roofs.[28]

This part of the discussion necessarily ends with a note of uncertainty and puzzlement, relating to the lack of clear evidence for a connection between industrial activity and land values. Tawney believed that industrial growth gave a stimulus to agricultural production, but we cannot be sure that this was always the case. In Cornwall conventionary rents, which were sensitive to market forces, were sluggish on manors with no great involvement in tinning or clothmaking, but a not dissimilar picture emerges from the manors where industrial employment was an important feature of the

26   The non-agricultural occupational sector is thought to have been 40 per cent of the population in the seventeenth century, though Tawney found the figure much higher in Gloucestershire in 1608: E. A. Wrigley, 'Country and Town: The Primary, Secondary and Tertiary Peopling of England in the Early Modern Period', in *Peopling of Britain*, ed. Slack and Ward, p. 226.

27   M. Hayward, *Rich Apparel: Clothing and the Law in Henry VIII's England* (Farnham, 2009), pp. 213–21; D. D. Andrews and G. Milne, eds, *Wharram: A Study of Settlement on the Yorkshire Wolds*, 1, *Domestic Settlement, Areas 10 and 6* (Society for Medieval Archaeology, Monograph series, 8, 1979), pp. 73, 94–5, 115.

28   For example at Oakham, Long Melford and Sudbury in 1522: J. Cornwall, ed., *The County Community under Henry VIII* (Rutland Record Society, 1, 1980), pp. 76–9; J. F. Pound, ed., *The Military Survey of 1522 for Babergh Hundred* (Suffolk Records Society, 28, 1986), pp. 19–29, 83–7.

locality.²⁹ The only study of agricultural output, using tithe records, comes from a region with a good deal of industry, County Durham, but grain production did not increase at the end of the fifteenth or in the early sixteenth century.³⁰ On the other hand, in the clothing county of Suffolk rents and manorial profits seem to have been rising at the end of the fifteenth century, with evidence for larger units of production. Rents were moving upwards in the period of recovery in the late fifteenth century in Wiltshire, another county with rural clothmaking. Tax records measure wealth, usually in goods, rather than rents which depend so much on the variability of administration and the politics of lord–tenant relations. A long-term movement in the yield of direct taxation is revealed when the ranking of counties in the lay subsidies of the early fourteenth century are compared with those of the first quarter of the sixteenth century. The textile-making counties in the south-east and the south-west, and in counties benefiting from the relative prosperity of London, moved to prominent positions in the league table of tax payment, reflecting not just the profits of the cloth makers, but also the advantages to those in agriculture who were supplying foodstuffs to towns and industrial districts.³¹

Industrial activity cannot be connected simply and directly with an increased demand for land, but the rising output from clothmaking and the extraction and working of metals provides us with the main dynamic element in the economy, which, as Tawney believed, influenced the rising trend in land values found in rents and tax yields in some districts.

III

The internal movements and tensions of peasant society can be investigated through manorial court records and wills, and these sources also provide insights into the mentality of the peasantry. Tawney knew that peasants offered resistance to enclosure by drawing on the collective energy of the community, and he put great emphasis on communities as the managers of the open fields and the supervisors of the common pastures.

29 H. S. A. Fox and O. J. Padel, eds, *The Cornish Lands of the Arundells of Lanherne, Fourteenth to Sixteenth Centuries* (Devon and Cornwall Record Society, new series, 41, 2000), pp. ci–cxiii.

30 B. Dodds, *Peasants and Production in the Medieval North-East: The Evidence of Tithes, 1270–1536* (Woodbridge, 2007), pp. 110–15.

31   M. Bailey, *Medieval Suffolk: An Economic and Social History 1200–1500* (Woodbridge, 2007), p. 233; N. Amor, *Late Medieval Ipswich: Trade and Industry* (Woodbridge, 2011), p. 196; J. Hare, *A Prospering Society: Wiltshire in the later Middle Ages* (Hatfield, 2011), pp. 208–10; R. Schofield, 'The Geographical Distribution of Wealth in England, 1334–1649', in *Essays in Quantitative Economic History*, ed. R. Floud (Oxford, 1974), pp. 79–106.

We now appreciate the wider manifestations of village self-government, which is particularly apparent in the resourcefulness of the churchwardens in raising money for repair and building of the church fabric, and the effort and expense that went into furnishings, vestments and books of which parishes were clearly very proud.[32] As well as concerning themselves with repairs to roads and bridges, the management of the pinfold (pound), the well or stream and other communal facilities, the leading villagers were anxious to impose order and discipline on the inhabitants. The records of the manor courts and courts leet contain evidence for the efforts of the villagers, acting in coordination with the lord, and seeking to make use of his authority, to prevent hedge-breaking, eavesdropping, and similar anti-social behaviour, and to prohibit illicit sports and games.[33]

In a much-quoted phrase Tawney referred to the end of villeinage being followed by the beginnings of the poor law, which for him meant that one form of oppression by the lord was replaced by another at the hands of the state acting through the parish worthies. He emphasised the novelty of the poor law, and the connection between the poor law and the enforcement of labour discipline. The antecedents of the poor law, however, developed in the context of the growing responsibilities of the village leaders for tax collection and the maintenance of the 'common box' which went back to the fourteenth century. Private charity had a strong public dimension as endowments of land were administered by groups of villagers acting as feoffees in order to generate money for distribution, a century before the beginnings of national poor law legislation. We can see in the social policies of the community a striking combination of the public sphere and private interest which was also characteristic of the later poor law, as the elite villagers were much concerned with the labour problem and the need to deal with idleness and fecklessness which helped to reduce the supply of wage labour.[34]

Tawney knew about the peasant land market, which he saw as the mechanism by which holdings could be engrossed. He appreciated that peasants were profit-seeking and aware of the market. He called them 'Lilliputian capitalists', a striking phrase that deserves a wider currency. But he tended to categorise them as the opposite of the farmers and graziers with their enclosed pastures held on lease – the farmers were fully committed to commodity production, while peasants aimed at subsistence. Consequently

32   B. Kumin, *The Shaping of a Community: The Rise and Reformation of the English Parish c.1400–1560* (Aldershot, 1996).

33   M. McIntosh, *Controlling Misbehavior in England, 1370–1600* (Cambridge, 1998), p. 33; Tawney, *Agrarian Problem* (1912 edn), p. 46.

34   Christopher Dyer, 'The Political Life of the Fifteenth-Century English Village', in *The Fifteenth Century, 4: Political Culture in Late Medieval Britain*, ed. L. Clark (Woodbridge, 2004), p. 135–57.

peasants grew corn, while farmers could specialise in pasture.[35] We still know very little about the production strategies of demesne farmers, but there is enough evidence from the husbandry clauses in leases, inventories of farmers' livestock and equipment, and fragments of evidence in correspondence and in imaginative literature to show that despite its limited profitability much arable cultivation continued on leased demesnes. On many peasant holdings, however, while a proportion of the crop went to feed the household, there was much production for the market. The balance of a yardlander's incomings and outgoings calculated above does not show much peasant grain going for sale, though it was a different story for a substantial minority of peasants in the midlands and south who were holding two and three yardlands, and therefore had a larger disposable surplus of arable crops. Wool was an important marketed product of sheep and corn husbandry, and that was sold in its entirety. The accounts of a north Gloucestershire woolman show that half of his suppliers were shearing less than a hundred sheep each, which means that a good proportion of the wool trade was supplied by peasant-owned sheep. In that part of England the flocks were kept on the fallows and stubbles of open fields.[36] They belonged in a mixed farming system to which they contributed a cash crop to the peasant budget, and manure to the corn fields. Many sheep were kept in the champion country (to apply the language of landscape history), as well as the pastoral areas which Tawney emphasised. A high level of wool production in such areas was not just compatible with peasant economy; it was positively beneficial to cereal yields and contributed to peasant prosperity.

Traditional sheep-corn husbandry had allowed peasants in the thirteenth and fourteenth centuries to produce most of the wool that was exported in large quantities to the continent. Peasant farming was adaptable to new conditions in 1440–1520, as is demonstrated by the sizeable number of peasant holdings which can be shown to have been devoting acres of arable to fodder crops such as peas, beans and vetches. These crops were sometimes sown on inhoks taken out of the fallow field and therefore cropped in successive years in an important departure from the traditional open-field routine. Leys were often adopted, by which a proportion of land previously (for centuries) used for arable was put down to grass. There are hints of improvements to meadows by which strategically sited ditches irrigated the grass with an overflow of floodwater before the animals took their first bite, but the comprehensive grid of channels of the floated meadows

---

35   Tawney, *Agrarian Problem* (1912 edn), pp. 224–8.
36   Christopher Dyer, *A Country Merchant: Trading and Farming at the End of the Middle Ages, 1495–1520* (Oxford, 2012), pp. 155–62.

were an innovation of the seventeenth century.[37] The further stage of improvement took the form of piecemeal enclosure, which could sometimes take over the whole village territory, in Devon for example, but usually consisted of partial enclosure: parcels could be taken out of the common field behind the tofts in which the peasant houses stood.[38] This process of enclosure by peasants themselves was appreciated by Tawney and analysed by him at some length.[39]

In a well-ordered village, changes in rotations and common grazing were coordinated and agreed among the villagers. A key to the management of the system was the agreement on a stint, often in the midlands limiting access to the commons for the tenant of a yardland or virgate of about thirty acres to three or four cattle and horses, and thirty sheep. This was supported by rules that no more livestock could be kept on the commons in the summer than could be supported on the peasant's own resources in the winter. In addition, rules against agistment (that is, the renting out of pasture) prohibited the sale to strangers (outsiders) of access to the common grazing. Not all of these rules were respected, as their constant repetition suggests. The 'Lilliputian capitalists' gave priority to their selfish interests, and broke the rules by overburdening the commons, ignoring the rotation, fencing off their strips, shutting their neighbours out of closes which were supposed to be made available to the whole community in the 'open time', and generally disrupting the agreed routines. The behaviour of these awkward individualists, combined with the disreputable conduct of the gamblers, prostitutes and wastrels who were believed to congregate at the ale houses, and the quarrels which led to accusations of theft, ill treatment of livestock, affrays, assaults and drawings of blood with sticks and knives, all provide an antidote to any idealisation of the cohesive peasant community.

For twenty-first-century historians the 'agrarian problem' which occupied Tawney's attention – the struggle over the commons, the competition between public good and private interest, and the clash between subsistence and commercial priorities – was at least in part a conflict within the village, in which insiders rather than the farmer or grazier eroded common-field husbandry. Nothing demonstrates this better than the history of deserted villages. Tawney did not believe that many villages had been depopulated in the course of the conflicts that he described, though he did illustrate *The Agrarian Problem* with a copy of a remarkable map of 1620 from All Souls College Oxford which depicted the township of Whatborough

37   H. Cook, K. Stearne and T. Williamson, 'The Origins of Water Meadows in England', *Agricultural History Review* 51 (2003), 155–62.

38   H. S. A. Fox, 'The Chronology of Enclosure and Economic Development in Medieval Devon', *Economic History Review*, second series, 28 (1975), 181–202.

39   Tawney, *Agrarian Problem* (1912 edn), p. 147–72.

in Leicestershire as a series of enclosed fields consisting of former arable land: 'Theise grounds have likewise beene arable' was written on one field. At the centre of the territory was a close surrounded by ridge and furrow labelled 'The place where the towne of Whatborough stoode.'

Beresford, writing forty years later, showed that many hundreds of villages had been deserted, most of them, he believed, in the period 1450–1520. He almost forgave Tawney his lapse in not noticing these abandoned settlements because Beresford was an admirer of the great man, and took up many of Tawney's arguments in explaining the removal of the villagers.[40] Both Beresford and Tawney emphasised the role of the acquisitive lord, aided and abetted by the farmer and the grazier who used various methods such as overstocking of grazing and enclosures of common pastures to make life unbearable for the peasantry, drove them away and then enclosed the former fields. We would focus more attention on the weakening of the village by migration and neglect of building repairs, the engrossing of neighbours' holdings, and the internal disruptions of the field systems by selfish individuals, which made the encroachments and appropriations of outsiders much more easily accomplished. Often the accumulation of land in the hands of a few tenants, the ruinous state of buildings and the grassing over of arable were not part of some deep laid plot, but the unintended consequences of demographic shrinkage and flows of migration. The conversion of fields to pasture and their enclosure were remedies for decay, which proved profitable. The creation of large enclosed pastures in the period 1440–1520, often on former village sites, were not a response to a surge in market demand, but rather should be set in a context of expensive labour and plentiful land, in which efficiency and reductions in the costs of production were rewarded.

At the same time that some villages were falling apart and being overwhelmed by their enemies, others were able to keep the open fields functioning. Their peasants faced the problems of migration and the challenges of acquisitive neighbours, and successfully produced for the market. In some respects they competed with the large-scale farmers and graziers by supplying the wool market with their cumulatively large quantities of fleeces. Much is revealed about peasant society from the land market, which Tawney interpreted in rather one dimensional terms as the means by which divisions were created between labourers and the 'middle class' with larger holdings. Now transfers of land are discussed in terms of the cohesion of the family and inheritance strategies pursued by peasants. There was still some life and energy in the old peasant economy which survived the threats of the sixteenth century.

---

40   Beresford, *Lost Villages of England*, 4th edn (Stroud, 1998), pp. 197–9.

IV

Tawney correctly identified the enclosure of open-field land and its conversion to pasture as a significant trend which was active in the period 1440–1520. The economic background was not conducive to profitable investment as conventionally imagined, as population was not growing and prices and production were sluggish. Clothmaking and tin extraction expanded, much of it to satisfy overseas demand, and industrial growth had repercussions for the profits of agriculture. The enclosed pastures represent a technical development in a period of slow agrarian change. Some villages decayed internally and attracted the enclosers, but others adapted, and the trade in wool helped to strengthen the peasant economy.

Tawney's model assumed that a significant number of landlords and farmers were driven by acquisitive instincts to destabilise traditional peasant society. Twenty-first-century historians would distance themselves from Tawney's overt application of moral judgements, but his identification of profit-seeking as a source of social change is in tune with modern thinking about commercialisation. The tendency since Tawney's time to understand trends in population, prices, wages and rents – which has here been called conjunctural history – leaves yet more intractable problems to resolve, such as the failure of the population to grow, and the differences of experience between England and parts of continental Europe. Tawney was probably right to locate the origins of change in the ambitions of entrepreneurs, for which the explanation could be found in cultural changes which are still imperfectly understood. There was an agrarian problem in the years around 1500, but there is also an academic problem of interpretation and explanation which troubles historians a century after Tawney's book.

2

Common Law and Manor Courts

Lords, Copyholders and Doing Justice in Early Tudor England[1]

HAROLD GARRETT-GOODYEAR

Introducing *The Agrarian Problem of the Sixteenth Century*,[2] R. H. Tawney characterised the 'problem' of his title as a struggle between copyhold and leasehold. The ultimate triumph of the latter is confirmed by our familiarity with the terms of leasehold and leases: neither legal nor historical training is required to use the term in general conversation to refer to contractual tenures held for fixed terms and for fixed rents. Copyhold, on the other hand, belongs to a past era, an era in which tenures were 'free' or 'unfree', in which lords of manors held courts for their tenants, and in which custom within the manor was acknowledged as authoritative, independent of the common law enforced within royal courts. Emerging in the fifteenth century as the most common form of peasant tenure, copyhold acquired its name from the practice of giving a tenant a copy of the entry from the manorial court roll, which described terms on which the lord admitted the tenant and his heirs to the landholding. Those terms by the sixteenth century were routinely phrased 'at the will of the lord, according to the custom of the manor', and differences over interpretation of the copyhold title were, at least before the mid-sixteenth century, settled within the lord's manorial court, not in one of the common law courts presided over by the king's justices.

At stake in a struggle between leasehold and copyhold, then, was the security a copyholder might rely on against his lord; and for Tawney, the long-term outcome of this struggle – the displacement of copyhold by leasehold – reflected the ultimate victory of a landed aristocracy powerful enough to defeat not only peasant communities relying on custom to defend their holdings but also their (admittedly erratic) allies among

---

1 References to pleadings in common law or other royal courts are to TNA, Kew: Common Bench plea rolls CP 40, King's Bench plea rolls KB 27, Chancery files of pleadings C 1, Star Chamber files of pleadings STAC 2.
2 Tawney, *Agrarian Problem*.

Tudor monarchs and their councillors. In mapping the competition between leasehold and copyhold – roughly equivalent in his analysis to
conflict between landlords and their peasant tenants – Tawney depended
heavily on evidence from the king's equity and prerogative courts, especially Star Chamber and the Court of Requests. Complaints submitted in
those courts by copyholders, and decisions there protecting the interests
of copyholders against lords hostile to customary rights, provide much
of the support for Tawney's conclusion that royal governments offered
some resistance to the transformation of agrarian relations in which customary tenure and 'collective' agriculture dominated, to those in which
a tripartite relationship of lord–farmer–landless labourer characterised
agrarian production.

The weight Tawney put on the role played by courts in the transformation of agrarian production is evident in his observation that '[w]hat
made the new methods of agriculture not simply an important technical
advance in the utilisation of the soil, but the beginning of a social revolution, was the insecurity of the tenure of large numbers of the peasantry,
in the absence of which they might gradually have adapted themselves to
the altered conditions, without any overwhelming shock to rural life such
as was produced by the evictions and by the loss of rights of common'.[3]
Tawney is less than clear, however, about the role of common law courts
in the transformation of agrarian production and the emergence of new
social relations in the English countryside. He cites no common law
cases, either to illustrate the pressure from lords for curtailing customary
constraints on their economic exploitation of estates, or to demonstrate
royal restraints on lords' control over tenures long acknowledged as appropriate to the jurisdiction of lords and their manorial courts. To be
sure, he notes the expansion of common law jurisdiction to copyhold,
but his reference is vague; and, on one of the few occasions when Tawney
explicitly refers to the content of proceedings in the common law courts,
his citations include no references to the records of either Common Pleas
or King's Bench.[4]

Tawney's neglect of evidence from the king's common law courts is
easy to understand. Given the wide-ranging scope of his book, the ac-
cessibility and nature of legal records from the sixteenth century at the
time he wrote, and the state of scholarship when Tawney tackled *The
Agrarian Problem*,[5] I would prefer not to criticise what he did not use,

3   Tawney, *Agrarian Problem*, p. 406.
4   Ibid., pp. 294–5.
5   What follows can only be a selection of the recent scholarship on lords and peasants
in late medieval England relevant to interpreting common law cases regarding copyhold
in the early Tudor period: Christopher Dyer, *An Age of Transition? Economy and Society
in England in the Later Middle Ages* (Oxford, 2005); E. B. Fryde, *Peasants and Landlords*

but to praise the clarity and elegance with which he integrated political and economic history into an admittedly provocative, but immensely illuminating study of a transformation embracing agrarian life and both 'national' and local political institutions. It was, after all, a transformation that arguably created the very categories of 'politics' and 'economics' which, accepted uncritically, may have obscured for less perceptive and less adventurous historians a deep connection between state formation and the development of agrarian capitalism in the sixteenth and seventeenth centuries.[6]

Engaging critically with the process by which the common law courts incorporated customary tenures within their ordinary jurisdiction, I suggest in this essay, may afford a clearer analysis of the connection between 'politics' and 'economics' that Tawney so vigorously tried, with only partial success, to demonstrate and explain. Records of the earliest pleas offered by copyholders, or by parties challenging claimants of copyhold in Common Pleas,[7] will not 'solve' an 'agrarian problem' which continues to provoke the curiosity and speculation of historians across a wide range of historical fields and approaches; but early Tudor cases that invoked title 'by copy of court roll at the will of the lord according to the custom of the manor' may enable us to understand more fully what was at stake for each of the parties – lords, their tenants, and the king and his justices – engaged in controversy over customary rights in late medieval and early modern England. These parties were re-negotiating the character of rights to land, but they were also re-thinking authority and power over people; and the re-negotiation, which was far from painless for those involved, extended to the administration of justice, and to new practices and new conceptions of justice itself.

<hr />

in Later Medieval England (New York, 1996); C. J. Harrison, 'Manor Courts and the Governance of Tudor England', in *Communities and Courts in Britain, 1150–1900*, ed. Christopher W. Brooks and Michael Lobban (London, 1997); H. R. French and R. W. Hoyle, *The Character of English Rural Society: Earls Colne, 1550–1750* (Manchester, 2007); J. A. Raftis, *Peasant Economic Development within the English Manorial System* (Stroud, 1997); Z. Razi and R. M. Smith, eds, *Medieval Society and the Manor Court* (Oxford,1996); Whittle, *Development of Agrarian Capitalism*; L. R. Poos and Lloyd Bonfield, *Select Cases in Manorial Courts 1250–1550: Property and Family Law* (Selden Society, 114, London, 1998).

6 On this point, see Brenner, 'Agrarian Class Structure' and R. W. Hoyle, 'Tenure and the Land Market in Early Modern England: Or a Late Contribution to the Brenner Debate,' *Economic History Review* 43:1 (1990), 1–20.

7 The much smaller number of cases in King's Bench that include pleadings on copyhold title (no more than twenty at most, either bills or writs of trespass, and two writs of error to Common Pleas) would not, I am reasonably certain, alter the argument here.

I

Thanks to John Baker's work both in editing the sources of legal history for the early Tudor legal period and in explaining them to readers not familiar with the procedural complexities of common law courts,[8] a pivotal moment in relations between common law and customary rights associated closely to tenure by copy of court roll is much less opaque today than when Tawney wrote. Much remains obscure about the circumstances, and certainly much is obscure about motives, which led English common law justices to accept responsibility for hearing disputes over copyhold titles, a responsibility they had refused, or denied themselves, for at least two centuries. Nonetheless the more than 200 entries (perhaps as many as 240)[9] in which tenure 'at the will of the lord according to the custom of manor' is mentioned explicitly between Henry VII's accession and his son's death in 1547, and the contrast between roughly eighteen of these cases appearing on the plea rolls of Henry VII's Common Pleas and the remaining 200-plus heard by Henry VIII's Common Pleas justices, argue that a major shift had occurred in judicial thought and practice in the first half-century of Tudor rule. As Baker emphasises,[10] the king's justices were not, at least in the first half of the sixteenth century, prepared to make a complete break from the traditional view that the lord's fee simple in a manor ruled out a direct challenge in the king's ordinary courts from tenants holding 'at his will'. The phrase 'according to the custom of the manor' in the description of their tenure made a lord's grant of copyhold a legitimate defence in proceedings against a copyholder in Common Pleas. Copyholders, from early in the sixteenth century, could plead copyhold against lords or others, but a copyholder was still denied the right to challenge at common law his lord's seizure of or re-entry on the holding, almost surely until after Henry VIII's reign.

Since Tawney attempted to puzzle out the 'agrarian problem', discussions of common law protection afforded customary tenures, and the decision to abandon a doctrine which had denied access to common law remedies by customary tenants, have focused on the copyholder and his security: when and how did copyhold tenants secure protection against

---

8   John Baker, *The Oxford History of the Laws of England, 6: 1483–1558* (Oxford, 2003), pp. 644–50; John Baker, ed., *Reports of Cases by John Caryll, 2: 1501–1522* (Selden Society, 114, London, 2000), hereafter cited as 2 *Caryll*; John Baker, ed., 'Cases from the Notebook of William Yelverton (1526–1550)', in *Reports of Cases from the Time of King Henry VIII, 2* (Selden Society, 121, London, 2004), hereafter cited as *Yelverton's Cases*.

9   The higher number would include all cases in which copyhold figures, including the roughly forty entries alleging debts, broken covenants, or actions of *assumpsit* arising from sales or promises to convey title to copyhold.

10   Baker, *Oxford History of the Laws of England*, p. 648.

eviction by their lords? Implicit in this question was another, perhaps more fundamental question: when and how did lords lose or surrender their right and obligation to do justice to their copyhold tenants? Modern attention to customary tenures, focused on a copyholder's security and the lord's ability to oust that copyholder, is consistent with the terms in which early Tudor reporters described debates over pleas by copyholders impugning the lord's freedom to dispose of copyhold at his pleasure.

In John Caryll's report of *Tropnell v. Kyllyk*,[11] a 1505 case (reported with a similar case of the following year), the chief justice 'thought that the prescription was good enough to bind the lord so that he could not oust his customary tenants'. Despite an argument from a lawyer for the plaintiffs – who were in both of these cases lords of manors – that copyholders lacked 'the thing which would enable them to prescribe [against the lord himself], namely the interest of the lord in the seignory',[12] all of the justices are reported as sympathetic to the position announced by the chief justice. To judge from the exchanges reported by Caryll, copyholders were presented as claimants to a new entitlement, challenging long-established characteristics of lordship, and threatening freehold estates. The affirmative response of the chief justice and his fellow justices in 1505 suggests that the assertion of customary title, even against the copyholder's lord, no longer appeared absurd; but hesitation to entertain pleas of customary tenure, indeed, the apparent need to argue for accepting such pleas, can and has been interpreted as favourable to lords, and a continuing handicap for copyholders in search of security against arbitrary ousting by their lord.

This interpretation is by no means ungrounded, but there may be some value in re-focusing the inquiry into common law jurisdiction over copyhold to ask whether it was indeed copyholders whose interests in security most fully explain why Common Pleas, from the last years of the fifteenth century, increasingly heard disputes in which copyhold title figured explicitly. Whatever the importance of judicial attention to the nature of the copyholder's estate and his entitlement to plead manorial custom in proceedings at common law, the cases which prompted the debate over copyhold title were initiated, not by copyholders pursuing a remedy against greedy landlords, but by landlords themselves. Anne Tropnell's lordship, to judge from her recourse to common law, was ineffective on its own to enforce her will against Kyllyk, who claimed to occupy the disputed tenement where the alleged trespass occurred by a demise of customary tenure by an earlier lord of the manor. The king's common law justices debated the legitimacy of copyhold title as a bar to her action; but by pursuing

---

11   2 *Caryll*, pp. 489–94; CP 40/974, m. 445 (1505).
12   2 *Caryll*, p. 490.

trespass before justices at Westminster, Tropnell had in effect conceded that she would not, or could not, oust Kyllyk on her own authority and by her own power as lord. Even if she or her lawyer counted on blocking the defendant's possible invocation of copyhold title to bar her action, she had nonetheless turned to the common law in the exercise of her manorial lordship.

Tropnell's lawyer demurred to the defendants' plea of a customary title for their occupation of the land in debate; despite the reported consensus in the defendant's favour among the king's justices, he likely succeeded in blocking the case. No judgement is recorded, and the aftermath of her suit is not known. Tropnell's common law initiative against a copyholder was not, however, an exceptional event in the first decade of the sixteenth century. When William Syll, lord of Cheverston (Devonshire), sued three of his tenants in 1505, he encountered a defence based on his demise to them, by 'copy of court roll according to the custom of the manor at the will of the lord', of a fee simple in the disputed pasture; he denied that such demises were customary in the manor, and on this issue, the parties agreed to accept a jury's verdict.[13] And in the term immediately preceding *Tropnell v. Kyllyk*, the Prioress of Ambresbury complained that Thomas Bryne, a husbandman, had downed trees belonging to her. Bryne countered that the prioress, as lord of Wigley manor (Hampshire), as well as her predecessors, had been accustomed to demise the property in question to tenants by copy of court roll, to hold of the lord at will according to custom, and that her steward had, also by long custom, authorised the cutting of trees for repair of buildings on the property.[14]

One further case in the term following Tropnell deserves notice, as further evidence that lords around 1505 were exploring the advantages of common law litigation in defence of their own stake in manorial custom – and in doing justice to their manorial tenants. Sir John Arundel brought an action of trespass against John Squire, a Devonshire husbandman, alleging that Squire had pastured his animals on Arundel's land. Squire denied that he had committed a trespass, since the land where the trespass allegedly occurred was a customary tenement of the manor of Stokeley Lucomb, of which John Arundel was the lord. This entitled the tenant 'for life or years at the lord's will according to the custom of the manor' to enjoy uninterrupted occupancy so long as accustomed rents and services were paid and performed and so long as they did nothing contrary to the custom of the manor. Arundel conceded in his response that the defendant indeed held in reversion to his father, to whom Arundel had made the original grant of the customary tenement. But he then invoked on his own behalf the custom

13   *Syll et al. v. Aylmer et al.*, CP 40/972, m. 329d (1505).
14   *Prioress of Ambresbury v. Bryne*, CP 40/973, m. 550 (1506).

of the manor to insist that the particular custom in this instance entitled the manor's lord to seize any customary holding should the tenant make his primary habitation elsewhere, especially should that tenant refuse to obey the lord's (or his steward's) explicit command to occupy the holding in person. Arundel explained that Squire's refusal to reside on the holding, despite admonitions to do so, forced him as lord to take the tenement back into his own hands. The issue for Arundel was not whether the defendant had title by custom of the manor, but whether the lord could exercise a customary right to enforce the residency of a copyhold tenant. Arundel's plea, invoking his manor's court rolls, indicates that when the authority of his manor court failed to support his goals, he found another route to success through the king's Court of Common Pleas. He had, that is, placed in the determination of a common law jury his right to re-occupy a holding granted at his will, but also by the custom of the manor.[15]

II

Throughout the remainder of Henry VII's reign and that of his son, lords of manors would continue to initiate proceedings in the king's common law courts against persons who, in defending the conduct complained about by these lords, relied on grants by those same lords or their stewards. Or to describe this stream of suits in the Common Bench a little differently, from 1506 to the end of Henry VIII's reign, few years passed in which we do not find at least one example of a defendant in trespass pleading that the site of the alleged trespass belonged to the customary lands ordinarily granted as copyhold by the lord of the manor, and that the act described by the plaintiff as a trespass was simply an exercise of the defendant's copyhold title. In a majority of these cases, the plaintiffs who initiated them were the lords to whom defendants attributed the concession by which they justified the alleged trespass, a concession of copyhold usually made on behalf of the lord by a manor's steward.[16] Plaintiffs in

---

15 *Arundel v. Squire*, CP 40/975, m. 355 (1506).

16 *Prior of Nostell v. Wrayth*, CP 40/978, m. 416 (1506); *Prior of Avecote v. Gardener et al.*, CP 40/1002, m. 526 (1514); *Abbess of Syon v. Moigne*, CP 40/1007, m. 331 (1514); *Rector of Ashridge v. Hawkins*, CP 40/1022, m. 632 (1518); *Prior of Hospital of St John of Jerusalem v. Swale*, CP 40/1022, m. 419 (1518); *Seyntmer v. Westborne & wife*, CP 40/1029, m. 402 (1520); *Drury v. Doke et al.*, CP 40/1040, m. 611 (1523); *Abbot of Bruton v. Grace*, CP 40/1041 (1523); *Nashe v. Yong*, CP 40/1046, m. 447 (1525); *Kervyle v. Gansell*, CP 40/1046, m. 429 (1525); *Tyrell v. Kyng et al.*, CP 40/1046, m. 407d (1525); *Frost v. Dyuker*, CP 40/1052, m. 720 (1526); *Master of Holy Cross College, Attleborough qui tam rex v. Aleyn et al.*, CP 40/1056, m. 319 (1527); *Abbot of Ramsey v. Skecher et al.*, CP 40/1067. m. 94 (1530); *Dean & Chapter of Wells Cathedral v. Somer*, CP 40/1070, m. 354 (1531); *Levett v. Kynatt*, CP 40/1091, m. 514 (1536); *Forster v. Maiden*, CP 40/1099, m. 607 (1538);

these cases – usually lords of the manors to which the copyholds belonged, according to defendants – responded to defendants' copyhold titles either by denying that the land in question belonged to the manor, or by insisting that no grant of copyhold had been made by them or, in a handful of cases, denying that the lands in question were customary or parcel of the manor. But even if the plaintiffs denied that copyhold or customary tenure was at stake, they surely did not initiate actions in Common Pleas without an awareness that their suits would open to common law determination copyhold titles pleaded by defendants. Plaintiffs, that is, even if planning to deny the customary nature of a defendant's tenures, submitted their claims of freehold – in most cases, equivalent to claims of manorial lordship – to common law determination.

But as *Arundell v. Squire* in 1506 illustrates, lords of manors might well have good reason to acknowledge customary tenures, at least in those cases in which manorial custom favoured the lord's claims on contested holdings. The numbers of cases over the half-century after *Arundell v. Squire* is not overwhelming, but neither is it trivial: at least nine lords of manors sued trespass against defendants whom they acknowledged as their customary tenants – but as tenants who had, through violations of manorial custom, forfeited their copyholds, or who invoked customs rejected or denied by their lords.[17] Custom, this small but steady stream of cases demonstrates, could work for lords in common law litigation with their tenants, even as copyholders found themselves newly entitled to invoke manorial custom to challenge what otherwise might have been an exercise of seigniorial will. From the end of the fifteenth century, copyholders also brought actions against freeholders and other copyholders, taking for granted that they were entitled to bring trespass on the basis of their customary tenures. And even if uncertainty remained for several decades after 1505 over copyholders' entitlement to sue directly lords whom they accused of unjustly ousting them from their customary holdings, a least a small handful of

---

Coffyn v. More & husband, CP 40/1121, m. 550 (1544); *Wade, Rector of Northlewe, v. Bowder et al.*, CP 40/1121, m. 518 (1544); *Wolacomb v. Jule*, CP 40/1125, m. 570 (1545).

17   *Abbot of Pershore v. Celles et al.*, CP 40/1037, m. 412 (1522); *Long v. Long & wife*, CP 40/1045, m. 411 (1524), the plaintiff alleging forfeiture by the copyhold tenant for the wife's remarriage contrary to custom of the manor; *Blyaunte v. Bacon*, CP 40/1052 (1526), plaintiff alleging forfeiture by copyhold tenant for demise without lord's license; *Saintlowe v. Mogridge et al.*, CP 40/1065, m. 413 (1530), plaintiff alleging forfeiture as a result of waste committed by the copyholder; *Bedyll v. Avery & wife*, CP 40/1067, m. 760 (1530), plaintiff alleging forfeiture of copyhold for waste by copyholders; *Unton v. Mawre*, CP 40/1069, m. 541 (1531), plaintiff alleging that best beast belonged to lord on tenant's death; *Danvers v. Henne*, CP 40/1071, m. 796 (1531), plaintiff alleging failure to reside on copyhold resulted in its forfeiture; *Dean & Chapter of Exeter v. Tree*, CP 40/1114, m. 602 (1542), plaintiff alleging failure to occupy copyhold resulted in its forfeiture; *Colyer v. Hothley*, CP 40/1121, m. 691 (1544), plaintiff alleging forfeiture by copyholder, for waste.

customary tenants initiated litigation on behalf of their copyholds by suing manorial officials.

An early example occurred in 1506 when a plaintiff, contending that he
held land conveyed by the Bishop of Norwich as copyhold and therefore enjoyed protection against expulsion so long as he paid his rent and rendered
customary services, sued agents of the bishop for entering to seize grain
on 'his' land; the bishops' servants responded that they entered to seize the
grain sown after the bishop had discharged the plaintiff from occupation
of the holding, granted to him only at will.[18] In this case, the defendants
demurred to the plaintiff's plea of copyhold, which included not only an
assertion of customary tenure but an elaborate description of constraints
on the lord's collection of rents in arrears. John Baker speculates that this
demurrer may signify continuing uncertainty in the first decade of the century about how far 'custom' in customary titles qualified a lord's 'will'.[19]
Given the proximity of this case to discussion among justices prompted by
Tropnell v. Kyllyk, the demurrer is not surprising, although contrary to the
consensus among justices that copyholders could rely on custom to defend
their holdings against the freehold of their lords. Not until the 1520s do
plaintiffs dependent on copyhold tenure once again challenge encroachment on their holdings by seigniorial agents – but in these later suits, the
lords' men did not invariably resort to demurrers.[20] Issue in several pleadings was joined on whether a holding had been demised as copyhold, or if
demised as copyhold, to whom, or on what conditions.[21]

In the two decades after justices and lawyers in *Tropnell v. Kyllyk* argued
at length whether copyholders should be permitted to sue their own lords
for unjustly ousting them, these justices and lawyers acquired increasing
familiarity with actions and pleas in which customary title to holdings
was the central matter for adjudication, a matter previously determined
exclusively in manorial courts – or simply decided by lords of manors and

---

18   *Bastard v. Johnson et al.* (servants of Bishop of Norwich, lord of Gaywood manor),
CP 40/978, m. 599 (1506).

19   Baker, *Oxford History of the Laws of England*, p. 648. A demurrer is the defendant's
denial that a basis in law exists for the claim or charge made against him, even if the facts
alleged by the plaintiff are accurate.

20   The plaintiff in each of the cases following was a copyholder: *Grace v. Gryffyn* CP
40/1041, m. 502d (1523), but see also *Abbot of Bruton v. Grace*, CP 40/1041, m. 502 (1523);
Dynghurst v. Barlowe at al., CP 40/1044, m. 457 (1523); *Howe v. Eme*, CP 40/1044, m. 316
(1524); *Rogers v. Beknold*, CP40/1045, m. 602 (1524); *Chapel v. Nichols & Whytyngton*),
CP 40/1047, m. 306 (1525); *Gatacre v. Dean and chapter of Lichfield*, CP 40/ 1049, m. 631
(1526); *Chylly v. Hyllys et al.*, CP 40/1062, m. 414 (1529); *Berkeley v. Woode et al.*, CP
40/1069, m. 552 (1531); *Marten v. May*, CP 40/1111, m. 530 (1541); *Alegh v. Shergold et al.*,
CP 40/1113, m. 417 (1542); *Breche v. Taylor*, CP 40/1115, m. 444 (1542); *Howster v. Belsen*,
CP 40/1125, m. 449 (1545); *Morefewe v. Blomefeld et al.*, CP 40/1130, m. 718 (1546).

21   See for instance: *Alygh v. Shergold*, CP 40/1113, m. 417 (1542); *Alygh v. Shergold*, CP
40/1117, m. 583 (1543); *Mills et al v. Wild*, C 1/1181/30.

their counsellors. Cases in which copyhold title figured centrally were, not surprisingly, initiated in some cases by copyholders; and copyholders who sued their lords' officers and agents for seizures of or intrusions into customary holdings hint at a strong and perhaps growing pressure to extend to copyholders security against arbitrary ouster by lords, the security supported by justices in the debates over *Tropnell v. Kyllyk* in 1505, but still more an ideal than practice in the 1520s. Less expected, given Tawney's concern and that of other historians with the insecurity of copyholders and the presumed readiness of their lords to take advantage of such insecurity, are the cases initiated by lords themselves who, in turning to common law to assert claims over holdings their tenants defended by copyhold titles, simultaneously reinforced and compromised their jurisdiction over copyhold tenants whose titles depended on the very manorial courts that underpinned lords' authority over property held 'at will of the lord according to the custom of the manor'.

A small handful of cases during Henry VIII's reign, moreover, illustrate yet another source of interest among the king's justices of Common Pleas both in copyhold titles but also, and perhaps more significantly, in the manorial courts where those copyhold titles were accustomed to determination. These actions, pursued at common law but intended to rectify abuses or defects within manorial courts in which custom, not common law, should prevail, included alleged maintenance in manor courts;[22] a false presentment by jurors in Queen Katherine's manor of Dedham Hall;[23] trespass on the case against a manorial understeward for refusing to enrol a plea in the manor court of Langley Abbots;[24] trespass on the case for fabricating a fraudulent copy to support an unjust claim to a customary holding in the manor of Tittenhanger and Park;[25] false judgement in pleadings over title to two customary holdings in the court of Morehall and Chilternhall, Gnosall, Staffordshire;[26] and a *recordare* (used to transfer the record of proceedings in a manorial or other local court to trial before royal justices) in an action of dower sued in the Abbot of Halesowen's manorial court of Harborne and Smethwick.[27] The appearance of these actions on the plea

---

22   *Rolle v. Stalworthman et al.*, CP 40/1022, m. 573d (1518) and 1024, m. 516 (1519), regarding a manor court of the Prioress of Ickleton; *Roos et Rex v. Hurleston et al.*, CP 40/1042, m. 446 (1524), regarding a manor court of the Abbot of St Albans.

23   *May v. Cransen et al.*, CP 40/1024, m. 426 (1519), regarding Queen Katherine's manor of Dedham Hall.

24   *Ewer v. Elys*, CP 40/1029, m. 659 (1520); 1031, m. 60d (1521); 1032A, m. 407d (1521); 1033, m. 304 (1521); the manor court belonged to the Abbot of St Albans.

25   *Purs v. Kylby*, CP 40/1067, m. 1 (1530).

26   *Wolriche v. Robyns*, CP 40/1113, m. 352 (1542). For litigation between these same parties in Chancery, see C 1/1083/36–37.

27   *Pryste v. Hoggetts*, CP 40/1052, m. 543 (1526); and see also two chancery cases on administration of justice to copyholders within Harborne and Smethwick, C 1/581/159–63

rolls of Common Pleas confirms a willingness by common law justices to afford remedies to litigants complaining of injustices within manorial courts, while illustrating a readiness on the part of those same common law justices to affirm and on occasion reinforce the jurisdiction exercised by manorial lords over copyhold tenants.

III

By the 1520s, justices and lawyers in common law courts, as well as lords and their copyhold tenants, were increasingly willing to regard the common law courts as a useful venue in which to resolve disputes over copyhold titles. But we find also in the records of such common law proceedings that copyholders were not yet able to challenge their own lords directly. A few years after a copyholder's suit against the Dean and Chapter of Lichfield once again demonstrated refusal to admit customary tenants to a common law remedy against lords who ousted them, and roughly a quarter-century after *Tropnell v. Kyllyk*, contrasting interpretations of the estate conferred by a grant 'at the will of the lord according to the custom' were once again reported, and once again, despite a more extensive or more fully recorded debate, this time among newly admitted serjeants at law, no definitive answer emerged to the question 'May the lord oust his tenant by copy of court roll?'[28] Between *Tropnell v. Kyllyk* and the *Serjeants' Case* in 1531, pleading copyhold, whether against other copyholders, claimants to freehold, or lords' officers, had become established practice in Common Pleas. But changes in practice had not yet overwhelmed a reluctance among justices and lawyers to imagine lordship divorced from a lord's full discretion when dealing with his customary tenants. From the case which generated the debate among serjeants in 1531, and from a glimpse into this exercise of lordship afforded by subsequent pleadings in Chancery, a possible explanation emerges not only for change in judicial responses to pleas of copyhold, but also for the continuing uncertainty over copyhold and the status of copyholders before common law justices despite greater receptivity to pleas of copyhold title.

Newly admitted serjeants were given a 'hard' case to debate, and the action of replevin between Thomas Cheynell and William Parson, to judge from the report in Yelverton's Notebook, offered a wide range of substantive and formal problems for analysis and judgment by lawyers. Cheynell

---

and 897/11.
28 *Gatacre v. Dean and Chapter of Lichfield*, CP 40/1048A, m. 617d, and 1049, m. 631 (1525 and 1526); *Yelverton's Cases*, pp. 294–309; for the original pleadings: *Cheynell v. Parson*, CP 40/1067, m. 547 (1531).

initiated his action with a demand that William Parson explain why he took a bullock and two cows at Aldbury (Surrey). Parson's defence or avowry was that he took the animals into custody when he found them doing damage in his tenement, a tenement which he held, at the will of the lord according to the custom of the manor, by virtue of a concession to him and his heirs by Edmund, Lord Bray, following a surrender into the lord's hands by William at Mere, who, Parson declared, had earlier received the grant to him and his heirs from Bray as lord of the manor. The plaintiff Cheynell admitted that the land was indeed held of Lord Bray's manor, and at Lord Bray's will, according to custom; indeed, a major piece of his argument would be Bray's lordship. Cheynell's narrative of events further coincided with the defendant's in describing the concession by Bray on 27 March, 13 Henry VII, on which Parson relied, but with one major variation: the concession was to both William at Mere and his wife Joanne. This variation became significant in light of the next episode recounted by both plaintiff and defendant: William at Mere surrendered the holding to Bray, to the use of Parson and his heirs. If, as Cheynell claimed, Bray had demised the holding to both William at Mere and his wife, then a surrender by William at Mere alone to Parson's benefit left open challenge from Joanne, William at Mere's wife. Cheynell's narrative in support of his action argues strongly that Joanne disregarded, or regarded as null, the surrender by her husband, entering on the holding despite the lord's concession to Parson and precipitating suits and discords within the manor which forced Lord Bray to intervene. Presumably while awaiting the outcome of those suits in his manorial court, Bray turned the land in question over to Cheynell, on a one-year lease renewable from year to year which, Cheynell pleaded, he had occupied and used peacefully until Parson seized livestock from the holding. Parson demurred to Cheynell's plea, and the Common Plea entry ends without a judgement, much as the *Serjeants' Case* ends with congratulations to the participants, but no definitive conclusion regarding a lord's freedom to oust customary tenants.

The pleadings summarised above gave the serjeants several matters to debate, including the possible 'doubleness' of the plaintiff's bar to the defendant's avowry: could he present an argument which put in issue not only the nature of the surrender by William at Mere, but also the seizure of the land in question by the lord? To judge from the space allocated to this and other points of pleadings, the serjeants found them no less interesting than the substantive question, whether a lord could oust a tenant holding at his will, but according to custom. Still, Roger Yorke, the puisne serjeant whose opinion is the first recorded, identified the question 'may the lord expel his copyholder' as the 'principal matter' in this case. Custom, he insisted, bound the lord, and the tenant on such terms should 'have the land provided he observes the custom'.[29] On the other side of the debate, emphasis fell on the first part of the phrase *ad voluntatem domini secundum constuedinem manerij* ('at the will of the lord according to the custom of the manor'). Serjeant Knightley, for example, pointed to 'express mention in the copies themselves that the tenant shall have it *ad voluntatem domini*' to support his position that lords could not dispossess their copyholders.[30] Parsing the seemingly contradictory conditions on which a lord granted and the copyholder accepted land by copy of court roll, most of the participants appear to have seen the principal matter as a choice: either a concession which could be revoked at the lord's will, or a grant secured by manorial custom restricting the lord's discretion. Those placing emphasis on the lord's will also denied the possibility of two fee simple estates in the same land, whereas advocates for custom that bound the lord as well as the tenant saw no obstacle to acknowledging freehold in both lord and copyholder, a freehold in each case worthy of protection at common law.

Almost obscured by the attention given a choice between will and custom on the one hand, the contradictory nature of fee simples in both lord and copyholder on the other, brief allusions to the politics of justice at the level of manorial administration introduce further complexity to the serjeants' debate. Two participants referred, briefly, to the lord's administration of justice. Hynde agreed with those arguing that the lord may oust his tenant, 'for he is but tenant at his will', and elaborated the point by noting that the copyholder shall have no remedy to recover land from which he had been ousted, 'for if the lord will not keep his court, or accept a surrender, the tenants shall have no remedy'.[31] On the other side of the debate, Baldwin conceded that 'the lord may choose whether he will keep his court or not', but continued by insisting that such conduct 'does not take away the tenant's inheritance. For if the king will not keep any of his courts that does not take away the common law; but by common right and justice he is bound to keep them, and so is the lord.'[32]

In the longest of the commentaries included in the report, senior serjeant Thomas Audley hinted at a way out of the seeming impasse between will and custom, explicitly referring to the lord's responsibility for administering justice:

Also when he [a copyholder] surrenders to the lord to the use of someone else, the lord may not withhold it, for he is only an instrument to cause it

29 *Yelverton's Cases*, p. 298.
30 Ibid., p. 299.
31 Ibid., p. 303.
32 Ibid., p. 304.

to pass, and if he withholds it I shall have an action upon the case against him, notwithstanding that he is a lord who has the administration of justice; for the king, who is the head of justice, will punish him and see that redress is provided in this matter.[33]

Audley, no less than his fellow serjeants, addressed the vexing dilemma faced by common lawyers: if the lord held the freehold in the manor, how could tenants who claimed their estates as parcel of the manor also enjoy the security of freeholders, should the lord exercise his own freehold? But by recognising that a lord was not simply or even primarily a landlord, and that his 'property' in a manor included administration of justice, Audley, intentionally or not, brought the legal debate a little closer to the complex struggle taking place in Bray's manor of Aldbury, and probably in many other manors throughout England.

Cheynell had turned to Common Pleas because Lord Bray, his court, and his officers in Aldbury had failed to secure peaceful occupation of the land held by lease renewable yearly. From the plaintiff's perspective in this particular copyhold case, the 'problem', if not the legal issue, was the effectiveness of manorial administration. To succeed in his action before Common Pleas justices, Cheynell's attorney had to convince those justices to uphold a lord's freedom and ability to intervene in a dispute between rival claimants to the copyhold, and to dispose of the contested property at his discretion while he and the parties sorted out the various claims. His action, that is, sought a remedy from Common Pleas, a remedy for Lord Bray's inability to administer justice within the manor of Aldbury. The *Serjeants' Case* includes strong arguments for extending the jurisdiction of the king's justices to contests over copyhold titles, an extension that would appear to challenge a lord's jurisdiction over the customary tenants of his manor. The record of the proceedings that generated these arguments, however, leaves little doubt that the pressure in this case for extension of royal jurisdiction came not from the claimant to copyhold title, but from the lord and his leaseholder.

Whatever their precise motives or interests, parties to the *Serjeants' Case* found no resolution in Common Pleas and each pursued their interests in other judicial venues. The plaintiff at common law, Cheynell, found himself defendant in the manor court of Aldbury, sued by heirs of Joanne at Mere (Thomas Parson's rivals for title to the customary holding). It is very likely the suit was collusive, since immediately upon a verdict in favour of the plaintiffs by a manorial jury, Cheynell purchased their interest and was admitted to it by Lord Bray. And we know about these proceedings in the manorial court, and the subsequent purchase by Cheynell, confirmed by

33   Ibid., p. 309.

grant of the lord, from Parson's petition against Lord Bray and Cheynell in Chancery.[34]

Who ultimately triumphed is not known, but the dispute in Aldbury illustrates well the risks of over-simplifying relations between lords and their customary tenants. Lord Bray may have been the villain from Parson's perspective; but records from the several courts in which his actions towards his tenants were scrutinised argue for a more generous interpretation, one that takes seriously Serjeant Audley's conviction that lords were entitled and obligated to do justice within their manors. That Bray, and other lords of customary tenants, may have vigorously exercised responsibility for doing justice does not mean, however, that they were indifferent to their self-interests; nor does it mean that their interests did not often differ from the interests of their customary tenants. Another petition to Chancery, this one by Bray himself, reveals a lord entirely ready to avail himself of royal authority to frustrate what he described as an attempt by customary tenants to free themselves of copyhold status, in order to enjoy the advantages of freehold within his manor of Dunstaple Houghton.[35] The frequency with which lords or their agents initiated actions in Common Pleas against copyhold tenants who had, their lords alleged, violated manorial custom, is itself an argument that they saw no inevitable conflict between such custom and their self-interest. To construe Bray's intervention in controversy among his tenants in Aldbury as an exercise of lordship does not require that we attribute to him altruistic or disinterested motives, either in that conflict or in others on his estates, but it does encourage caution in interpreting this and similar struggles over copyhold as evidence for lords' aggressive greed.

Whatever the potential advantages to copyholders of common law recognition of their titles, the lords who granted their lands to be held by custom may have feared the implicit concession of jurisdiction to the king's courts less than they welcomed the support those courts might afford when their manorial courts proved ineffective. When, for example, in the manorial court of Hindringham held on behalf of Martin Hastings, farmer to the Dean and Chapter of Norwich Cathedral in 1539, jurors refused to deliver a verdict against William Clerk for cutting down and selling oaks on his holding without the lord's license, fines were levied against each of the jurors so refusing. The manor's court rolls do not tell us whether Hastings or his officers collected the fines.[36] But the action of

34 The Chancery proceedings are found in C 1/867/8–11, *Parson v. Lord Bray and Thomas Cheynell.*

35 C 1/728/20–22, *Edmund Braye, Lord Braye, v. Thomas, son and heir of Richard Barbour.*

36 BL, Additional Roll 19084, m. 1, Court in Lent, 1539, of Hindringham Manor, Norfolk.

trespass begun by Hastings in Common Pleas a few years later,[37] against three individuals for pasturing their livestock and cutting trees on his land, argues that he stood to gain more by suing at Westminster than by holding court in Hindringham. The three defendants pleaded customary tenure that included a tenant's entitlement to the trees on his holding; Hastings, whose recourse to Common Pleas originated in his conviction that the lord, or the lord's farmer, was entitled to the timber on customary lands, joined issue over existence of the particular custom invoked by the defendants. What was decided in this case is not known, but we do know what the defendants and very likely other customary tenants of the manor thought of Hastings's resort to Common Pleas. In a petition to the chancellor, they complained vigorously that Hastings' suits at common law were intended to wear down their defence of customary rights.[38]

IV

Within the framework of the manor, clear distinctions between a lord's interests and the interests of his copyholders could often prove elusive. Is it possible to decide now, in disputes of this sort, who benefited most from access to common law remedies, and whose interests were best served by proceedings within the lord's manorial court? The manor court, however imperfectly it worked in practice, constituted a site and a process for integrating self-interest with justice, offering lords and their tenants a means to preserve their respective interests, hardly equal, but equally essential to production and social stability in manorial economies and manorial polities. Historians today may be tempted to separate a lord's interests as landlord from his role as a governor responsible for maintaining social order and assuring justice for all of his 'subjects' or tenants, as Tawney was surely tempted; but confrontations between lords and their tenants before the early Tudor Common Bench make no clear distinctions between a lord's self-interested assault on copyholders and his enforcement of custom to the advantage of all members of the manorial community.

   Certainty about the motives of individuals engaged in litigation over copyhold, whether in common law courts, Chancery, or prerogative courts of the king, is a goal likely to elude us today, as it eluded Tawney, whatever his admirable intention to fit those individuals into a bigger picture of a transition from 'feudal' lords and their customary subjects to 'modern'

---

37   *Hastings v. Mason*, CP40/1124, m. 417 (1545).
38   C 1/1145/30, *William Mason and others v. Martin Hastynges, esq.* For an earlier complaint by the same tenants, with Hastings' answer, see C 1/1029/17–18. For a similar dispute in Sussex see *John Abroke v. Robert Holbeme et al.*, CP 40/1083, m. 614 (1534); *Robert Holbeme v. Bishop of Chichester & John Abroke*, C 1/811/8.

landlords, farmers and farmers' landless employees. The cases examined here can help map the early route by which common law justices accepted jurisdiction over copyhold title; they do not explain why such acceptance occurred, nor can they fully explain why litigants pressed common law justices to hear cases long regarded as appropriate for manorial courts. They can, however, in conjunction with continued investigation of those manorial courts at the onset of agrarian capitalism, give us insight into how lords of manors, their copyholders, and the king's justices and serjeants were re-imagining their world, and re-framing the categories with which they interpreted both self-interest and justice in their dealings with each other.

Tawney may have been readier than are we today to assign greed a prominent role in the gradual erosion of both customary tenure and the communal character of agricultural production he associated with copyhold and common lands; but he grasped the integral nature of property and justice, economics and politics, 'private' interest and 'public' welfare in late medieval and early modern England. More importantly, Tawney understood well the importance of a moment in which the English were deconstructing a world in which lords oversaw administration of justice in their own courts, to construct a world in which landlords left matters of justice to the king's (or the nation's) courts, confident that such courts would more effectively protect their economic power than the 'private' jurisdiction of manor courts.

3

Negotiating Enclosure in Sixteenth-Century Yorkshire

The South Cave Dispute, 1530–1536[1]

BRIONY MCDONAGH

Writing a hundred years ago, R. H. Tawney recognised the complexity of the term 'enclosure'. In the first few pages of *The Agrarian Problem* he asks, 'what exactly did enclosing mean?' and the book goes on to draw attention to the wide range of agricultural changes conventionally labelled as enclosure.[2] His most significant contribution in this vein was probably to document the efforts of the peasantry to enclose land, but the book also discusses a huge variety of modifications to existing agricultural practice.[3] Thus he makes reference to piecemeal enclosure and the exchange of open-field strips to create consolidated holdings, to the enclosure and reallocation of fields and meadows 'by agreement', to encroachment on commons and meadows, to the enclosure and improvement of wastes and pastures, and to depopulating enclosures and engrossment.[4] More than fifty years later, in her classic chapter on the subject, Joan Thirsk echoed a great deal of what Tawney had said. For her, enclosure was 'a very loose general term' which meant different things in different places. While primarily focusing on the enclosure of Midland arable and its conversion to pasture, Thirsk nevertheless highlighted the varying regional experiences of enclosure with a clarity Tawney had not.[5] Later scholars have added much to our knowledge of these different types of enclosure and their regional histories, but the quotation remains a valuable reminder that the

---

1 This chapter builds on a more general discussion of the Star Chamber papers for the Yorkshire Wolds which includes a summary of the South Cave dispute published in B. McDonagh, 'Subverting the Ground: Private Property and Public Protest in the Sixteenth-Century Yorkshire Wolds', *Agricultural History Review* 57:2 (2009), 191–206.

2 Tawney, *Agrarian Problem* (1912 edn)p. .

3 Ibid., pp. 147–73.

4 Ibid.

5 Joan Thirsk, 'Enclosing and Engrossing', in *Agrarian History*, 4, pp. 200–55, quotation from p. 200.

term enclosure is shorthand for a wide variety of agricultural changes which differed in their form, purpose and impact.[6]

Tawney's choice of words is also interesting. In asking what enclosing – as opposed to enclosure – means, he draws attention to enclosure as a process rather than an outcome. This helps us move away from thinking about enclosure as the inevitable result of new ideas about space, property and the individual, and instead encourages a recognition of enclosure as a contested practice. In so doing, it also prompts important questions about what the enclosure of common fields, wastes and meadows meant to people at the time. While Tawney did not see it in these terms, this chimes well with the recent emphasis in social history on the negotiations, mediations and everyday politics taking place within local communities.[7] Also important are ideas currently circulating within cultural geography and archaeology which argue that the landscape is never finished, but instead constantly unfolding. While themselves influenced by distinct philosophical perspectives, Barbara Bender, Tim Ingold and Chris Tilley have all been influential in encouraging archaeologists to explore the ways that places and landscapes are brought into being through people's everyday encounter with the world.[8] Thinking about landscapes which are – in Barbara Bender's words – 'always in the making' focuses attention on the role ordinary people played in shaping the world around them, as well as drawing attention to the multiple and continually shifting practices of

6   See, for example, J. A. Yelling, *Common Field and Enclosure in England, 1450–1850* (London, 1977); Thirsk, *England's Agricultural Regions*. For more on the regional histories of enclosure, see C. Thomas, 'Enclosure and the Rural Landscape of Merioneth in the Sixteenth Century', *Transactions of the Institute of British Geographers* 42 (1967), 153–62; M. Reed, 'Enclosure in North Buckinghamshire, 1500–1750', *Agricultural History Review* 32:2 (1984), 133–44; J. E. Martin, 'Sheep and Enclosure in Sixteenth-Century Northamptonshire', *Agricultural History Review* 36:1 (1988), 39–54; K. B. Stride, 'Engrossing in Sheep-Corn-Chalk Areas: Evidence in Norfolk 1501–1633', *Norfolk Archaeology* 40:3 (1989), 308–18; D. Hayter, 'Pastures and Profits: Sheep and Enclosure in Sixteenth-Century Kings Sutton and Chipping Warden Hundreds', *Cake and Cockhorse* 15 (2003), 255–74 and 304–11.

7   Keith Wrightson, 'The Politics of the Parish in Early Modern England', in *The Experience of Authority in Early Modern England*, ed. Paul Griffiths, Adam Fox and Steve Hindle (Basingstoke, 1996), pp. 10–46; Michael J. Braddick and John Walter, eds, *Negotiating Power in Early Modern Society: Order, Hierarchy and Subordination in Britain and Ireland* (Cambridge, 2001); Wood, *Riot, Rebellion and Popular Politics*.

8   B. Bender, 'Introduction: Landscape – Meaning and Action', in *Landscape: Politics and Perspectives*, ed. B. Bender (Oxford, 1993), pp. 1–17; J. Thomas, 'The Politics of Vision and the Archaeologies of the Landscape', in *Landscape: Politics and Perspectives*, ed. Bender, pp. 19–48; T. Ingold, 'The Temporality of the Landscape', *World Archaeology* 25:2 (1993), 152–74; C. Tilley, *A Phenomenology of Landscape: Places, Paths and Monuments* (Oxford 1994); A. M. Chadwick, ed., *Stories from the Landscape: Archaeologies of Inhabitation* (Oxford, 2004).

power which underpinned early modern society, an idea which borrows from Foucault as much as from Ingold.[9]

All these ideas influence the approach taken here to enclosure and in particular enclosure protest, the chapter's central theme. Tawney wrote in some detail about contemporary commentaries on enclosure and depopulation, weighing them up against the statistical evidence of evictions drawn from the Inquisitions of Depopulation.[10] At the same time, he actually said relatively little about enclosure protest. For him, enclosure protest was aimed squarely at manorial lords and large graziers. Encroachment, piecemeal enclosures and enclosure by consent did not run into opposition: instead, rioting was prompted only by the activities of large landowners.[11] In much the same way as the pamphlet literature of the period laid the evils of enclosure, engrossing and conversion to pasture at the door of large farmers and landlords, so historians like Thirsk saw enclosure as a profit-orientated process driven by manorial lords, and later by capitalist farmers, who 'clearly wanted the hills to themselves, and disliked accommodating themselves to communal rules of husbandry'.[12] Hence protest primarily focused on the activities of the wealthy.

More recently, historians such as Andy Wood, Steve Hindle and Steve Hipkin have done much to complicate this account of early modern protest, drawing attention to the community politics, customary practices and local personalities which lay behind episodes of enclosure.[13] In a similar vein, this chapter explores the complexities of enclosure protest, paying particular attention both to the variety of changes which were labelled as 'enclosure' and to the ways seemingly diverse groups might be brought together by their opposition to enclosure. Using material from the Star

---

9   B. Bender, 'Introduction: Contested Landscapes', in *Contested Landscapes: Movement, Exile and Place,* ed. B. Bender and M. Winer (Oxford, 2001), pp. 1–18, quotation from p. 3. For Foucault's arguments on power relations, see M. Foucault, *Foucault Live (Interviews, 1961–1984),* ed. S. Lotringer, trans. L. Hochroth and J. Johnston (New York, 1996), pp. 209–10; M. Foucault, *The History of Sexuality, 1: An Introduction,* trans. R. Hurley (Harmondsworth, 1981), p. 93.

10   Tawney, *Agrarian Problem* (1912 edn), pp. 261–5.

11   Ibid., pp. 154 and 179.

12   Thirsk, 'Enclosing and Engrossing', pp. 239 and 254, and 'The Farming Regions of England', in *Agrarian History,* 4, pp. 1–112, quotation from p. 34.

13   See for example, Steve Hindle, 'Persuasion and Protest in the Caddington Common Enclosure Dispute, 1635–1639', *Past & Present* 158:1 (1998), 37–78; H. Falvey, 'Crown Policy and Local Economic Context in the Berkhamsted Common Enclosure Dispute, 1618–42', *Rural History* 12:2 (2001), 123–58; S. Hipkin, ' "Sitting on His Penny Rent": Conflict and Right of Common in Faversham Blean, 1595–1610', *Rural History* 11:1 (2000), 1–35; Andy Wood, 'Subordination, Solidarity and the Limits of Popular Agency in a Yorkshire Valley c.1596–1615', *Past & Present* 193:1 (2006), 41–72; N. Whyte, *Inhabiting the Landscape: Place, Custom and Memory, 1500–1800* (Oxford, 2009).

Chamber and Chancery courts, it explores how one particular Yorkshire community, South Cave in the East Riding, reacted to the threat of agricultural change in the decade immediately prior to the dissolution of the monasteries and the Pilgrimage of Grace. Such a microhistorical analysis allows for an exploration of the local circumstances surrounding enclosure protest at the same time as setting these events within their wider regional and national contexts.

I

South Cave was a large village at the southern tip of the Yorkshire Wolds where a market had been held from at least the twelfth century.[14] There were probably between one hundred and one hundred and twenty houses in the village in the late fourteenth century and around the same number at the Hearth Tax in 1672.[15] The village itself stood at the foot of the Wolds so that to the north and east the land rose above 150 metres. Between the village and the Humber estuary to the south was an area of low-lying marshes, carrs and sands, while to the west lay Wallingfen, an uncultivated tract of fen and marsh regularly inundated by the waters of the Humber. In the early sixteenth century, the arable land was arranged in three fields with additional common grazing in the marshes to the south and west of the village. There had certainly been some rearrangement of the common fields before the early seventeenth century when the name 'New Field' was first recorded, and the court documents used here suggest that the early sixteenth century may also have seen changes to local agricultural practice.[16]

South Cave was not alone in this. While the changes to the East Riding economy were probably not on the same scale as those seen in the Midlands – where the conversion of tens of thousands of acres to pasture in counties like Northamptonshire, Leicestershire and Warwickshire led to widespread unrest culminating in the failed uprising of 1596 and the Midland Rising of 1607 – the sixteenth century was nevertheless an important period of change.[17] Enclosures and evictions are recorded in the

14   A. H. Smith, *The Place Names of the East Riding of Yorkshire and York* (Cambridge, 1937), p. 223.
15   VCH, *East Riding*, 4:43.
16   Hull University Library (hereafter HUL) DDBA/4/3. Copy of 1633 lease of the parsonage.
17   E. F. Gay, 'The Midland Revolt and the Inquisitions of Depopulation of 1607', *TRHS*, new series, 18 (1904), 195–244, especially p. 236; J. E. Martin, *Feudalism to Capitalism: Peasant and Landlord in English Agrarian Development* (Basingstoke, 1983), p. 181; Martin, 'Sheep and Enclosure', 39–54; John Walter, 'A 'Rising of the People'? The Oxfordshire

high wolds at places like Wharram Percy, Thirkleby, Hanging Grimston and Caythorpe, all of them linked to the expansion of sheep walks or warrens.[18] Further south, detailed local investigation reveals evidence for an expansion of privatised land ownership as deer parks were extended, open-field systems reorganised or enclosed, and demesnes consolidated. Several large sheep walks are recorded in the vicinity of South Cave at places like Hunsley, Ripplingham and Hesslekew – often on the sites of abandoned hamlets – and new deer parks were laid out at Leconfield, Scorborough and Risby.[19] The latter is 6 miles (10 km) north-east of South Cave and here the deer park was created in c.1540 at the same time as the local landowner enclosed one of the common fields and created a consolidated block demesne. The new enclosures were almost certainly for grazing rather than arable, but while there is no evidence that the tenants at Risby objected to these changes, moves to enclose land for pasture at nearby South Cave ran into highly organised and sustained opposition.

Sometime around 1530, Richard Smetheley leased the manor house and eighteen oxgangs at South Cave as under-tenant to Elizabeth London, whose son John London had left her a share of the manor in his will.[20] Elizabeth died in November 1534 and a dispute over Smetheley's tenancy of the manor farm seems to have begun almost immediately. In early February 1535, the servants of another local landowner, Sir Robert Constable of Flamborough – who was renting lands in South Cave from John London's widow, Kathryn – stormed in to the manorial complex and attempted to evict Smetheley. According to Smetheley, they threatened his servants, menaced his tenants and drove his sheep and cattle out of the closes in which they were grazing.[21] Smetheley sued Constable in the Star Chamber,

---

Rising of 1596', *Past & Present* 107 (1985), 90–143; Steve Hindle, 'Imagining Insurrection in Seventeenth-Century England: Representations of the Midland Rising of 1607', *History Workshop Journal* 66:1 (2008), 21–61.

18   I. S. Leadam, 'The Inquisition of 1517: Inclosures and Evictions' (in two parts), *TRHS*, second series, 6 (1892), 167–314, and 7 (1893), 127–292, especially pp. 247–9; VCH, *East Riding*, 2:315; 8:138; Maurice W. Beresford, 'The Lost Villages of Yorkshire', *Yorkshire Archaeological Journal* 38 (1954), 344–70; J. W. Clay, ed., *Testamenta Eboracensia, or, Wills Registered at York*, 6 (Surtees Society 106, 1902), pp. 106–7.

19   VCH, *East Riding*, 4:13, 150 and 159–60; Leadam, 'Inquisition' (part 2), 248; Beresford, 'Lost Villages of Yorkshire', 67; Borthwick Institute of Historical Research, University of York, CP G 2654. See B. McDonagh, 'Manor Houses, Churches and Settlements: Historical Geographies of the Yorkshire Wolds before 1600' (unpublished PhD thesis, 2007), pp. 201–4 for more discussion of these examples.

20   *North Country Wills* (Surtees Society 116, 1908), pp. 118–19; TNA STAC 2/26/139; C1/894/38.

21   TNA STAC 2/26/139. The surviving bundle consists of Smetheley's bill, Constable's answer, the interrogatories against Constable and the other defendants, and the answer of another defendant, William Walker.

presenting the case as a violent and riotous dispossession, but one that hinged on the question of how the manor should be best managed for the profit of the Londons' heir, to whom Smetheley's daughter was married.[22]

The South Cave case was one of a number litigated between Smetheley and the executors of John London in the two decades after London's death in 1525. As the father-in-law of London's only son Oswold, Smetheley had taken on leases of property at South Cave and Beswick, another Wolds village 12 miles (19 km) to the north-east. Disputes subsequently arose over both properties. In the mid-1530s, Smetheley complained to the Chancery that Elizabeth London's widower Edward Askew had wrongfully sued him in the Court of Common Pleas for a debt of £40 owing on the lease of South Cave and that Askew had packed the jury who found against him.[23] A few years later, John London's widow Kathryn and her new husband James Packe sued Smetheley in the Chancery over the Beswick property, arguing that Smetheley was obliged to render the profits of the land to London's executors for the benefit of Oswold's sister, Cassandra. Smetheley denied this and claimed the profits in Oswold's name. The Beswick dispute had twice been referred to mediators, but only after Oswold's death in June 1538 did the case finally appear before the Chancery.[24] Neither of the Chancery cases is endorsed with a decree and their outcome is therefore unknown, although the pleadings give a strong flavour of the difficult relationship which existed between the executors and their lessee. Together the two Chancery cases offer context to the South Cave dispossession and Constable's role in it: in his answer to the Star Chamber bill, Constable claimed to be acting on behalf of James and Kathryn Packe in evicting Smetheley, and the dispossession could be interpreted as an early attempt by the executors to rid themselves of an unhappy choice of tenant.

Yet there was certainly much more to the events in South Cave than a simple property dispute. After driving the animals out of the close, Constable's men had set about ploughing up Smetheley's pastures. Smetheley recorded neither the number nor the names of the rioters in his bill of complaint, but eighteen or nineteen ploughs were said to have been used, a fact that implies the villagers were almost certainly involved alongside Constable's men. Mobilising even a small number of ploughs would have required days of planning and a significant level of community involvement, much as in hedge-breaking incidents.[25] Although

22   TNA STAC 2/26/139.
23   TNA C1/894/38. Bill, *Richard Smetheley v. Edward Askew*.
24   TNA C1/1048/8–9. Bill and answer, *James Packe v. Richard Smetheley*.
25   Both Christopher Dyer and Nicholas Blomley make a similar point about the protracted nature of enclosure riots: Christopher Dyer, 'Conflict in the Landscape: The Enclosure Movement in England, 1220–1349', *Landscape History* 29 (2007), 21–33; N. Blomley,

Smetheley was careful to state that he had sown corn on at least some of his farm, the actions of the rioters show that they thought that this was land wrongfully removed from the open arable fields and illegally converted to pasture.[26] The timing of the riot was also significant: it took place on 1 February, just as the first strips were being ploughed for the spring crops. Much as hedge-breaking might take place in association with a perambulation of the bounds – as was the case at Old Buckenham (Norfolk) in 1619 and at Otmoor (Oxfordshire) in 1831 – so too land taken from the common fields without the community's consent might be ploughed up by them at the beginning of the agricultural year.[27] Other incursions on existing agricultural practice might be tackled at the same time: thus, for example, Constable's men were also accused of pulling down the banks surrounding a new furlong of arable land belonging to Smetheley, most likely lying in the sands and marshes near the River Humber and representing an infringement on common grazing rights.[28]

Similar incidents were recorded elsewhere in the Wolds at South Kettlethorpe, Bishop Burton, Speeton and West Heslerton, though they seem to have occurred more commonly in this than other regions.[29] There are clear parallels between this kind of enclosure riot – perhaps best described as a mass ploughing – and incidents in which hedges were pulled down and common rights reasserted by grazing animals on the land. As with hedge-breaking, ploughing up pasture visibly inscribed the disputed land with a new use as well as making it difficult and costly to return the land to its former use: the individual sods would have to have been righted by hand in order to restore the land to grazing. Rather than a spontaneous incursion on private property, this was a carefully planned communal action which aimed to bring back into cultivation land which Smetheley had enclosed from the common arable fields and put down to pasture.

'Making Private Property: Enclosure, Common Right and the Work of Hedges', *Rural History* 18:1 (2007), 1–21, especially 11–12.

26   Smetheley's bill referred to 'new corn being newly put in the grownd' and his interrogatories asked witnesses whether Smetheley had sowed and fallowed (in other words, ploughed) any part of the premises before 1 February (TNA STAC 2/26/139).

27   VCH, *Oxfordshire*, 5:71–2; N. Whyte, 'Landscape, Memory and Custom: Parish Identities c.1550–1700', *Social History* 32:2 (2007), 166–86; Wood, *Riot, Rebellion and Popular Politics*, pp. 102–3.

28   TNA STAC2/26/139. This accusation appeared in the interrogatories but not in the pleadings, and was probably added relatively late in the proceedings.

29   Yorkshire Star Chamber Proceedings (hereafter YSCP) (4 vols, Yorkshire Archaeological Society Record Series, 41, 45, 51, 70 (1909–27)), 2:104 and 147; YSCP 4:16–17; Yorkshire Archaeological Society, H49. Analysis of the STAC 2 cases for Northamptonshire revealed only one mass ploughing in the county.

II

At the same time as the case against Constable was rumbling through the Star Chamber, Smetheley was being sued in the Chancery courts by a group of South Cave tenants. The principal litigant was a man named Michael Ledall who sued Smetheley both individually and as one of a group of twenty-two tenants who claimed to be acting on behalf of the community more generally.[30] The tenants' cases related back to events in the early 1530s at around the time Smetheley first took on the lease of South Cave. The case had previously been litigated in the local Assize courts where the tenants said Smetheley had been ordered to make recompense for his actions, something he had subsequently refused to do. It was no doubt his refusal to abide by this judgement that landed him in the equity courts.

The tenants' bills listed numerous wrongs done to them by Smetheley, but their principal complaint was that Smetheley had disturbed them in taking their common. They said he had wrongfully impounded their sheep and cattle as they grazed on the stubbles in the common fields and in the marsh at Wallingfen. There are clear parallels here with other disputes both within the Wolds and further afield in which enclosing landlords tried to extinguish common rights by impounding the sheep and cattle of commoners.[31] The tenants said Smetheley charged them unreasonably high sums of between 1 and 3d for the release of each animal and there were also allegations of mistreatment: after finding Michael Ledall's sheep grazing on the stubbles, Smetheley had reportedly driven them to a private sheepfold where he had kept them for six days and treated them so badly that they later died.[32] The implication was that Smetheley had acted outside the bounds of local custom: in charging such excessive sums for poundage and in keeping the sheep in a private sheepfold – where they manured his land rather than the common fields – Smetheley accrued benefits to himself which were due to the community as a whole.

The tenants also claimed that Smetheley had disturbed them in taking their common in Wallingfen where they had rights to graze animals and cut turves for fuel. Estimated at five thousand acres when it was enclosed in the 1770s, Wallingfen was a low-lying area of marsh and fen stretching between the Humber estuary in the south and the River Foulness in the north.[33] It was intercommoned by the surrounding five parishes and managed by five surveyors and forty-eight jurors appointed by the

---

30 TNA C1/839/21 and C1/845/35–36. The surviving Chancery papers include two bills of complaint and one answer relating to the case.
31 McDonagh, 'Subverting the Ground'.
32 TNA C1/839/21.
33 East Riding Archives, AP/3/26.

townships.[34] Rights to grazing and turbary extended to all those living
on ancient tofts, but the lords of South Cave had periodically and largely
unsuccessfully tried to claim superior jurisdiction over the marsh.[35]
Sometime between 1518 and 1525, John London had sued the parishioners and surveyors in the Chancery, claiming that they had obstructed him
in his rights to strays, fishing, fowling and other profits from the marsh.[36]
He argued that the tenants had recently elected surveyors to manage the
marsh and thereby deprived him of rights exercised by his ancestors,
though it is clear from other sources that the court had been in existence
since at least 1425.[37] This then was part of long-running dispute which
flared up again at a time of tension between the tenants and the manorial
lessee.

While the tenants were perhaps intentionally vague about the exact geography of the dispute, a close reading of the documents reveals the key
sites. In his answer, Smetheley argued that he had impounded the animals not in the common fields but at Weedley, a deserted medieval village
in the extreme north-east of the parish which had been abandoned at an
unknown date before the early sixteenth century.[38] He said that the tenants had turned large numbers of sheep – estimated by him at between
three and four hundred animals – onto his pastures on several occasions,
thereby deliberately destroying his grass and wood.[39] Smetheley claimed
to hold the pastures and woodland there in severalty for his private use
'at all tymes of the year', a statement which seems to imply that this was
a landscape in which field closes were not unknown even whilst denying that such an arrangement existed at Weedley. He said he had therefore been within his rights to impound the sheep which he had charged
only a halfpenny an animal to release. The tenants clearly considered
Weedley to be part of the common field system and by turning their
animals onto the land, they tried to reassert grazing rights which had
been recently extinguished by Smetheley, probably in conjunction with
the area's physical enclosure. Hedges certainly existed at Weedley by the
1570s and Smetheley's insistence that his pastures were 'open upon the
feelds of Cave' suggests an arrangement so impractical as to question his

34   HUL, DDBA/10/1.
35   Calendar of Patent Rolls, *Edward II*, 1: *1307–13* (London, 1894), p. 261; VCH, *East
Riding* 4:48.
36   TNA C1/535/21 Bill, *John London gent. v. Sir Robert Constable and others*. A Star
Chamber suit lodged before 1513 in which London denied being 'an extorcioner and
oppressor of his neybors' may also relate to the long-running dispute about rights in
Wallingfen (YSCP 4:56–9).
37   HUL, DDBA/10/1.
38   VCH, *East Riding* 4:51; Beresford, 'Lost Villages of Yorkshire', 70.
39   TNA C1/845/36.

truthfulness to the Court at the same time as revealing his determination to deny all charges of enclosing land.[40]

Conversely, grazing animals on arable crops might sometimes function as a means to promote – rather than resist – enclosure and agricultural change. The tenants complained that Smetheley had grazed his animals on their crops in the common arable fields on numerous occasions. They said he had ordered his shepherd to turn four hundred sheep onto a part of the common field known as Cold Wold, thereby destroying peas and corn the tenants had sown there.[41] Smetheley denied this, saying that when his sheep had sometimes 'by chance . . . fortuned to graze into the fields' he had always paid the money demanded of him by the town pinders for these infringements.[42] Cold Wold had, moreover, previously been a scrub-covered manorial pasture in which the tenants had only limited grazing rights until it had been cleared and ploughed up for the first time five years previously. Not surprisingly, the tenants presented a very different history of the site, arguing that Cold Wold was a long-standing part of the open-field system in which they had had common rights 'without condition time out of mind'.[43] Neither party mentioned the Star Chamber case, but it is possible that Cold Wold was the site either of the 1535 mass ploughing or another similar – but unrecorded – incident.[44] Thus by the mid-1530s, if not before, Cold Wold was a highly contested space, the site of an ongoing dispute about customary rights and ownership that was played out through grazing animals, trespassing humans and 'riotous' plough teams.

While there is little explicit mention of new boundaries and none of hedge-breaking, the Chancery and the Star Chamber cases clearly relate to tensions over agricultural change and enclosure. Here enclosure meant the conversion of arable land to sheep pasture and to woodland, and was accompanied by attempts to curtail the tenants' common grazing rights in the open fields and in the marshes and carrs of Wallingfen. Like many others in the Wolds and further afield, this was a dispute about the rights of landowners – or in this case, a manorial lessee – to remove land from the common fields and put it down to more profitable uses. Converting land to pasture was a lucrative undertaking whilst grain prices were low and wool prices high in the first two decades of the sixteenth century. Although the

40 HUL DDBA(2)/6/42; TNA C1/845/36.
41 TNA C1/845/35.
42 TNA C1/845/36.
43 TNA C1845/36.
44 The Chancery cases are undated, although given that Smetheley's answer makes no mention of Constable's involvement in the Pilgrimage of Grace, it was almost certainly filed before the autumn of 1536. Yet the chronology of the events recorded in the bills and answer and their relation to the incidents detailed in the 1535 Star Chamber case remain unclear.

price of wheat rose more steeply than wool in the 1520s and early 1530s, conversion to pasture seems to have continued in many places with well documented social and economic consequences.[45] The early Tudor Acts and statutes legislated against the conversion of land to sheep pasture and the related practice of engrossing holdings, which was alleged to lead to the depopulation of villages, the destruction of churches, unemployment, criminality and the weakening of England's defences, as well as the grain shortages in the capital.[46] Contemporary literature and pamphlets put it even more colourfully: sheep were said to eat men and 'devour whole fields, houses, and cities'.[47]

The inhabitants cast Smetheley's actions in a similar light. They argued that as a consequence of impounding their animals and grazing his beasts on their crops, 'the said town is not only now greatly decayed within the four or five years as well in plowes & other substance but is also depopulate of people'. Where there had previously been thirty ploughs in the village, there were now only twenty-two, and the tenants would soon be forced 'to forsake the said town to their utter undoing in the world'.[48] Here the tenants utilised the familiar rhetoric of Star Chamber litigants – that the plaintiffs would be utterly undone unless remedy was made by the court – at the same time as tapping into wider commentaries on enclosure and depopulation. Thus the wording of the Chancery bills echoes much that appears in the 1515 Act against depopulating enclosures and the pream- ble to Wolsey's subsequent inquiry. In all probability, the South Cave ten- ants felt encouraged in their opposition to Smetheley's enclosures by the cases which reached the courts in the aftermath of the 1517 Inquisitions of Depopulation, the 1529 proclamation that all enclosed grounds should be laid open before the following Easter and the 1533 Act which legislated against engrossing and the keeping of large sheep flocks.[49]

In framing their complaints in terms of a threatened depopulation, the tenants underlined the seriousness of Smetheley's actions to the court. South Cave was a large village split between two main manors and, as such, both Smetheley and the tenants would have recognised the impos- sibility of total depopulation and wholesale conversion of the common fields to sheep walk.[50] Where families had previously been displaced and arable land converted to sheep pasture in the vicinity of South Cave, this had primarily taken place in smaller townships with low populations, and

45   Bowden, 'Agricultural Prices, Farm Profits, and Rents', pp. 593–695; Clay, *Economic Expansion and Social Change, 1: People, Land and Towns*, p. 43.
46   Thirsk, 'Enclosing and Engrossing', pp. 214–15.
47   T. More, *Utopia*, ed. E. Arber, trans. R. Robinson (London, 1869), p. 41.
48   TNA C1/845/35.
49   Thirsk, 'Enclosing and Engrossing', pp. 216–17.
50   VCH, *East Riding*, 4:43–5.

in most cases probably long before 1500.[51] Yet unemployment and the resultant fall in population would have been foreseen side-effects of the decision to convert demesne and common-field arable to pasture. By destroying the tenants' crops, impounding their animals and pursuing them through the courts with 'wrongfull vexaciones and suytes', Smetheley was presumably attempting to make their tenancies unviable and rid himself of those tenants who most vehemently opposed his plans for enclosure.[52]

Like Smetheley, the tenants combined direct action like animal trespasses and the mass ploughing with litigation in the common law and central equity courts, much of which couched Smetheley's 'wrongs' in the language of depopulation, ruin and decay. Intriguingly, there is also a hint that the tenants offered Smetheley money to leave South Cave, perhaps an attempt to buy out the remaining years on his lease of the manor farm: in their bill to Chancery, the inhabitants said they had 'diverse & sundry times offered & tended to give & pay Smetheley 40 l for to departe & dwell x miles out of the said town of South Cave', presumably on the Beswick farm.[53]

III

As was usual for anyone suing a bill of the equity courts, the tenants cast Smetheley as a powerful landowner. In reality, he was a medium-sized farmer who rented the manor house and a relatively small parcel of land of perhaps 250–300 acres. In turn, Smetheley claimed that he was being victimised by a much bigger local landowner, Sir Robert Constable of Flamborough. It was Constable's men he identified as leading the enclosure riot and in his answer to the Chancery bills, Smetheley claimed that the tenants' cases were also brought about by the 'malice and evell wyll' of Constable.[54] This no doubt underplayed the tenants' role in opposing enclosure, but Constable's involvement in the dispute is interesting nonetheless.

Constable was an important local landlord who owned considerable estates in the East Riding centred on his manor house at Flamborough in the north-east Wolds.[55] It is unclear whether Constable held freehold land in South Cave, but he was one of the tithe-holders and rented land from the widow of the previous lord of the manor.[56] He also seems to have

---

51 Beresford, 'Lost Villages of Yorkshire'.
52 TNA C1/839/21.
53 TNA C1/845/35. Interestingly, the figure here was the same as that said to be owing to Elizabeth London's widower, Edward Askew, in the later Chancery case (TNA C1/894/38).
54 TNA C1/845/36.
55 'Constable, Sir Robert (1478?–1537)', *ODNB* online.
56 TNA C1/563/27.

managed an estate in nearby North Cliffe on behalf of the young son of a cousin, and Constable's opposition to the land use changes introduced by Smetheley was certainly underpinned by his own property interests in the area.[57] At the same time, in ploughing up Smetheley's pastures Constable aligned himself with the tenants and supported them in their opposition to an enclosing landowner. There was, moreover, a history of alliance between Constable and South Cave villagers: in the 1520s, Constable had been chosen by the inhabitants of South Cave as one of the surveyors and rulers of Wallingfen and he later acted on their behalf when John London sued in Chancery for manorial rights in the marsh.[58] Yet relations between Constable and the South Cave inhabitants were not always friendly: at around the time of the Wallingfen case, he was accused by the local clergyman of withholding money owed on tithes and of maintaining a clerk 'against the will of all the parishioners'.[59] Constable was, nonetheless, an important asset to the tenants in their fight against Smetheley and his policy of enclosure and estate improvement. As a member of the king's Council of the North, Constable had access both to the royal court and to the legal machinery at Westminster, and it's tempting to suggest that he advised the tenants on bringing the equity court cases or even helped them to access lawyers.

Constable was also involved in anti-enclosure riots elsewhere in the Southern Wolds. In 1533, another local landowner, Marmaduke Monkton, complained that Constable and around seventy riotous persons had unlawfully entered into closes at nearby South Kettlethorpe and ploughed up the pastures, manuring and sowing them with seed so as to convert the land to arable.[60] A year later, Constable was accused of sending more than forty men to North Cave where they dug up and burnt the hedge enclosing a pasture and turned horses, oxen and cattle onto the land.[61] It is unclear from the bills how many of those involved were Constable's household servants and tenants, but the large number of people and ploughs involved in these incidents again imply a significant degree of community involvement. These were mass actions in which small tenants and a powerful local landowner acted together against freeholders and manorial tenants who tried to enclose land for their own profit. But if Constable acted as a champion for the local cause at places like South Cave, North Cave and South Kettlethorpe, he was by no means always an anti-enclosure figure. At nearby Arras, he tried to evict the villagers in an attempt to depopulate

57   'Constable, Robert (late 1450s–1501), Lawyer', *ODNB* online.
58   TNA C1/535/21.
59   TNA C1/563/27. Bill, *William Rypplyngham v. Sir Robert Constable*.
60   YSCP 4:16–17.
61   Yorkshire Star Chamber Proceedings, 3:68–9.

the hamlet and extend pastoral husbandry in the area, just as Smetheley had hoped to do at South Cave.[62]

IV

In examining events at South Cave, this chapter has pointed to the complexity of the term 'enclosure'. At South Cave, tensions over enclosure centred on the conversion of arable land to sheep pasture but also touched upon other changes to existing agricultural practice including the fencing off of land for woodland at Weedley, the reclaiming of small plots in the sands and marshes, and attempts to restrict rights to graze the open-field stubbles and to gather fuel in the marshes. Enclosure clearly meant very different things in different places, even on the micro-scale within a single Yorkshire parish. Definitions of enclosure might become still more complicated where convertible husbandry helped to keep the land fertile or temporary field closes existed, as was perhaps the case at Cold Wold. Yet if the changes labelled as enclosure varied in their form, purpose and impact, the South Cave tenants nevertheless framed their complaints with reference to the various early Tudor Acts on the decay of tillage, choosing to present this diverse bundle of agricultural changes to the Chancery as a depopulating enclosure. This decision was highly strategic, and is good evidence of the ways individuals and groups below the gentry might play a key part in negotiating enclosure and agricultural change, as well as an important reminder of the inherent difficulties of making sense of the multiple and conflicting accounts presented to the courts.

The chapter has also explored enclosure as a contested practice, paying particular attention to the relationships between the key figures in the South Cave dispute. Here a large and almost certainly non-resident landowner supported smaller tenants in their opposition to agricultural changes introduced by a medium-sized farmer, himself the tenant of another absent landowner. The same was true at South Kettlethorpe and North Cave where protest was focused on enclosures that had been put in place not by manorial lords, but by medium-sized freeholders and manorial tenants. This then is a rather more complicated model of landlord–tenant relations than either Tawney or Thirsk imagined to be the case in the enclosure disputes they studied.

Landlord–tenant relations were certainly by no means always adversarial, although where large landowners lent their support to groups of tenants in opposing enclosure, such alliances might be relatively short-lived. At South Cave, Constable's property interests aligned with the tenants'

---

62   TNA STAC 2/1/42. Bill, *Thomas Alderson and others v. Sir Robert Constable.*

objections to enclosure and the result was a coalition between Constable and the tenants, potentially underwritten by quite different concerns. At the same time, Constable's response to enclosure varied on the micro-scale: thus he supported the local anti-enclosure movement at South Cave while at the same time moving forward with his plans for the enclosure and depopulation of nearby Arras. Such decisions no doubt depended on the precise economic gains each potential enclosure offered and while the reasons behind Constable's support of the South Cave tenants are not fully recoverable, the case is a reminder of the importance of local politics, as well as culture and custom in determining enclosure responses, a point also made by both Hindle and Hipkin.[63]

It is only through microhistorical studies such as this that we can begin to reveal the dense social networks and complex local circumstances within which enclosure took place. Rather than the inevitable result of new ideas about individualised property rights, enclosure was an ongoing process contingent on a complex array of factors. For the people on the ground, the outcome of each episode of enclosure was as yet unknown and could thus be negotiated via both the courts and a range of more direct measures including animal and human trespasses, mass ploughings and hedge-breaking incidents. These were landscapes 'in the making' and in recognising them as such, we open up space for alternative readings of agricultural change and enclosure which recognise the agency of ordinary people and the influence of village-level politics in the unfolding histories of the English landscape.

63   Hindle, 'Persuasion and Protest', 42–3, 75–6; Hipkin, 'Sitting on His Penny Rent', 2.

4

The Politics of Enclosure in Elizabethan England

Contesting 'Neighbourship' in Chinley (Derbyshire)*

Among the numerous examples of 'aggressive landlordism' that R. H. Tawney cited in *The Agrarian Problem* are the nefarious activities of Godfrey Bradshaw in Chinley (Derbyshire) in 1569, which had first been brought to light in an article published in the *Derbyshire Archaeological Journal* in 1899.[1] Tawney's discussion of the unrest provoked by Bradshaw's estate management is based exclusively on the Star Chamber interrogatories issued on Bradshaw's behalf, sources which, by their very nature, present a partisan and adversarial version of the episodes.[2] Tawney nonetheless assumed the veracity of the narrative implied by Bradshaw's attorneys and explained the story as a series of attempts by dispossessed inhabitants to regain 'the rights of pasture which they had hitherto enjoyed'. He also drew attention to a particularly tantalising aspect of the alleged events at Chinley: local men were said to have conferred with the mysterious 'Master Bircles of the Countye of Chester' and consulted 'bookes of prophesie' – the latter far more politically dangerous than mere enclosure rioting.[3] Keith Thomas further explored this aspect of the events at Chinley, identifying 'Master Bircles' as John Birtles, who in about 1584 was one of those involved in an alleged conspiracy against the queen, he being found in possession of 'a certain old book of prophecy . . . [which] sheweth when this realm of England shall be subverted'.[4] Krista Kesselring has even suggested

---

* Thanks to Derek Brumhead, Roger Bryant, Steve Hindle, Bill Shannon, and the staff of the Lichfield Record Office, the Sheffield Archives and the National Archives for their help in preparing this chapter, and to Mandy de Belin for drawing the schematic maps.

1 Tawney, *Agrarian Problem* (1912 edn), pp. 327–9; C. E. B. Bowles, 'Enclosure Riots at Chinley, AD 1569', *Derbyshire Archaeological Journal* 21 (1899), 61–8.

2 The original interrogatories are held at the Sheffield Archives: Sheffield Archives (SA) Bowles Deeds (BD) 101.

3 SA BD101, interrogatories 27 and 28.

4 K. Thomas, *Religion and the Decline of Magic* (London, 1971), p. 404, citing L. O. Pike, *A History of Crime in England*, 2 (London, 1873–6), p. 23. The original description of Birtles and his alleged activities is now too faint to read: TNA SP12/175/90.

that, in their combination of social unrest and political prophecy, the riots at Chinley were precursors of the Northern Rebellion of 1569.[5]

All these discussions of the events at Chinley are, however, based on a misinterpretation of their dating. Charles Bradshaw Bowles, who wrote the original article and owned the manuscript interrogatories, misread the only specific date mentioned therein. The twenty-fifth interrogatory concerns events that allegedly took place 'a bout the tenth daye of Aprill in the xv[th] yere of the Quenes Ma[jes]ties Reigne that nowe is' (i.e. 10 April 1573). Bowles, misreading 'xv' as 'xi', interpreted the year as 11 Elizabeth (1569), hence his assumption that the riots took place in 1569. Furthermore, neither Bowles nor Tawney were aware of the existence of relevant Star Chamber pleadings which also challenge the interpretation that the Chinley riots occurred in 1569: Bradshaw's bill of complaint, which specifically mentions events that took place in July 1574 and January 1575, was presented in January 1576; some of the accused returned their answers later that month.[6] The interrogatories would accordingly have been issued after this (i.e. in early 1576) and, since most of the offences were alleged to have happened during the year 'last past', they must have occurred in 1575, some six years *after* the Northern Rebellion. A draft version of Bradshaw's bill has also survived, which when read in conjunction with the final version that was presented in court, provides fascinating insights into how a complainant might embellish his account of events in order to strengthen his suit and to bring the dispute within the cognisance of the Star Chamber.[7]

As the majority of documents relating to Chinley were generated during the course of various legal actions, it is difficult to unpick the conflicting narratives, particularly when several suits refer to various 'agreements' and leases which appear to be either overlapping or contradictory, or both. But perhaps the most impenetrable aspect of the Chinley dispute is exactly why protagonists were arguing so fiercely over enclosures within an area of only six hundred acres that was situated in thousands of acres of upland commons, wastes and moorland. This chapter will first outline the events that were alleged to have occurred at Chinley in the early 1570s; secondly place Chinley in its economic, demographic and geographic contexts; and thirdly attempt to identify the social status of those involved to

---

5 K. Kesselring, *The Northern Rebellion of 1569: Faith, Politics and Protest in Elizabethan England* (Basingstoke, 2007), pp. 14–15. Tawney had also identified a possible link with the Rebellion: *Agrarian Problem* (1912 edn), p. 329.

6 TNA STAC5/B93/31, document 2, catalogued as bill of complaint of *Godfrey Bradshaw v. Edward Kirk* [sic] *et al.*, endorsed 'Oct Hillary 1575' (octave of Hilary 1575 = 20 January 1575/6); STAC5/B93/31, document 1, answers of Edward Kirke et al., sworn 26 January 1575 [1575/6].

7 SA BD102 and 103. The folios that comprise the draft bill are jumbled with the folios of another document.

ascertain whether Tawney's heroes, and Bradshaw's victims, really were 'Derbyshire peasants'.[8] Finally, since most of the events occurred in 1575, the putative links with the 1569 Northern Rebellion suggested by Bowles, Tawney, Thomas and Kesselring are re-evaluated, for the Chinley riots can no longer be viewed as precursors of that upheaval.

I

In the sixteenth century the area of ground known as Chinley, situated in the High Peak some 3 miles (5 km) to the north-west of Chapel-en-le-Frith, comprised about six hundred statute acres. During the early 1570s, according to Godfrey Bradshaw, some of his neighbours and other inhabitants not only destroyed his enclosures there but also erected cottages and made their own enclosures to the detriment of other users.[9] The numerous attacks on his property, including at least one under cover of darkness were, Bradshaw alleged, well organised and violent, and occurred in the very teeth both of injunctions issued by the court of the Duchy of Lancaster and of a Queen's Bench warrant to keep the peace. In particular, Bradshaw singled out a physical assault at Hayfield on 10 July 1574 on the bailiff and high constable when attempting to arrest one Richard Shore under the terms of the warrant.[10] Having set Shore free, his armed rescuers evaded arrest and pursued Bradshaw and the court officials for several miles, putting their quarries in fear of their lives.

As in many Star Chamber suits, the victim alleged that his opponents had raised a common purse and had riotously gathered together armed with various weapons, such as 'bowes pytche Forkes clobbes staves swords and daggers drawen'. He also named those who had allegedly given land in Chinley to William Bearde in return for his support against Bradshaw and for supplying, as and when required, 'ydll ryotouse persons' to assist them in their 'yll doinge'. Bradshaw even suggested that Edward Kyrke had planned to hire an arsonist. Matters apparently came to a head in the early summer of 1575. Despite an alleged agreement that Bradshaw should be allowed to enclose part of Chinley, his opponents forsook that bargain and, together with their associates, chose May Day to destroy the enclosure. Bradshaw also alleged that on about the same date, a notoriously lawless time of year, Reynold Kyrke had consulted Master Bircles 'concerning prophesies by noble men' and together the two had perused 'bookes of prophesie'. After this

---

8   Tawney, *Agrarian Problem* (1912 edn), p. 329.
9   Unless otherwise stated, events in this section have been reconstructed from the thirty interrogatories that comprise SA BD101.
10   TNA STAC5/B93/31, document 2.

putative consultation, large companies of men, including William Bearde
and Ralph Bradley, had assembled at 'the Lords yate', apparently inspired
by the prophecies and so, by implication, were guilty of treason.[11]

Of the forty-four men whom Bradshaw summoned to appear in Star
Chamber, only six answered his bill of complaint.[12] They admitted nothing;
nor did they make any statement concerning their rights within Chinley.
They did, however, assert that the account of the violent release of Richard
Shore from custody was a blatant falsehood, since Shore had already died
before the alleged offence had been committed and thus impugned the
veracity of Bradshaw's complaints. Nonetheless, the court considered it
necessary to investigate them, and accordingly issued interrogatories to be
administered to witnesses.

Here then, apparently, is a classic tale of an enclosing landowner, who by
denying access to land wherein other inhabitants had previously enjoyed
customary usage so antagonised those inhabitants that they took violent
action in order to recover their access. This tale, however, hangs on the
assumption that Chinley was an area of common land that Bradshaw had
illegally and damagingly appropriated for his own use; in fact its legal status was altogether different, and thus our interpretation of the unrest must
also deviate from Tawney's norm of resistance to aggressive landlordism.

II

In the medieval and early modern periods 'Chinley', often referred to as
'Mainstonfield alias Chinley', was an ancient herbage within the royal
forest of High Peak.[13] Originally many herbages were designated areas in
the royal forests, which were held directly from the Crown by religious
houses.[14] Most were vaccaries (cattle pastures) but Chinley, which had been
granted to Merevale Abbey, Warwickshire, included cultivated land as well
as pasture.[15] By 1392 all of the herbages in High Peak had come into the

---

11   For the significance of prophecy as a catalyst for dissent, see K. Kesselring, 'Deference
and Dissent in Tudor England: Reflections on Sixteenth-Century Protest', *History Compass*
3 (2005), 1–16, especially 7–11; T. Thornton, *Prophecy, Politics and the People in Early
Modern England* (Woodbridge, 2006), pp. 24–5.

12   TNA STAC5/B93/31, document 1.

13   Both names have several spelling variants.

14   Very little has been written about these herbages. See, for example, D. Brumhead and
R. Weston, 'Seventeenth-Century Enclosures of the Commons and Wastes of Bowden
Middlecale in the Royal Forest of Peak', *Derbyshire Archaeological Journal* 121 (2001),
244–86, 256. Somerville says nothing about their origins or management: R. Somerville,
History of the Duchy of Lancaster 1: 1265–1603 (London, 1953) and *History of the Duchy
of Lancaster, 2: 1603–1965* (London, 1970).

15   *Rotuli Litterarum Clausarum, 1: 1204–1224* (London, 1833), p. 563, 13 September

possession of the Duke of Lancaster and were being leased out.[16] By 1436 the herbage of Chinley was being let to farm for an annual rent of £10 13s 4d, providing the Duchy with a guaranteed income and lessees with sole rights over the soil and pasture in that herbage.[17] This rent remained unchanged until the late sixteenth century, Chinley being the most lucrative of the Duchy's herbages within the manor of High Peak.[18] This herbage, therefore, was emphatically not part of the common waste of the royal forest, but was instead an estate legally separated from the forest and leased directly from the Duchy. It was not subject to common rights, but if the lessee so chose he might sublet all or part of it to others, who would accordingly have individual grazing rights proportionate to their lease.

The exact location of Chinley herbage is now difficult to pinpoint. On two contemporary sixteenth-century representations of High Peak, the various herbages are clearly marked and are represented very differently from the hamlets, villages and small towns round about (see figures 4.1 and 4.2). The purpose of the map in figure 4.1, from the Duchy of Lancaster archive, is now obscure because it has been detached from the documents to which it relates; nevertheless it appears that the herbages are the map's main focus since they are coloured vermilion in the original.[19] The map in figure 4.2 is closely connected with Bradshaw's Star Chamber suit since the original is drawn on the back of the manuscript interrogatories that he owned.[20] No herbages are indicated on Burdett's map of Derbyshire, published in 1791. The north-west of the county, marked 'High Peak', is an area of dispersed settlement; north of Chapel-en-le-Frith there are landmarks called 'Chinley Head', 'Chinley heys' and 'Chindley Churn' [sic], and (some distance to the west) a small cluster of buildings marked 'Chinley Houses'.[21] A detailed map of the modern parish of Chinley, Bugsworth and Brownside shows old field names and other features, but does not indicate the extent of the herbage.[22]

1223 [7 Henry III]; *Close Rolls of the Reign of Henry III, 1227–1231* (London, 1902), p. 259, 8 November 1229 [14 Henry III]. Translations of the documents cited here and in the two following notes were kindly supplied by Roger Bryant.

16 TNA DL29/22/373, Receiver's account, 1391–92.

17 TNA DL29/22/377, Bailiff's account, 1435–36.

18 TNA DL43/1/25, sixteenth-century transcripts of three rentals of the manor of High Peak.

19 TNA MFC 1/53. The original map, now conserved as a composite, was formerly in three fragments, under the references MPC 7 (previously DL 31/7), MPC 37 (previously DL 31/7) and MPC 44 (previously DL 31/44).

20 SA BD101v.

21 *Burdett's Map of Derbyshire*, introduction by J. B. Harley, D. V. Fowkes and J. C. Harvey (Derbyshire Archaeological Society, 1975).

22 C. M. Tattersfield, *The Parish of Chinley, Bugsworth and Brownside: A Map and Historical Guide of a Derbyshire Peak District Parish* (Chapel-en-le-Frith, 1992).

Figure 4.1: Schematic map of High Peak herbages, sixteenth century, based on TNA MFC 1/53. (The original map, now conserved as a composite, was formerly in three fragments under the references MPC 7 (previously DL 31/7), MPC 37 (previously DL 31/7) and MPC 44 (previously DL 31/44).

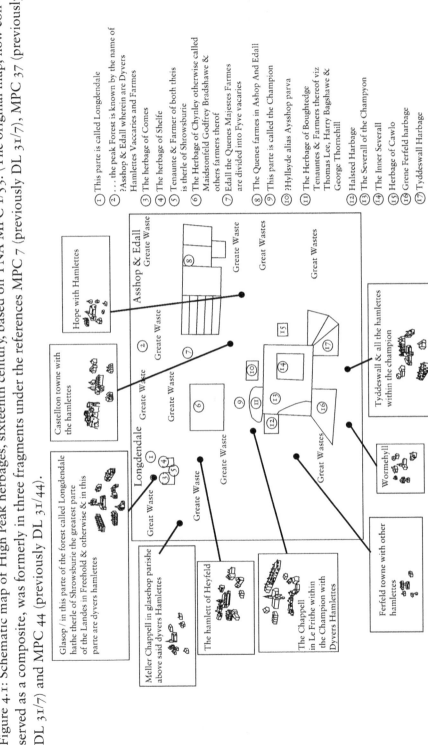

1. This parte is called Longdendale
2. ... the peak Forest is known by the name of Asshop & Edall wherein are Dyvers Hamlettes Vaccaries and Farmes
3. The herbage of Comes
4. The herbage of Shelfe
5. Tenaunte & Farmer of both theis is therle of Shrowsburie
6. The Herbage of Chynley otherwise called Maidstonfeild Godfrey Bradshawe & others farmers therof
7. Edall the Quenes Majestes Farmes are divided into Fyve vacaries
8. The Quenes farmes in Ashop And Edall
9. This parte is called the Champion
10. ?Hyllsyde alias Aysshop parva
11. The Herbage of Boughtedge Tenauntes & Farmers thereof viz Thomas Lee, Harry Bagshawe & George Thornehill
12. Halsted Harbage
13. The Severall of the Champyon
14. The Inner Severall
15. Herbage of Cawlo
16. Grene Ferfeld harbage
17. Tyddeswall Harbage

Castellton towne with the hamlettes

Hope with Hamlettes

Asshop & Edall Greate Waste

Greate Waste

Greate Waste

Greate Wastes

Greate Wastes

Greate Waste

Greate Waste

Longdendale Greate Waste

Greate Waste

Greate Waste

Great Waste

Great Waste

Great Wastes

Great Wastes

Glasop / in this parte of the forest called Longdendale hathe therle of Shrowsburie the greatest parte of the Landes in Freehold & otherwise & in this parte are dyvers hamletes

Meller Chappell in glasshop parishe above said dyvers Hamlettes

The hamlet of Heyfeld

The Chappell in Le Frithe within the Champion with Dyvers Hamlettes

Ferfeld towne with other hamlettes

Wormehyll

Tyddeswall & all the hamlettes within the champion

Figure 4.2: Schematic map of High Peak herbages, c.1569, based on SA BD101v

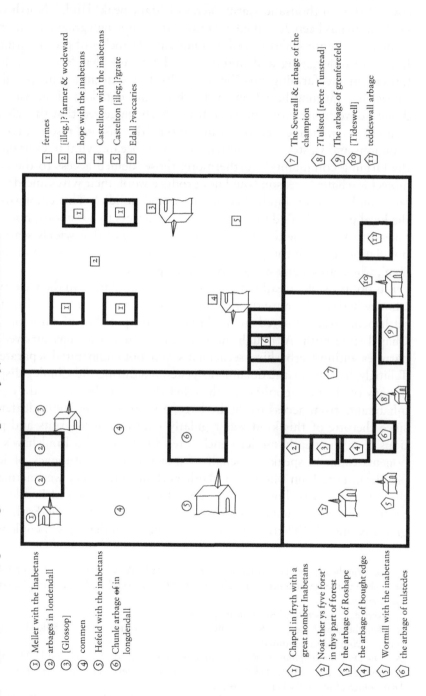

1   fermes
2   [illeg.]? farmer & wodeward
3   hope with the inabetans
4   Castellton with the inabetans
5   Castelton [illeg.]?grate
6   Edall ?vaccaries

7   The Severall & arbage of the champion
8   ?Tulsted [recte Tunstead]
9   The arbage of grenferefeld
10 [Tideswell]
11 teddeswall arbage

1   Meller with the Inabetans
2   arbages in londendall
3   [Glossop]
4   commen
5   Hefeld with the inabetans
6   Chunle arbage of in longdendall

1   Chapell in fryth with a great nomber Inabetans
2   Noat ther ys fyve forst' in thys part of forest
3   the arbage of Roshape
4   the arbage of bought edge
5   Wormill with the inabetans
6   the arbage of tulstedes

From medieval times this region of Derbyshire was included in the administrative and fiscal division known as Bowden Middlecale, which covered sixteen thousand statute acres of 'dark peak' land.[23] North-west Derbyshire has been described as 'a vast extent of rough grazing', suffering from 'harsh winters, short, cool summers, and 60 inches of precipitation'.[24] It was an unforgiving and unpromising landscape that 'set severe limitations on the farming possibilities'.[25] By the sixteenth century mixed subsistence farming based on cattle, sheep and oats had given way to a domestic woollen textile industry. It has been suggested that this change of direction in the local economy meant that 'the pastoral resources of the commons and wastes for the grazing of sheep became vital to everyone in the farming community'; furthermore, those 'denied access to the commons for whatever reason could not produce wool, their wives and daughters could not spin, [and] their looms would lie idle'. This emphasis on the local population's desperate reliance on access to commons, however, takes into account neither the relatively small size of that widely scattered population, nor the comparatively vast areas of 'Great waste' and 'commen', which are clearly marked on contemporary maps.

It is not possible to estimate the size of the population in the vicinity of Chinley herbage because the numerous isolated farmsteads and dispersed settlements were situated in the large upland parishes of Glossop and Chapel-en-le-Frith. Although the 1563 'diocesan census' has survived for parishes within Derbyshire, settlements were not enumerated separately.[26] Tellingly, in none of the documents generated during the Chinley dispute did any of the protagonists cite the relief that might be obtained by poor inhabitants from access to the herbage, a silence all the more deafening since rhetoric of this kind was regularly rehearsed in lawsuits and petitions contesting early modern enclosures. Only once did Bradshaw's opponents claim to speak on behalf of a significant constituency of local people: in 1572 John Manners and others claimed that they were acting 'in the name of Fourtie householders, and of others tenauntes of Landes and tenementes in the saide parishes [of Glossop and Chapel-en-le-Frith] to A greate Number'.[27] There is, however, no suggestion that these people were

---

23   D. Brumhead, 'Social Structure in Some "Dark Peak" Hamlets of North-West Derbyshire in the Seventeenth and Eighteenth Centuries', *The Local Historian* 28:4 (1998), 194–207, 194.

24   Kerridge, *Agricultural Revolution*, p. 166.

25   Brumhead and Weston, 'Seventeenth-Century Enclosures', 253; the following quotations are from the same source.

26   *The Diocesan Population Returns for 1563 and 1603*, ed. A. Dyer and D. M. Palliser (London, 2005), p. 108; P. Riden, 'The Population of Derbyshire in 1563', *Derbyshire Archaeological Journal* 98 (1978), 61–71.

27   TNA DL1/93/M15, *Manners et al. v. Bradshaw*, undated but endorsed 'Pasch' xiiij', i.e. Easter term 14 Elizabeth (1572).

poor householders and tenants. This contrasts directly with the situation at Greenfairfield, a herbage to the south of Chapel-en-le-Frith, to which in 1585 some six hundred inhabitants had access, of whom – it was claimed – a great number would be 'driven to extreme povertye & beggerey' if it were enclosed.[28] Clearly, the demographics at Chinley were significantly different from those at Greenfairfield, which lay on the edge of the Peak lead mining district.

On one contemporary map (see figure 4.1), Chinley is represented as a disproportionately large rectangle, with the legend 'The Herbage of Chynley otherwise called Maidstonfeld Godfrey Bradshawe & others farmers thereof'. As well as leasing the rights of pasture in the Chinley herbage, the lessee was also entitled to cultivate its soil and let the cottages built thereon; the woods, underwoods and watermill continued as Crown property.[29] When in 1628 the whole of Chinley was enclosed, surveyors produced a detailed description of the land in the herbage, which ranged in nature from cultivable land through open pasture, wood pasture and woodland, to meadow, marsh, peat bog, bole hills and slate-ground.[30] The surveyors' report indicates that Bradshaw had not been utilising the entire area of the herbage but only the most fertile six hundred acres. Some contemporary documents stated that Chinley covered about three hundred acres;[31] however these were 'forest acres' or 'Cheshire acres', which were just over twice the size of statute acres.[32] The key to understanding the disputes over Chinley lies in Godfrey Bradshaw's management of these six hundred statute acres that he had leased from the Duchy.

The Crown's policy towards leasing its lands was based on 'its perception that the estate was both a source of income and the means by which its servants could be rewarded'.[33] Leases were frequently granted in reversion. Such a lease was 'the lease of a future right in a property, usually at the end of a current lease . . . Normally the property would not be taken up by the lessee in reversion, who would simply sell the right to the reversion, usually to the current lessee'.[34] In the case of Chinley, the lessees in reversion did indeed sell the right of reversion, but to a third party rather than to the

28 TNA DL6/34, fols 139–62, draft decree concerning Greenfairfield, suit heard 6 November 1585, quotation from fol. 152.
29 SA Bagshawe Papers, Bag C/2907.
30 TNA DL44/1087, bundle of documents including a commission dated 20 May 1628.
31 For example, TNA DL1/70/A8.
32 Bowles, 'Enclosure Riots at Chinley', p. 62, note added by editor.
33 D. Thomas, 'Leases of Crown Lands in the Reign of Elizabeth I', in *The Estates of the English Crown, 1558–1640*, ed. R. W. Hoyle (Cambridge, 1992), pp. 169–90, quotation at p. 169.
34 TNA catalogue, introductory note to the class DL14: Duchy of Lancaster, drafts and particulars for leases, pp. 2–3.

current lessee. This complicated matters to the point where two groups of
'lessees' were claiming legal access to the herbage as a result of agreements
with different purchasers. By a 31-year lease dated 10 May 1548, Edward
VI had leased Chinley to George Grymsdiche, gentleman.[35] In a subsequent lease, dated 28 May 1568, Elizabeth granted the same herbage in
reversion to Laurence Mynter, gentleman of London, for thirty-one years,
following the expiry in 1579 of Grymsdiche's lease.[36] Almost immediately
Mynter sold his interest in Chinley to Richard Celey, also of London, who
in turn on 2 October 1568 sold it on to Godfrey Bradshaw.[37] The rapid
progression of Chinley through the hands of Grymsdiche, Mynter and
Celey is the sequence of leases on which Bradshaw based his claim to the
herbage. However, some of his opponents rehearsed a rather different sequence, and further claimed that *every* tenant of lands or tenements in the
parishes of Glossop and Chapel-en-le-Frith should have the 'herbage and
pasturinge' of Chinley with their 'cattall according to certeine Auncient
Customes and Rates agreed upon amongst them'.[38] No other such claims
concerning 'ancient customs' practised in Chinley were ever made.

Articles of agreement drawn up by Bradshaw in April 1569, just six
months after he acquired the herbage, indicate how Chinley was to be
managed.[39] The area was divided into forty portions, each known as a
'neighbourship', those holding such portions being known as neighbours.[40] A neighbour paid 5s 4d per annum in rent, one-fortieth of the
herbage's annual rent of £10 13s 4d.[41] Considering the detailed nature
of the 1569 agreement between Bradshaw and the neighbours, it might
be inferred that these articles actually instituted the role of 'neighbours'.
However, in a lease dated 15 November 1568 Godfrey Bradshaw had
transferred to his sons, Francis and Leonard, and his brother, Anthony, a
specific piece of ground in Chinley comprising 'one neighbourshipp and
A halfe neighbourshipp', indicating that the herbage was already so divided.[42] 'Neighbourship' was probably a loose translation of the word
'vicinage', from *visenage*, old French for 'neighbourhood'.[43] 'Common
of vicinage' implied rights claimed by owners of adjacent properties.[44]

---

35   TNA DL42/32, fols 52–52v.
36   TNA DL42/33, fols 747v–748v.
37   See for example TNA DL1/93/M15a; DL1/98/M3a.
38   TNA DL1/93/M15; SA BD 102, fol. 5.
39   TNA DL1/98/M3b.
40   The number of neighbourships is not mentioned in TNA DL1/98/M3b, but is clearly
stated in subsequent documents, such as DL1/93/M15a.
41   TNA DL1/98/M3b, article 1 (my numbering).
42   SA BD100, 15 November 1568.
43   *Oxford English Dictionary sub* 'vicinage'.
44   D. Hey, *The Oxford Companion to Local and Family History* (Oxford, 1996), *sub*
'vicinage, common of'.

Neighbourships might be subdivided into halves or quarters, so that the total number of neighbours usually exceeded forty. Far from being excluded from Chinley, those 'Fourtie householders' whom John Manners et al. claimed to represent in 1572 were evidently 'neighbours' in this tenurial sense, for Bradshaw's own copy of their bill is endorsed 'A Bill agaynst the Tenant of Chynley by dyvers neygbors adioyning', the term 'neygbors' conveying a very specific meaning in this context.[45]

From the articles of 1569 it is clear that from thenceforward the 'neighbours' of Chinley would hold some of their portion of land in common with all other neighbours and the remainder in severalty. The 'owt grownd' of Chinley would be agisted at the rate of sixteen 'beastes' for a neighbourship, eight for a half and so on proportionately.[46] Penalties for overgrazing indicate that a 'beast' was equivalent to one head of cattle, one horse or ten sheep. In addition, every neighbour would occupy four (forest) acres of enclosed herbage 'in severaltie', a half-neighbour two acres and so on. The most logical explanation for allocating four forest acres (or eight statute acres) to be held in severalty is that these distinct areas of the herbage were, or would become, cultivated land: if they too were pasture, there would be no benefit in holding such small closes in severalty.

Since Chinley was already divided into neighbourships when Bradshaw acquired the herbage in 1568, such division alone cannot be the explanation for the subsequent riots. Although ostensibly the cause and targets of the riots, Bradshaw's enclosures were not the only ones in Chinley. Neighbours had already been building cottages in Chinley and erecting enclosures – perhaps to supply the cottages with four acres of land – before their agreement with Bradshaw.[47] Perhaps the unrest occurred because the 1569 articles altered significantly the terms of 'neighbourship': cultivation was now to be in closes of eight statute acres, the fences of which would, by their very existence, limit access to both cultivable land and pasture in the herbage. Since Bradshaw had retained some neighbourships for himself he was entitled to enclose his proportion of the herbage: he had erected some thirteen hundred 'quyckesettes willowes and willowe stackes' around his land.[48] Of the forty-four men in Bradshaw's bill of complaint

45 SA BD102, fols 4, 5, 7–10 is a partial version of the bill; the full version is TNA DL1/93/M15.

46 Unless otherwise noted, details in this paragraph are taken from TNA DL1/98/M3b.

47 TNA DL1/70/A8, undated but calendared under 9 Elizabeth [Nov 1566–Nov 1567], *Attorney General v. [eight named individuals]*; DL1/75/A6, undated but calendared under 10 Elizabeth [Nov 1567–Nov 1568], *Attorney General v. [ten named individuals]*.

48 SA BD101, interrogatory 25. It is not clear how many neighbourships Bradshaw had retained. Bowles mistranscribed the number of quicksets as 'XLIII hundredth' (4,300); the numeral, now very faint, is 'xiij hundredth' or possibly 'xviij' (i.e. 1,300, or 1,800).

accused of destruction, rioting and intimidation in Chinley, twenty-three were parties to the 1569 agreement, ten of whom the Duchy had previously accused of erecting cottages and enclosures, and of cutting down wood there. Presumably these twenty-three neighbours were attacking Bradshaw's property because he was enclosing quite literally more than his share. Doubtless some rioters who were not neighbours were renting cottages within the herbage: access arrangements previously agreed with the cottages' owners had been curtailed by the new agreements. Nicholas Blomley has suggested that Bradshaw had hedged pastureland, causing 'villagers' to be 'denied their rights of pasture'.[49] But the dispute in Chinley was more complex: access to common land was not the issue, rather it was access to pasture and cultivable land for which neighbours and their subtenants were paying rent.

Although located geographically inside the forest of High Peak, by virtue of its status of designated herbage, Chinley was exempt from forest law;[50] thus it is reasonable to suggest that in the 1560s it already displayed the characteristics of improved and enclosed forests.[51] Theoretically, forest law imposed severe limitations on neighbouring communities, creating 'the equivalent of a nature reserve, in which the use of land must not be changed without permission, so as to offer free movement, shelter and food for game and hawks. Permission was required to enclose or plough open land and to fell tree or bush even on privately owned land'.[52] Contemporary arguments advanced in favour of disafforestation, or the removal of forest law, therefore, must convey something of the attractions of Chinley for the neighbours and their subtenants. When, in 1634, the process of disafforestation was commenced in the Peak, the freeholders and tenants in the communities affected petitioned the Crown apparently in support, wishing to be 'freed from the severity, trouble and rigor of the forest laws and customs', from the inconveniences of 'deer lying and feeding in their corn and grass . . . [and] of hunting and riding over their corn and grass, and pulling down their fences'.[53] Although probably a

49   Blomley, 'Making Private Property', 14.
50   For the forest of High Peak, see J. C. Cox, *Royal Forests of England* (London, 1905), chapter 14, and 'The Forest of the High Peak', in *Victoria History of the Counties of England: Derbyshire 1*, ed. W. Page (London, 1905–7), pp. 397–413; R. Somerville, 'Commons and Wastes in North-West Derbyshire – the High Peak "New Lands" ', *Derbyshire Archaeological Journal* 97 (1977), 16–22.
51   For early modern forests, see, for example, J. Langton and G. Jones, eds, *Forests and Chases of England and Wales c.1500–c.1850* (Oxford, 2005); P. A. J. Pettit, *The Royal Forests of Northamptonshire: A Study in their Economy, 1558–1714* (Northamptonshire Record Society, 23, 1968), especially pp. 37–95.
52   G. Hammersley, 'The Revival of the Forest Laws under Charles I', *History* 45 (1960), 85–102, quotation at 88.
53   Brumhead and Weston, 'Seventeenth-Century Enclosures', 249, quoting 'State of the

rhetorical device, nevertheless this petition conveys the likely benefits of disafforestation; and they did apparently ensue. A parliamentary survey of 1649–50 reported that, within a few years of enclosure, land in the Peak Forest had become 'verie fruitfill'[sic], supporting 'many good sheep' and 'much very good Corne'.[54] Thus a neighbourship in Chinley provided easy, although not free, access to an oasis of both good pasture and fertile, cultivable land within a desert of extensive rugged moorland that was technically still subject to forest law; indeed, during Elizabeth's reign forest courts were still being held in High Peak.[55]

III

When attempting to identify various protagonists in the Chinley dispute, research is hampered by the paucity of local records. The only available probate material is from the extensive upland parish of Glossop, although many testators requested burial at Chapel-en-le-Frith.[56] To most of the wills are appended details of debts owed both to and by the testator; perhaps rather than signalling an impoverished community, the large number and low value of most of these sums, or in some cases goods, indicate a remote community where inhabitants were interdependent. Using the few wills and inventories that can be ascribed (tentatively) to men named in the Star Chamber papers and to other parishioners, it is possible to trace various loops of association amongst some of the protagonists.

The claims and counterclaims regarding ownership and access to Chinley made in the Duchy court between 1572 and 1575 by John Manners et al. and Godfrey Bradshaw et al. are connected with the 1576 Star Chamber suit and indicate high status opposition to Bradshaw's activities.[57] Manners was the second son of Thomas, first earl of Rutland; his interest in Chinley was, ostensibly, via an alleged reversionary lease of the herbage and a disputed indenture between Bradshaw and the neighbours dated 1571.[58] Since such a man would hardly be dependent on access to that herbage, perhaps there existed some personal animosity between Bradshaw and Manners

title of the King's Majesty to the timber, woods, mines of coal within the disafforested Forest of High Peak' (1773), p.62, held in the Duchy of Lancaster Office.

54 Brumhead and Weston, 'Seventeenth-Century Enclosures', 250, quoting J. C. Cox, *Notes on the Churches of Derbyshire*, 4 (London, 1879), pp. 508–9.

55 Cox, 'The Forest of the High Peak', pp. 411–12.

56 Chapel-en-le-Frith parish was an ecclesiastical peculiar from which no probate material survives before the seventeenth century; nor are there any relevant wills from the Prerogative Court of Canterbury held at TNA.

57 See, for example, TNA DL1/93/M15 (April 1572); DL1/98/M3 (23 November 1575).

58 TNA DL1/93/M15; SA BD102, fol. 5.

of which the neighbours took advantage. Of his nine associates named in
the Duchy court, six were esquires and gentlemen. Neither Manners nor
any of these were mentioned in the Star Chamber papers; the other three
– Thomas Rawlinson, William Ridge and Reignolde (or Reynold) Kyrke
– were neighbours of Chinley and were named defendants in Bradshaw's
Star Chamber suit. Rawlinson and Kyrke had previously been accused
of erecting cottages in Chinley. From the 1560s onwards these two were
named as witnesses, appraisers or overseers in various probate documents
from the parish of Glossop, suggesting that they were amongst the better
sort of the parish at the time of the unrest.[59] William Ridge may have been
younger as his name does not appear in parish documents until the 1580s;
he was alleged to have been particularly active during the riots.

In addition to the forty-four men subpoenaed to appear and answer
the charges laid by Bradshaw, fourteen others were identified in the interrogatories as participants in assorted illegal activities.[60] Not unexpectedly,
of these fifty-eight, as well as Rawlinson, Kyrke and Ridge, twenty-three
others were neighbours.[61] Only six do not appear in any of the available
probate material. The will and inventory of the rioter James Carrington of
Chinley Houses are particularly illuminating. Carrington leased various
properties, including 'three quarters of a neighbourshipp in the Arbage
of Chindley', which he assigned to his eldest son John.[62] Three of his
four supervisors were neighbours; five men named in Star Chamber were
debtors to him; and two of the four men who appraised his goods were
neighbours. Of the thirty-two people accused in Star Chamber who were
not neighbours, just eight do not appear in any local documents. As noted
above, some of the thirty-two were doubtless legitimate subtenants who
had negotiated access to the herbage with the owner of their cottage. At
least three of the thirty-two only appear in probate documents as debtors
to others. Less shadowy is Richard Shore, the man who Bradshaw claimed
had been sprung from the clutches of the bailiff, under the very nose of the
constable.[63] Defendants had alleged that this incident in 1574 was fictitious
since Shore had died by then.[64] Probate was indeed granted to the will of

---

59   See, for example, the following documents: Lichfield Record Office (LRO) B/C/11,
Nicholas Garlecke, probate 14 February 1566/7; Henry Bayley, probate 29 April 1568;
James Carrington, probate 12 April 1564; Thomas Oliver, probate 17 September 1568;
James Carrington of 'Chindlehowses', probate 30 April 1579.
60   One of the fourteen may have been a woman (?Em' Moult). The badly damaged final
interrogatory may include further names.
61   TNA DL1/98/M3b.
62   LRO B/C/11, James Carrington of 'Chindlehowses', probate 30 April 1579. Perhaps
surprisingly this is the only will that specifically bequeaths a neighbourship.
63   TNA STAC5/B93/31, document 2.
64   TNA STAC5/B93/31, document 1.

'Rycharde Shower of the Brownesyde' on 16 April 1572.[65] Whatever his involvement in the riots, Shore's probate documents also disclose links with seven men named in the Star Chamber papers. Perhaps the man seized by the bailiff was actually his son, also Richard: four of his eight appraisers were named in the Star Chamber papers.[66]

Although some of the thirty-two 'non-neighbours' accused of rioting were poor, others were men of substance who, lacking a formal interest in Chinley, had presumably antagonised Bradshaw in some way. Charles Lingard rented a farm from George Bowden, one of the neighbours; one neighbour witnessed his will; and another appraised his inventory; three other witnesses and two other appraisers were named in the Star Chamber papers.[67] Even more substantial was William Bearde, the man allegedly given a half-neighbourship in return for 'maynteyning' Reynold Kyrke, Thomas Rawlinson and others against the queen and against Bradshaw.[68] William Bearde of Bearde Hall, gentleman, was appointed supervisor by several testators. His own very detailed will confirms his status: he requested burial before the choir of Glossop church and settled £300 on each of his three daughters.[69] Bearde also allegedly supplied 'ydll ryotouse persons' on occasions to assist Kyrke, Rawlinson and others.[70] Those rioters named in bills of complaint or interrogatories were people whose activities attracted the attention either of the authorities or of witnesses; most of the remaining participants, often encompassed by such umbrella phrases as 'very many as yet unknown', were the early modern equivalent of 'rent-a-crowd'. This particular interrogatory confirms that rioters might indeed be procured or supplied upon request.

Following Bowles, Tawney (and Thomas and Kesselring after him) assumed that the Star Chamber suit was initiated by the authorities in 1569 and therefore that the suggestions of dabbling in prophecies might indicate that, to quote Tawney, 'all in authority had that autumn an unusually bad attack of nerves' concerning any outbreak of unrest in the North.[71] The error in dating notwithstanding, perceived links between Chinley and the Northern Rebellion would be more convincing were there any evidence of unrest in Derbyshire during the Rebellion. Unrest might plausibly have occurred since Mary Queen of Scots, a prisoner of the Earl of Shrewsbury

---

65 LRO B/C/11, Rycharde Shower of the Brownesyde.
66 LRO B/C/11, Richard Shore of the Brownesyde, probate 21 December 1583.
67 LRO B/C/11, Charles Lingard of the Chappell Milne, probate 29 February 1575/6.
68 SA BD101, interrogatory 15.
69 LRO B/C/11, William Bearde of Bearde, probate 8 August 1580.
70 SA BD101, interrogatory 15.
71 Tawney, *Agrarian Problem* (1912 edn), p. 329. Thornton notes that 1569–70 'may itself have been the highpoint of rebellion in part because of prophecy relating to Elizabeth's twelfth year' (*Prophecy, Politics and the People*, p. 25).

between 1569 and 1584, was held in various properties in and around Derbyshire and was, at least according to government fears, a constant focus for discontent.[72] However, no such evidence is forthcoming.[73] That it was Bradshaw, rather than the authorities, who initiated the suit in early 1576 gives the suggestions of dabbling in prophecies a rather different complexion.

During the period between 1569 and early 1576, local relations had become so acrimonious that objections to divisions within the herbage had been transmuted into treasonous activities. Witnesses were to be asked whether Reynold Kyrke had confederated with Master Bircles 'concerning prophesies by noble men or otherwise'; and what 'bookes of prophesie' they had seen or heard of; and what they contained.[74] Furthermore, it was suggested that as a result of such prophetic consultations, companies had assembled at 'the Lords yate', including William Bearde of Bearde, gentleman, and Ralph Bradley of Haughe, yeoman.[75] In 1580 Bradley was one of Bearde's appraisers, as was one Hugh Byrtells.[76] Here, perhaps, is a familial link with the 'troublemaker' John Birtles identified by Keith Thomas.[77] By including interrogatories that contained accusations of consulting prophesies, Bradshaw's counsel was attempting to implicate his opponents in treasonous crimes, in which participants in the Northern Rebellion had *already* been implicated and therefore to define these local riots as aftershocks of the Rebellion.[78] Far from prefiguring that unrest, the Chinley riots were fashioned into the spectre of its continuation, a ghost that so haunted the authorities that, Bradshaw hoped, it would bring down their full wrath upon the offenders. Such a strategy was also attempted in the aftermath of the so-called Midland Rising of 1607, when in order to discredit enclosure rioters, landlords and their counsel portrayed them as rebels and 'levellers', and their activities as later manifestations of the Rising, even in areas not associated with it.[79]

In the absence of corresponding depositions, it is impossible to know

---

72 S. E. Kershaw, 'Power and Duty in the Elizabethan Aristocracy: George, Earl of Shrewsbury, the Glossopdale Dispute and the Council', in *The Tudor Nobility*, ed. G. W. Bernard (Manchester, 1992), pp. 266–95, 268; Kesselring, *Northern Rebellion*, pp. 76–7, 159–63.

73 The majority of the rebels came from North Yorkshire and County Durham: Kesselring, *Northern Rebellion*, pp. 61–74.

74 SA BD 101, interrogatory 27.

75 SA BD 101, interrogatory 28.

76 LRO B/C/11, will and inventory of William Bearde of Bearde.

77 Thomas, *Religion and the Decline of Magic*, p. 479.

78 For prophecies at the time of the Rebellion, see: Kesselring, *Northern Rebellion*, pp. 44, 45–6, 112; Thornton, *Prophecy, Politics and the People*, pp. 24–5.

79 R. B. Manning, *Village Revolts: Social Protest and Popular Disturbances in England, 1509–1640* (Oxford, 1988), pp. 83, 84, 235.

whether any witnesses ever responded to those interrogatories that linked the riots with treasonous prophecies; however, although the outcome of the Star Chamber suit is unknown, there are several indications that nothing came of Bradshaw's vindictive strategy. Firstly, he continued to live at Bradshaw Edge, just a few miles from Chinley, until his death in 1607.[80] Secondly, local men continued leasing neighbourships from him, confirming that these remained desirable properties and, at the very least, suggesting that he modified his enclosing activities within the herbage.[81] It would, however, be false to conclude that unfettered neighbourliness reigned thereafter in Chinley since subsequent minor lawsuits in Chancery indicate otherwise.[82] Furthermore, this local system clearly worked: in 1628 the Duchy court ratified the enclosure of the whole of Chinley and its continued division into forty neighbourships.[83]

IV

The underlying theme of this study has been the importance of placing 'expressive actions' such as enclosure riots in their local context.[84] Since Tawney wrote, our understanding of the pattern of participation in riots has become more nuanced as rhetorical strategies used by both sides have been unpacked. Records of early modern crowd actions were usually created by or for the authorities, consequently these convey much about elite preconceptions concerning crowds and rather less about the crowds themselves. It was reassuring for contemporaries to be able to attribute such outbreaks of lawlessness to 'the rude multitude', that part of local society that 'most propertied contemporaries would have thought of as "naturally" given to disorder'.[85] The alternative was unpalatable: any rioters who were persons of quality 'were cankers at the heart of society; renegades of power, position and wealth were much more dangerous than the desperate poor'.[86] Nevertheless, recent studies of enclosure riots, including the one presented here, have demonstrated that participants

---

80 He died intestate; the Bowles Deeds catalogue, pp. 187–90, records verbatim letters of administration, dated 23 April 1607.

81 For example, SA Bag.C/2907, 13 August 1617, which recapitulates previous 21-year leases of the herbage; SA BD110, indenture dated 9 April 1578.

82 For example, TNA C2/Eliz/B10/17.

83 TNA DL44/1087.

84 W. Te Brake, *Shaping History: Ordinary People in European Politics, 1500–1700* (Berkeley, 1998), p. 11.

85 John Walter, *Understanding Popular Violence in the English Revolution: The Colchester Plunderers* (Cambridge, 1999), p. 238.

86 B. Sharp, *In Contempt of all Authority: Rural Artisans and Riot in the West of England, 1586–1660* (London, 1980), p. 131.

might come from all levels of local society.[87] Perhaps most relevant is John Walter's study of the 'rising of the people' in Oxfordshire in 1596 which failed to materialise because a lack of authoritative leadership prevented the leap from discontent to action, yet the very act of planning the rising terrified the authorities into awful reaction.[88] Here is the likely explanation for Godfrey Bradshaw's strategy in linking the unrest at Chinley to the government's latent fears of a continuation of rebellion in the North, a strategy which, as already noted, was employed by victims of riots after the Midland Rising in 1607. Interestingly, in three consecutive sentences in *The Agrarian Problem*, in his broad sweep of 'the last great age of the peasant uprisings' (1500–1650), Tawney linked the riots at Chinley with the planned rising in Oxfordshire and the Midland Rising, both of which have also recently preoccupied historians.[89] In doing so he was guilty of the kind of 'stepping-stone history' derided by Walter, a misrepresentation that can only be avoided by close contextual reading of riots.[90] To be sure, from this perspective these episodes appear more complex and somehow less satisfying than they appeared to Tawney, but they reflect more accurately the complexities of rural social relations than simple models of aggressive landlords and truculent peasants ever did.

87   For example, Falvey, 'Crown Policy and Local Economic Context'; Hindle, 'Persuasion and Protest'; Hipkin, ' "Sitting on His Penny Rent" '; McDonagh, 'Subverting the Ground'.
88   Walter, ' "Rising of the People"?'.
89   Tawney, *Agrarian Problem* (1912 edn), p. 320; Walter, ' "Rising of the People"?; Hindle, 'Imagining Insurrection'.
90   John Walter, 'Public Transcripts, Popular Agency and the Politics of Subsistence in Early Modern England', in *Negotiating Power in Early Modern Society*, ed. Braddick and Walter, p. 146.

5

The Loss of Athelstan's Gift

The Politics of Popular Memory in Malmesbury, 1607–1633[1]

ANDY WOOD

A century after its publication, R. H. Tawney's *The Agrarian Problem in the Sixteenth Century* remains as imaginative, spirited and passionate as ever. For a long time, the book was neglected by early modern historians. The dismissal of *The Agrarian Problem*, often by those unacquainted with it, grew from Eric Kerridge's denunciation of it in 1969. Adopting a schoolmasterly tone, Kerridge chided Tawney for spending too little time in the archives ('Time which he might have given to studying history was devoted instead to the Fabian Society and the Labour Party') and condemned *The Agrarian Problem* as mere socialist propaganda.[2] More recently, the tables have turned.[3] The last twenty years have seen a flowering of work on customary law, much of it conducted under the influence of E. P. Thompson's 1991 book *Customs in Common*.[4] This work has recaptured some of the qualities of *The Agrarian Problem*, most notably its recognition of the political characteristics of custom. Tawney characterised the politics of custom as follows:

> The custom of the manor is a body of rules which regulates the rights and obligations of the peasants in their daily life. It is a kind of law. It is a kind of freedom. And since it is the custom [of the manor] which most concerns the mass of the peasantry, it is not the state, or the law,

1   The research on which this chapter is based was funded by the Arts and Humanities Research Council and the Leverhulme Trust. I am grateful to Dave Rollison and Keith Wrightson for their comments on an earlier draft.
2   Kerridge, *Agrarian Problems*, p. 15.
3   See the respectful tone adopted in Wrightson, *Earthly Necessities*, pp. 4, 5, 17. See also P. Withington, *Society in Early Modern England: The Vernacular Origins of Some Powerful Ideas* (Cambridge, 2010), pp. 45–8.
4   E. P. Thompson, *Customs in Common* (London, 1991). See also Wrightson, 'The Politics of the Parish', pp. 22–5. My own attempt to assess the politics of custom opens with an acknowledgment of Tawney's contribution: Andy Wood, 'The Place of Custom in Plebeian Political Culture: England, 1550–1800', *Social History* 22:1 (1997), 46.

but the custom of the manor which forms their political environment and from which they draw their political ideas. They cannot conceive the state except as a very great manor. Their idea of good government is the enforcement of the idealised customary.[5]

Informed by a grittily materialist sense of the importance of customary entitlements, recent work has followed Thompson and Tawney in focussing upon rural communities.[6] The result has been a sequence of deeply contextualised micro-histories of village politics.[7] There has been a growing recognition of the relationship between customary law and the wider world of popular memory: custom is seen as an organising force within broader popular senses of the past, providing ways of grounding collective identities, making sense of earlier conflicts and contextualising ongoing struggles.[8]

One unremarked consequence of the focus on rural England, however, has been an inattention to customary disputes and popular memory in the towns and cities of early modern England.[9] Just as there is very little work on urban common rights, so work on urban memory deals primarily with civic values, going no deeper than the middling sort.[10] This is characteristic of broader work on the urban polity, where the experience of the middling male citizen-householder is all too often taken as universal.[11] The ways in which poorer townspeople may have remembered the history of their communities, and the junction of such memories with customary arrangements, remains largely unexplored. Where poorer people are shown

5   Tawney, *Agrarian Problem* (1912 edn), p. 131.
6   See for instance Steve Hindle, *On the Parish? The Micro-Politics of Poor Relief in Rural England, c.1550–1750* (Oxford, 2004).
7   See, for instance, Hipkin, ' "Sitting on his Penny Rent"'; Falvey, 'Crown Policy and Local Economic Context'; Hindle, 'Persuasion and Protest'.
8   For an example, see S. Sandall, 'Custom, Memory and the Operations of Power in Seventeenth-Century Forest of Dean', in *Locating Agency: Space, Power and Popular Politics*, ed. F. Williamson (Newcastle, 2010), pp. 133–60.
9   The key exception is H. R. French, 'The Common Fields of Urban England: Communal Agriculture and the "Politics of Entitlement" ', in *Custom, Improvement and the Landscape in Early Modern Britain*, ed. R. W. Hoyle (Farnham, 2011), pp. 149–74.
10   R. Tittler, 'Reformation, Civic Culture and Collective Memory in English Provincial Towns', *Urban History* 24:3 (1997), 283–300; R. Tittler, *Townspeople and Nation: English Urban Experiences, 1540–1640* (Stanford, Calif., 2001), chapter 5.
11   See for instance M. Goldie, 'The Unacknowledged Republic: Office-holding in Early Modern England', in *The Politics of the Excluded, c.1500–1850*, ed. T. Harris (Basingstoke, 2001), pp. 153–94. In an admirable intervention which engages with 'the politics of remembering' in towns and cities, Phil Withington attempts to link urban custom with civic humanism, but has little to say about the role of borough custom in the regulation of economic affairs and ignores common rights: P. Withington, 'Agency, Custom and the English Corporate System', in *Identity and Agency in England, 1500–1800*, ed. H. R. French and J. Barry (Basingstoke, 2004), pp. 200–22.

exercising agency in urban communities, this is often fleeting and atom-
ised, part of a way of making ends meet, or as unconnected moments of
defiance.[12] The idea that the urban lower classes might assert themselves *as
an organised collectivity* remains under-explored.[13] This is curious, since
the archival evidence points to issues concerning customary entitlement
being the focus of urban social conflicts. These conflicts in towns were,
if anything, often even sharper than in rural communities.[14] This chapter
seeks to correct that absence. It also aims to add something to the literature on urban society and to that on custom and popular memory. Its
focus is primarily on those below the level of the middling sort and depicts
urban workers staking a claim to a place within the polity of the borough.
It locates struggles over customary entitlement and urban identity within
the broader pattern of social relations in one particular community:
Malmesbury, a small cloth-working town in Wiltshire.[15]

I

The dispute of 1607–13 which forms the core of this essay revolved around
a combination of economic and constitutional issues. It is therefore best to
sketch the development of the administration of the borough. As early as
the ninth century, Malmesbury enjoyed borough status. In reward for the
town's service against the Danes, King Athelstan extended its liberties and
granted it a wide common, King's Heath.[16] By the thirteenth century there
was a guild merchant and two other governmental bodies in the town: the
hundred and the half-hundred.[17] Whereas the guild merchant appears to
have originated in the self-organisation of wealthier cloth merchants, the
hundred and half-hundred emerged from loose groups of lesser traders
and artisans. Athelstan's charter was reconfirmed by the Crown in 1381.[18]
By the seventeenth century, authority was distributed across a number

12   See, most recently, the picaresque world vividly evoked in P. Griffiths, *Lost Londons:
Change, Crime and Control in the Capital City, 1550–1660* (Cambridge, 2008).

13   For two exceptions, see Walter, *Understanding Popular Violence*; D. Rollison, *Commune,
Country and Commonwealth: The People of Cirencester, 1117–1643* (Woodbridge, 2011).

14   For urban struggles over customary entitlements as a cause of insurrection in 1549, see
Wood, *The 1549 Rebellions*, pp. 13–14, 43–4, 49, 60, 62, 121, 124.

15   For brief mention of the 1607–13 Malmesbury dispute, see: Manning, *Village Revolts*,
pp. 104–5; D. Underdown, *Revel, Riot and Rebellion: Popular Politics and Culture in
England, 1603–1660* (Oxford, 1985), pp. 96, 280.

16   *Calendar of Patent Rolls, 1381–85*, 54. Luce estimates the date of Athelstan's charter
as AD 939: see R. H. Luce, *The History of the Abbey and Town of Malmesbury* (Minety,
1979), p. 91.

17   VCH, *Wilts*, 14:149.

18   VCH, *Wilts*, 14:131.

of bodies. The manor court retained jurisdiction over criminal matters and the two hundreds had multiplied into six. Each was made up of male householders who had been born in the town, those who had married a native Malmesbury woman, or those who had lived there for three years. The main purpose of entering a hundred was to gain common rights on King's Heath. Membership appears not to have required any property qualifications and so provided poorer householders with a legal basis to claims to common rights on King's Heath.[19]

Town government in the years before the dispute of 1607–13 had clearly undergone important change, but the nature of those changes, and their legitimacy, remains unclear. In the dispute of 1607–13, the leading men of Malmesbury claimed that back in the 1560s town government had been settled following a period of turbulence by the Bishop of Salisbury, John Jewell, who established a company of thirteen burgesses including an alderman and two stewards, three trade companies and a council of twenty-four landholders.[20] In the 1607–13 dispute, and in subsequent testimony collected in 1633, this claim was contested by the poorer inhabitants. They argued that Bishop Jewell had disrupted the earlier, legitimate mode of government, which had rested with a head bailiff, two constables, and a body of wardsmen, all of them elected annually at the court leet of the manor.[21] This popular faction based their claims on what they had 'crediblie heard': that is, upon oral tradition.[22] The poorer commoners wished to return the government of the town to what they saw as its customary form. In their account, Bishop Jewell's intervention, which they dated to 1566, had been 'unlawful' and had resulted in a narrowly illegitimate governmental structure, dominated by the rich men of the town.[23] As we shall see, these were more than mere quibbles over minor administrative arrangements.

The ambiguity of governmental forms in Malmesbury formed part of a wider crisis of legitimacy. Administration had evolved over the years through a combination of habit, compromise and long usage: that is, the classic blend that generated customary law in manors and parishes as well

---

19   Recent studies of common rights have ignored urban common rights. See Sara Birtles, 'Common Land, Poor Relief and Enclosure: The Use of Manorial Resources in Fulfilling Parish Obligations, 1601–1834', *Past & Present*, 165 (1999), 74–106; Leigh Shaw-Taylor, 'Labourers, Cows, Common Rights and Parliamentary Enclosure: The Evidence of Contemporary Comment, c.1760–1810', *Past & Present* 171 (2001), 95–126.

20   Luce, *History*, p. 96.

21   VCH, *Wilts*, 14:150–2.

22   Adam Fox, 'Custom, Memory and the Authority of Writing', in *The Experience of Authority*, ed. Griffiths, Fox and Hindle, pp. 89–116; Andy Wood, 'Custom and the Social Organisation of Writing in Early Modern England', *TRHS*, sixth series, 9 (1999), 257–69.

23   TNA STAC8/290/22.

as boroughs.[24] Within this, two issues were especially fraught: common rights on King's Heath; and participation in the election of town officers. By the beginning of the reign of James I, opinion on these matters had polarised on class lines: richer townspeople insisted upon a narrower definition of the franchise and sought to restrict common rights upon King's Heath to landed inhabitants. Poorer people, many of them weavers, took the opposite view. The conflict was partially fought out as a jurisdictional conflict between the clearly expanding powers of the borough authorities, dominated by the richer classes, and the manor court and hundreds, in which their poorer neighbours found a voice. These divisions came into public view in the years between 1607 and 1613. The conflict in Jacobean Malmesbury evoked conflicting ideas about order, governance, custom and entitlement, grounded upon opposed readings of local history.

Malmesbury was an industrial town. When John Leland visited it in 1542, he was told that three thousand cloths were produced there each year.[25] The site of the abbey had been purchased by a clothier, William Stumpe, who employed weavers in the former abbey outhouses. Fortunes were to be made in the Wiltshire cloth industry: by 1538, Stumpe held the commission of the peace. His son, James, was knighted and established a mansion house on the abbey site.[26] While there were rich cloth merchants and clothiers within Malmesbury, there were also a great many poorer people. This was a town whose inhabitants felt markedly comfortable in employing a dichotomous language in description of local society. In 1633, the 76-year-old weaver John Johnson said that Malmesbury was 'very full of poore people'. His neighbour William Brook agreed, claiming that many Malmesbury householders had been forced into poverty as a result of the illicit seizure of King's Heath by the wealthy men: 'they are much the poorer by reason the Alderman & Burgesses of the said Towne & doe deteyne & keepe the said hundred lands & Kings Heath to themselves from the poore people.'[27]

At the time of the 1607–13 dispute the same polarised language prevailed. The 'poore inhabitants' saw their opponents as 'the Richer sort' who were trying to 'debar and exclude . . . the greater parte of the poore inhabitants'. [28] A 70-year-old carrier felt that in dispossessing the poorer

---

24   For a useful overview, albeit one which places insufficient emphasis upon the organic evolution of urban custom, see A. Kiralfy, 'Custom in Medieval English Law', *Journal of Legal History* 9:1 (1988), 26–39.

25   L. Toulmin Smith, ed., *The Itinerary of John Leland, in or about the Years 1535 to 1543*, 1 (London, 1964), p. 132.

26   VCH, *Wilts*, 4:146–7; Luce, *History*, pp. 78–80; G. D. Ramsay, *The Wiltshire Woollen Industry in the Sixteenth and Seventeenth Centuries* (Oxford, 1943), pp. 17, 32–4.

27   TNA E134/9ChasI/Mich75.

28   TNA STAC8/138/8; TNA STAC 8/93/2.

householders, the aldermen sought only 'their owne private gaine'. His neighbours agreed, noting that the aldermen came from 'the wealthier sorte'.[29] Thus, the aldermen, who were 'men of greate estate' had driven 'poore men . . . ignorante of theire estates' off the common.[30] To the poor weavers of Malmesbury, it seemed self-evident that their livelihoods were threatened by 'householders of the Richer sorte'.[31] Nor was it only the poorer householders who saw things this way: in answer to complaints concerning their seizure of King's Heath, the aldermen noted contemptuously that their opponents were 'men and women of the meanest and basest sort of people' drawn from the 'Comon and inferior Company of the said Towne'.[32]

Of course, such language was rhetorical. For instance, we shall see that it was far from the case that the poor commoners were 'ignorante of theire estates'. As recent work on the language of legal complaint in local disputes has noted, 'such discourses were used creatively to justify different positions at different times'.[33] But language rarely floats wholly free of its signified subject. That both sides in Jacobean Malmesbury, like the old men of 1633, consistently described the dispute of 1607–13 in terms of a struggle between opposed social groups ought to tell us something important about social relations in the town.

In order to comprehend the issues at stake in Jacobean Malmesbury, we need briefly to reconstruct the course of events that generated conflict within the town. In 1607, the aldermen enclosed part of King's Heath and drove off the cattle of the poorer householders. That September, the weaver John Cowper (who was to assume a leading role in pressing the claims of the poorer commoners) claimed to have been attacked by the aldermen while asserting his common rights on King's Heath. Around the same time, the enclosures that the aldermen had made on King's Heath were broken down by a crowd led by Robert Terry, another significant leader of the poor commoners. In January 1608 John Cowper, claiming to speak on behalf of the poor inhabitants of Malmesbury, entered a suit against the aldermen in Star Chamber.[34] The following month, the alderman Humfrey Elkington and the stewards William Sparks and Thomas Pope initiated two counter-suits at the same court. In one complaint, they claimed that they had been assaulted on King's Heath in the previous November; in

29   TNA STAC8/130/3.1, 12.
30   TNA C78/174/5.
31   TNA STAC8/130/2.
32   TNA STAC8/290/22.
33   M. Clark, 'The Gentry, the Commons and the Politics of Common Right in Enfield, c.1558–c.1603', *Historical Journal* 54:3 (2011), 624.
34   For popular litigation at Star Chamber, see Steve Hindle, *The State and Social Change in Early Modern England* (Basingstoke, 2000), pp. 87–93.

another, they alleged that on 26 December 1607 their enclosures had been destroyed by a rioting crowd. On 12 March 1608, depositions were taken in these matters. Early the following month, the Star Chamber heard yet another complaint against the aldermen. That Easter, a further counter-suit was initiated, this time at Chancery. This came before Lord Ellesmere, who did his best to impose a compromise. On 20 October 1608, the opposing parties assembled in the Common Hall of Malmesbury to establish a commission which (according to the aldermen) agreed to the division of part of King's Heath. Nonetheless, enclosure rioting continued until 1611, allegedly involving crowds of up to two hundred, led in some cases by John Cowper.

The dispute involved not just entitlement upon King's Heath, but also the right to elect the governing bodies of the town.[35] As the aldermen explained to Star Chamber early in 1613, in October of the previous year John Cowper and his supporters had gone 'from house to house' to persuade the poorer inhabitants 'to be Rulers and governors within the said Towne'. Cowper and his faction held an election for thirteen new governors of the town. On 18 July 1612, they had publicly denounced the aldermen. The following Trinity Sunday, on the traditional day for the appointment of the new governors of the town, they assembled in the Common Hall and again denounced the aldermen. This explicit breach of governmental relations in the town appears to have forced the central authorities into decisive action, and on 22 June 1612, the Chancery dismissed John Cowper's case and ratified the aldermanic faction's authority both over the town and King's Heath. Further trouble followed, leading the aldermen to lodge a final complaint at Star Chamber in January 1613. Nothing is heard thereafter concerning the contested authority of the aldermen, or the extent of common right on King's Heath, until action was initiated over these matters at Exchequer in 1633. Depositions were taken in the matter that year, in which a sequence of aged weavers presented their bitter evidence concerning the events of 1607–13.

This action may have been the spur to the grant of a new charter in 1635, which (much in the authoritarian spirit of the Personal Rule) comprehensively shut down any institutional space for popular politics within Malmesbury.[36] A preamble to the charter stated the need for greater order in the town. The charter itself confirmed the authority of the corporation, adding the further provision that the aldermen were to act as magistrates,

35 Disputes over urban common rights sometimes raised broader issues about civic governance. For another example, see TNA STAC3/7/32.
36 It bears comparison with the Caroline charter of Colchester, which was similarly intended to shut down popular politics in the town. See: Walter, *Understanding Popular Violence*, pp. 82–3. Notably, like Malmesbury, Colchester was a weaving town with a history of trouble over adjacent common land.

coroners and the clerks of the market. There was to be a court meeting every three weeks to hear civil cases; the corporation, meeting in the Common Hall, was empowered to make regulations for the government of the town. The aldermen were to be self-selecting.[37] In concentrating authority in the hands of an oligarchic clique, the charter of 1635 solved the question posed by the 1607–13 conflict: that of the location of authority in the town. The history of early Stuart Malmesbury therefore provides clear evidence of the reassertion of urban oligarchy in the face of popular challenge. Notably, this linked issues of material and constitutional entitlement: the right for poorer people to select their governors was caught up with their right to exploit the resources of King's Heath. On both subjects, the poor commoners of the town were comprehensively defeated.

II

The poor commoners were adroit in their deployment of the traditions concerning King Athelstan. It was standard practice for defenders of popular claims to argue, as the Malmesbury commoners did, that they inhabited an 'Auncyent Towne' possessed of commons 'which in Tymes past hath lyen open'.[38] What the Athelstan tradition gave to the defenders of popular rights was a much more powerful and specific claim: that their commons had been given to them by the first monarch of a unified English realm in thanks for their service against foreign invaders. Both sides cited the Athelstan tradition in support of their case. They did so not only to different ends, but on the basis of opposed readings of local history. In their 1613 complaint to Star Chamber the aldermen noted that

> King Athelstan sometimes King of England for and in consideracon of the Aide and good service done unto the said kinge by the said Towne or burgesses in his warres or conflict against the Danes did by his highnes Charter of Lettes patents give and grant unto the said Burgesses . . . Five hid lands whereof part is and hath bene inclosed[.]

John Cowper and his friends answered by claiming that the Athelstan tradition did more than grant a body of land to the *borough* of Malmesbury: they suggested that the monarch had given rights and resources to its *people*. Citing Malmesbury's status as a royal borough, they argued that the aldermen's assumption of authority represented not just a breach of town custom, but was an abrogation of governmental relations that had

37   VCH, *Wilts*, 14:150; TNA E134/9ChasI/Mich75.
38   TNA STAC8/138/8.

been established by 'King Athelstan . . . of his bountie and grace by his l[ett]res pattents deed or other conveyances in writing'. Amongst these manuscripts, Cowper and his associates argued, lay not just sanction to an inclusive form of town government, but also their rights to King's Heath.

When the showdown came in the Common Hall on Trinity Sunday 1612, Cowper and his fellows began with a critique of their would-be rulers: they 'openly affirme[d] that . . . the Burgesses had noe authority within the said Towne . . . and did then . . . in contempt and disgrace and despight of . . . the said burgesses and of theire said authority sett themselves on the Bench or seat appointed for . . . the Alderman and burgesses.' Having physically occupied the seat of town government, 'the better to blinde and deceaive the multitude and meaner sort of people', Cowper

> did shew forthe a Boxe wherein he said there was sufficient to discharge . . . [the aldermen] from all theire power and authority and thereuppon used these . . . speeches . . . Mr Alderman and the rest of the burgesses your fellowes I discharge you and comand you by the authority I have here in my Boxe to forebeare to keepe anie Court or to decide anie further in the business of the . . . Towne.[39]

Within Cowper's box lay manuscripts which sustained the popular party's claim to a place in the government of the town, together with their rights upon King's Heath.

Athelstan's gift was central to Cowper's case. In denying the poor commoners their right to King's Heath and to their proper place in the government of the town, Cowper argued that the aldermen were breaching custom and undermining Athelstan's grant.[40] In Cowper's analysis, the aldermen intended to 'debar and exclude . . . the greater parte of the poore inhabitants' from their rights which they held 'according to the true meaning of the said auncient grante from . . . King Athellstane'.[41] In particular, he argued that the denial of popular rights on King's Heath represented an assault upon Athelstan's legacy. This was enabled, he argued in a cross-suit at Chancery, by the aldermanic faction withholding the 'deedes evidences letters patent charters and wrightings' of the borough, so ensuring that, for want of the said 'deeds charters letters patents wrightinge and evidence . . . [which] of right belonginge unto . . . the said burgesses and poore inhabitants', the poorer people of the town were unable to sustain their rights at law.[42]

39   TNA STAC8/290/22.
40   Ibid.
41   TNA STAC8/93/2.
42   TNA C78/174/5.

Contending versions of local history drawing upon local folkloric traditions concerning Athelstan were central to the Malmesbury dispute. Years
later, inhabitants of a sequence of Wiltshire villages drew the attention
of the Restoration antiquary John Aubrey to traces of Athelstan's regal
presence. He was told that the image of a king in a stained-glass window
at Corsham church was that of Athelstan. At Brokenborough, Aubrey was
shown both 'the Seate of Athelstan' and the ruins of Athelstan's palace,
located alongside the manor house. Reaching Malmesbury, Aubrey noted
that

> King Athelstan was a great Benefactor to this Borough . . . For the good
> service this towne did him against the Danes, he gave them a vast and rich
> common, called King's Heath, and other privileges to the Burghers, and
> also certain meadows near the town. By the Towne is a Hill called Danys-
> Hill. Winni is the name of the ground on which K. Athelstan vanquished
> the Danes.

Aubrey was shown the charter granted to Malmesbury by Athelstan,
'which is not above six lines, and very legible'.[43] Athelstan was seen as a
sufficiently authoritative grantor of borough freedom that the burgers of
Barnstaple went so far as to fabricate charters in his name.[44] Some other
signs of the ancient history of Malmesbury were pointed out to Aubrey. Just
as Athelstan's charter pointed to the long continuity in town government
(a continuity which Cowper and his faction argued had been fractured in
the 1560s), the ancient origins of its dominant industry were highlighted
by the name of a piece of meadow ground in the town. Aubrey was taken
to 'a meadow called St. Aldhelm's Mead', named after the founder of
Malmesbury Abbey. He noted that 'The Tradition here is that St Aldhelm's
father was a weaver'.[45]

In order to make sense of the tradition concerning St Aldhelm's father,
we need to locate it within collective memory, an element within a shared
set of beliefs about the past that was passed on because they were in some
form *usable*.[46] In a trail-blazing lecture in 1983, Keith Thomas suggested

43   J. E. Jackson, ed., *Wiltshire: Topographical Collections of John Aubrey, FRS, AD
1659–70* (Devizes, 1862), pp. 81, 210–11, 252. See also the examples quoted in Adam Fox,
Oral and Literate Culture in England, 1500–1700 (Oxford, 2000), p. 245.
44   S. Reynolds, 'The Forged Charters of Barnstaple', *English Historical Review* 84
(1969), 699–720.
45   Jackson, *Wiltshire*, pp. 253–4.
46   For the origin of the concept of the usable past, see H. S. Commager, *The Search for
a Usable Past* (New York, 1967). For influential overviews of collective memory, both of
which emphasise its utility, see P. Connerton, *How Societies Remember* (Cambridge, 1989);
J. Fentress and C. Wickham, *Social Memory* (Oxford, 1992).

that 'in sixteenth- and seventeenth-century England . . . the only respectable justification for the study of the past was that it could be of service to the present'.[47] This was as true of poorer and middling people as it was of the gentry. The commons of Tudor and Stuart England were anxious to hold onto local memories that had a meaningful function: the best example is that of customary law ('time whereof the memory of man is not to the contrary', or lying 'nowhere but in the memory of the people'), because of its basis for making claims to rights and resources in the present. But custom was not the only claim that gained legitimacy from the past. Collective identity, too, was vested in a sense of the past: the tradition concerning the livelihood of St Aldhelm's father implied a bigger narrative. What was being said here was that the weavers' story was the story of Malmesbury: that weaving preceded the foundation of the abbey, and so laid the basis for the town. In a culture in which the past was seen as the legitimate source of rights and entitlements, and in an economy in which the textile industry had a fundamental, material centrality, the sense of the past that was here being articulated was one which set weavers at the heart of local history.[48] Athelstan's gift, then, codified governmental practices for an *already existent* community: a community made by industrial labour, not by lordly, monastic or royal authority.

Malmesbury's traditions had a politics. In placing the weavers at the centre of the origins of the town, folklore legitimated the weavers' place in the small polity of the borough. The tradition concerning Athelstan's grant of King's Heath had a similar force. The story, as it was told to Aubrey, went like this: following his victory over the Danes, in which he had received the assistance of the people of Malmesbury, King Athelstan was riding along the Fosse Way (the great Roman road that runs from Cornwall to Scotland) when he encountered a beggar woman leading a cow. She complained to Athelstan that the town had no common. Queen Maud therefore asked that Malmesbury be given as much common as she could ride around on a bareback horse. Queen Maud's knight, Sir Walter, followed her in this first perambulation of what became King's Heath.[49] The tradition noted by Aubrey was hazy on one critical point: which part of King's Heath had

47 K. Thomas, *The Perception of the Past in Early Modern England* (London, 1983), p. 8.
48 On early modern senses of the longevity of the weaving trade, see: D. Rollison, 'Discourse and Class Struggle: The Politics of Industry in Early Modern England', *Social History* 26:2 (2001), 184.
49 For other traditions in which noblewomen or queens grant popular liberties within an area circumscribed by that which they could ride around, see M. D. Harris, ed., *The Coventry Leet Book*, 2 (Early English Text Society, new series, 135, London, 1908), p. 567; J. Dunkin, *The History and Antiquities of the Hundreds of Bullington and Ploughley*, 1 (London, 1823), p. 120.

been granted to Malmesbury and which to the nearby settlement of Long Newnton.

The assertion of Malmesbury's claim was marked with much ritualised commensality and rejoicing and, on at least one occasion, by the playfully violent assertion of their rights by the young men of the town. In the course of the celebrations concerning the grant of King's Heath, the processioning crowd was asked to

> pray to God that moved the hearts of King Athelstan & Dame Maud his good Queen to give this ground to our forefathers & to us, and to all them that shall come after us, and to all them that shall come after us in Fee for ever.[50]

These festivities traditionally took place on Trinity Sunday. It was on the Trinity Monday of 1613 that John Cowper and his comrades confronted the aldermanic faction in the Common Hall of Malmesbury. Perhaps some of the weavers' boots were still damp from tramping the muddy bounds of King's Heath on the previous day. On that Trinity Monday, John Cowper and his fellows laid claim both to King's Heath and to a place in the government of their town. King's Heath, like Malmesbury itself, formed a site for the ritualised assertion of a collectively remembered sense of belonging. Written into the landscape of Malmesbury was a distinct sense of the past, one stamped onto the ground in yearly perambulations and passed about by word of mouth as an oral tradition. In enclosing King's Heath, the aldermen were attacking not just a set of material claims, but a sense of entitlement: a way of belonging that was rooted in place, memory and tradition.[51]

III

John Cowper and his friends creatively exploited a founder myth, legitimating their struggle through the employment of a distinct sense of the

50   BL, Lansdowne 231, fol. 187v; Jackson, *Wiltshire*, pp. 272–3; for the riotous incident, see Wiltshire and Swindon Archives, Quarter Sessions rolls, A1/110, T.1641, fols 183v–5. This incident involved the deployment of rituals which are best analysed in A. Howkins and L. Merricks, '"Wee Be Black as Hell": Ritual, Disguise and Rebellion', *Rural History* 4:1 (1993), 41–53. It is important that Howkins and Merricks locate those rituals within local folklore.

51   For the invention of new rituals associated with Athelstan upon the enclosed King's Heath, see J. M. Moffatt, *The History of the Town of Malmesbury, and of Its Ancient Abbey* (Tetbury, 1805), p. 248. For landscape and belonging, see in particular: Tilley, *Phenomenology of Landscape*.

past, vested in local folklore. This was, then, a powerfully positive memory, one that legitimated subaltern agency in the present.[52] But none of this
prevented the ultimate triumph of the aldermen. What the old men who
gave evidence in 1633 concerning the history of entitlement upon King's
Heath remembered as 'the cause of the poore inhabitants' was eventually
defeated. Silence descends upon John Cowper as he reaches his most ar-
ticulate moment: the assertion of the poor commoners' rights on Trinity
Monday 1613.[53] Thereafter, all we know is that King's Heath was enclosed
and that, under Charles I, town government was closed down as a popular
space. The precise history of those processes lie beyond the archival record; but their outcome is not in doubt. From this moment a different kind
of popular memory emerges within the town which interlaced the folkloric
traditions concerning Athelstan's gift with a harsher, more immediate set
of memories: defeat, dispossession and exclusion. We gain historical access to these memories through the witness statements collected from old
men of the town in 1633. In that year, the Attorney-General began proceedings against the aldermen. As part of Caroline revival of ancient royal
liberties, the Attorney-General laid claim to King's Heath, arguing that it
was Crown land, and that the burgesses' hold upon it was illegal.[54] The
aldermen contested the case and so a commission of local gentlemen was
empowered by the Exchequer Court to take oral evidence from the aged
inhabitants of the town.[55]

The witnesses described in detail the gradual diminution, over some sixty years, of common rights on King's Heath. The evisceration of popular
entitlement on the Heath took place at the same time as the erosion of the
place of the poor commoners in the polity of the borough. In the memory
of the old men of 1633, this process had been initiated by Bishop Jewell
in the 1560s. At that time, Sir James Stumpe had sliced off part of the
common for himself. The erosion of King's Heath continued through the
reign of James I, encompassing the dispute of 1607–13 (which the old men
of 1633 remembered very well), concluding in the 1630s as the aldermen
took chunks of King's Heath for themselves. So far as the old men of 1633
were concerned, the aldermanic faction lacked legitimacy: the 76-year-

52 For memory as a source of subaltern agency, see R. Johnson and G. Dawson, 'Popular
Memory: Theory, Politics, Method', in *Making Histories*, ed. Centre for Contemporary
Cultural Studies (London, 1982), pp. 205–52; J. Rappaport, *The Politics of Memory:
Native Historical Interpretation in the Columbian Andes* (Durham, NC, 1998).
53 On silencing, politics and memory, see G. Sider and G. Smith, *Between History and
Histories: The Making of Silences and Commemorations* (Toronto, 1997); S. Narotzky and
G. A. Smith, '"Being Político" in Spain: An Ethnographic Account of Memories, Silences
and Public Politics', *History & Memory* 14 (2002).
54 TNA E178/5701.
55 TNA E134/9ChasI/Mich75.

old weaver John Johnson stated clearly that 'the compeines of fower &
twenty landholders have not any power in the orderinge & Gov[er]mt' of
Malmesbury.

The dispute threw up issues of social morality as well as institutional
legitimacy.[56] Thomas Pickringe contributed positive memories of one en-
closer which cast the more general process of enclosure in a harsh light.
He explained that back in 1624 Thomas Phillips had enclosed part of
Kings Heath but had subsequently given up this land because 'as he said
his conscience did give him that he did the poore of the said towne wrong
for holdinge & deteyninge the said enclosed lands from them & thereupon resyned & gave up his said place'. As Pickringe noted, other members of the town elite proved less morally discriminating. William Brook,
a 67-year-old weaver, was especially angry. He emphasised his own roots
in the town: he told the commissioners that he had been 'borne & bred
within the said towne [and] . . . hath from his childhood knowne . . . Kings
Heath & Hundred Lands . . . belonging to the . . . Towne'. This personal
acquaintance with the commons was underwritten by knowledge of the
history of those lands and the government of the town:

> Kinge Edward Eldar gave the hundred lands to all the inhabitants of the
> towne . . . in gen[er]all & his sonne Kinge Athelstone gave the said lands
> called Kings heath to the said towne as by the charter appeareth to the
> wch he referreth himselfe for the good service the Inhabitannts . . . against
> the danes[.]

Despite this grant by two great Anglo-Saxon monarchs to the general
population of the town, not only had the aldermen enclosed the commons,
but they had pocketed the cash that was paid by poorer householders for
pasturing their animals upon the enclosed land. For William Brook, the
corrupt administration of the enclosed lands was linked to a wider process
of expropriation such that 'the poore people are thereby debarred from
fetching a stick of wood out of the said Kings Heath & Hundred Lands &
are thereby likewise debarred of theire common'.

Remembering never invokes a lost, dead or inert past. Rather, it forms
an imaginative bridge between then and now.[57] It is therefore worth asking what was being remembered in Malmesbury in 1633. These were not

56   For the argument that the early modern English state rested on secure foundations of
broadly shared ideas about legitimate authority, see: Michael J. Braddick, *State Formation
in Early Modern England, c.1550–1700* (Cambridge, 2000), pp. 9, 90, 94. The material
deployed in this chapter suggests a different picture.
57   For a fuller discussion, see B. Jones, 'The Uses of Nostalgia: Autobiography, Community
Publishing and Working-Class Neighbourhoods in Post-War England', *Cultural and Social
History* 7 (2010), 355–74.

the positive, assertive memories that underwrote local custom and which guaranteed its continuance (so its claimants said) from time immemorial. There is nothing here of the 'idealised customary' that Tawney saw as the high ideal of what he called the 'peasantry'. Nor is there any of the organised, deliberate assertiveness that, in earlier work, I have argued informed the plebeian politics of custom.[58] All we find is bitterness and anger. A sense of loss runs through the recollections of the old men of Malmesbury: the loss of a collective resource, of shared entitlements, of a kind of social contract. None of this undermines Tawney's central argument about the importance of custom in popular political culture – if anything, it reinforces his point. Most importantly, the old men of 1633 remind us that custom was about more than the simple assertion of pragmatic material interests. For poorer people, grazing a cow or collecting fuel on King's Heath combined material need, common interest, memory, community, meaning and agency. Economics, culture and politics were entangled in custom.[59] And so, in places like Malmesbury, when custom was broken, what was also fractured was a shared way of *understanding* and of *being*. Histories of custom and popular memory need to engage with the complex entanglement of material life and remembered worlds: if we are truly to understand people such as the old men of Malmesbury in 1633, a history of popular politics is needed that gives equal weight to economics, culture, social relations and the endurance of structural inequalities of wealth and power.

58 Wood, 'Place of Custom'.
59 For the entanglement of production, reproduction and social relations, see I. Hodder, *Catalhoyuk: The Leopard's Tale* (London, 2006), pp. 186–95.

6

In Search of the Scottish Agrarian Problem

JULIAN GOODARE

Any one who turns over the Statutes and State Papers of the sixteenth century will be aware that statesmen were much exercised with an agrarian problem, which they thought to be comparatively new, and any one who follows the matter further will find the problem to have an importance at once economic, legal, and political.[1]

This was how R. H. Tawney introduced his seminal work on the 'agrarian problem' in sixteenth-century England. I would like to ask: could statements comparable to Tawney's be made about Scotland? The question is a difficult one – but, perhaps for that very reason, an inviting one. Hitherto, the agrarian history of sixteenth-century Scotland has seemed particularly hard to penetrate from an English viewpoint. Work that has been done on subsequent periods of Scottish agriculture, especially the later seventeenth century onwards, has enabled English historians to address it in familiar ways and to incorporate it in broader patterns of agrarian change; but the sixteenth century has remained 'frustratingly obscure'.[2] An attempt to lift some of this obscurity is surely worthwhile.

The search, as it proceeds, will indeed be 'economic, legal, and political'. The neglected legal and political aspects will be emphasised, but always with the purpose of relating them to the economy. The results, it will be suggested, indicate some significant parallel processes at work in the English and Scottish agrarian economies.

I

The single most visible development in Scottish landlord–tenant relations in this period was the feuing movement. It also elicited vigorous government action and social comment, so it is a natural point at which to begin. Feuing

1 Tawney, *Agrarian Problem*, p. 1.
2 Wrightson, *Earthly Necessities*, p. 16.

does not readily bring up a precise English equivalent, but English readers are urged to call to mind the dissolution of the monasteries, and then read on. In the early sixteenth century, there were three main categories of land-lord in Scotland: the Church, the Crown, and secular lords. Proportions of land in each category are not known precisely, but if it were suggested that the Church had up to half the land and that the Crown had one-tenth, these figures would at least be in the right order of magnitude. Church and Crown estates were not independent of secular lords; members of local aristocratic families were often their hereditary bailies or chamberlains, or (in the case of Church estates) actual bishops or heads of monasteries. For present purposes we need to concentrate on these different landlords' relationships with their tenants – and at the outset of the sixteenth century, they all rented their lands to peasant tenants in similar ways.

Into this traditional picture, feu-ferme tenure entered as something of a novelty. Legally, it was a perpetual lease rather than a feudal grant. Nevertheless, a feuar (the recipient of a feu) was effectively the full, herit-able proprietor of his lands so long as he paid his annual feu-duty, fixed in perpetuity and subject to considerable diminution in real terms during the inflation-ridden sixteenth century. Indeed, the feuar was in some ways privileged over traditional proprietors; although he owed feu-duties, he escaped most of the feudal 'casualties' that the Crown or other superiors could exact. Feu-ferme eventually eclipsed other tenures, remaining the basis of Scottish conveyancing law until 2000.

During the sixteenth century, and especially in its middle decades, most of the lands of the Crown and Church were feued. A good deal is known about the feuing of Church lands, thanks to the work of Margaret Sanderson.[3] Between the 1530s and 1580s, in a development comparable to the dissolution of the English monasteries, the Scottish Crown imposed heavy taxation on the Church, forcing churchmen to realise cash from their estates. They raised this, not by selling land (which was prohibited by canon law), but by feuing it. This was lucrative because, along with the annual feu-duty, churchmen could demand that feuars make a sizeable payment of cash up front. The Scottish bishops and heads of monasteries were thus alienating the direct control of their estates to the feuars.

Who, then, were the feuars of Church lands? Earlier scholars, guided by contemporary literary comment, had assumed that these were mainly existing nobles and lairds and their relatives – a new secular elite replacing the old clerical landlords. These were sometimes taken to be grasping and oppressive, possibly echoing English scholars of the time on the dissolution

3   See especially: Margaret H. B. Sanderson, *Scottish Rural Society in the Sixteenth Century* (Edinburgh, 1982) and *A Kindly Place? Living in Sixteenth-Century Scotland* (East Linton, 2002).

of the monasteries. Sanderson has highlighted the way in which a number of peasant tenants gained feus of their own holdings, thus rising in status. However, the proportion of the feued land area that they obtained was probably very modest.[4] The earliest actual figure for land held by small owner-occupiers comes from 1770 when they held 5.5 per cent of the land area.[5] Moreover, many small feuars failed to hold onto their lands. The initial cost of a feu was high. Down payments were usually many times the existing annual rent. There were legal costs. Crown confirmation was another large expense, also several times the rent. Finally, although the tenant was now a proprietor, he still had to pay his annual feu-duties, which were always set somewhat higher than the previous rent. In the long-term, feu-duties would be eroded by inflation – but that long-term could be generations away, and many small feuars did not last that long. Full statistics are lacking for this as for much else, but the impression is that many never recovered from the initial debts that they were forced to incur, and in due course they or their heirs had to sell up.[6]

It would, therefore, be a good thing if the welcome attention devoted by Sanderson to the small feuars could be paralleled by equally detailed investigation of the fate of those peasants, the large majority, who remained tenants. Later sections of this chapter will seek to open up this subject. Some of these peasants were tenants of secular lords, who rarely feued their lands; the remainder were those tenants of Church or Crown land – the majority, as we have seen – who saw their lands feued over their heads and who thus acquired new landlords. These new landlords have never received detailed study, and their dealings with their tenants are poorly documented. Yet the relationship between incoming feuar and sitting tenant of Church land formed one of the most pressing 'agrarian problems' of the 1550s and 1560s, from the policy maker's point of view, and this furnishes an entry point for the present investigation. To the question of Scottish land tenure, therefore, we now turn.

II

Scottish and English land tenures, despite their different terminology and legal traditions, were similar in practice. They were both based on

---

4   This is my conclusion from a careful perusal of the data in Sanderson, *Scottish Rural Society*, chapter 7 ('The feuars'), and some revisions thereto in Sanderson, *A Kindly Place*, pp. 20–2.

5   L. Timperley, 'The Pattern of Landholding in Eighteenth-Century Scotland', in *The Making of the Scottish Countryside*, ed. M. L. Parry and T. R. Slater (London, 1980), p. 142.

6   Sanderson, *Scottish Rural Society*, pp. 153–60; Sanderson, *A Kindly Place*, pp. 25–31.

a system of common law supplemented by statute. Laws in both countries were administered by a combination of private and royal courts: the Scottish equivalent of the English manorial court was the baron court, while the Scots had the Court of Session as their central civil court roughly paralleling the various Westminster courts.[7] What matters most here is a point that Sanderson has argued persuasively: that English copyhold tenure had a Scottish equivalent, 'rentalling'. The Scottish 'rentaller' had the terms of his lease enrolled in the lord's rental book, and was given a copy, known as a 'rental', to keep. Provided that he observed its conditions, a rentaller had legal security of tenure during the period specified in his rental. In the early sixteenth century, rentals were usually granted at least for life, and many were granted for more than one life – to a husband and wife conjointly, or even to a man and his heirs. Rentals that included heirs will be recognised as equivalent to English copyholds of inheritance. Rentals for terms of years were equivalent to copyholds for years, while rentals for life (the most common type) were equivalent to copyholds for life.[8] A rentaller was treated by the law as a species of lessee. The usual Scots term for a lease was a 'tack'. Tacks were usually granted for a term of years – typically three, five or nineteen years; tacks for life were also granted, which were often treated effectively as rentals. Legal sources speak more often of tacks than of rentals, but a rental was thought of as a species of tack that gave the tacksman (the lessee) additional or more clearly specified rights.

A further term relevant here is the 'kindly tenant' – the term 'kindly' meaning to do with kinship. As Sanderson helpfully puts it, 'kindly tenancy was not *how* the tenant held but *why* he held'.[9] A kindly tenancy was one that was, in principle, heritable – and, in the early sixteenth century at least, this seems to have meant most tenancies. A kindly tenant was either the actual heir of the previous tenant, or else was customarily treated as if he were; his 'kindness' meant his right or expectation of inheritance. Thus there was even the 'kindly' tenant at will, the son of the previous tenant, who expected to pass his tenancy on to his own son. These expectations of inheritance were often a matter of a shared understanding between landlord and tenant. It was partly in undermining such customary expectations that sixteenth-century developments would create an 'agrarian problem'. The issue of 'custom' will require further attention.

Thus, in descending order of legal security, we have heritable rentallers, rentallers for lives, rentallers for life, rentallers and other tacksmen for

---

7   Julian Goodare, *The Government of Scotland, 1560–1625* (Oxford, 2004), pp. 160–3 (Court of Session), 181–7 (baron courts).
8   Sanderson, *Scottish Rural Society*, pp. 51–7.
9   Sanderson, *Scottish Rural Society*, p. 58 (emphasis in original).

terms of years (from nineteen to three years), and tenants at will. In the early sixteenth century, what proportions of Scottish peasants were to be found in these different categories? And what proportions within each category thought of themselves as 'kindly', that is, as expecting to pass their tenancies on to their heirs? Unfortunately, as in England, these questions cannot be answered with any precision. Sanderson found quite a few estates on which rentallers were normal; usually these were rentallers for life, though their sons often inherited in practice. She also found numerous other 'kindly' tenants. Sometimes their 'kindness' (inheritance right) was such a specific legal quality that it could be bought and sold. But legal sources tend to tell us more about people who had legal rights than about people who had no rights. An educated guess would be that the descending order outlined above may have been a numerical pyramid, with larger numbers in each successively more insecure group. A further group of unknown size should also be mentioned here: the 'cottars', often subtenants, with small parcels of land and access to common grazing rather than a full peasant's holding. Less is known about them, and they do not feature directly in the 'agrarian problem', but their existence should be borne in mind.

III

One key issue of the English agrarian problem, for Tawney and those influenced by him, has been the way that the law treated copyholders. So how did Scots law treat rentallers? A full answer to this question would require a good deal of new research, but what follows may provide a working guide to the subject. The question is a crucial one. Even if, as is likely, rentallers were a minority of the tenants, their fortunes serve as a kind of barometer. We can track their legal position over time, and this provides a record of changes in the pressures felt by all Scottish tenants. If rentallers fared well in the courts, or were absent from the courts, this would indicate that landlords were not trying hard to put pressure on tenants. If, on the other hand, landlords were doing some of the grasping and oppressive things (or, if we prefer, modernising and entrepreneurial things) that attract historical attention – rack-renting and evictions being the most dramatic – then, precisely because the rentallers stood as a bulwark against such changes, the landlords would need to use the courts, especially the Court of Session, to attack the rentallers' position.

Most of the legal cases to be discussed here were not brought by peasants. The Court of Session was an expensive central court; the 'advocate for the poor' gave occasional help, but cases brought by poorer people were recognised to be few.[10] However, landlords might bring cases *against* tenants. Some cases were between a landlord and 'his tenants' collectively, though it is not always clear who had initiated the litigation. Many additional cases reached the courts because the 'tenant' litigants were not peasants, but members of the elite who happened to hold some of their lands by similar tenures. So the question of whether peasants could enforce their theoretical rights in court is a secondary one. Rentallers' and tacksmen's changing theoretical rights form a usable and important barometer of landlord–tenant relations.

Heritable tacks were apparently accepted by the court for most of the century. The court's 'acts and decrees' are unindexed and time-consuming to search, so the following investigation uses law reports, often known as 'practicks', compiled by lawyers interested in significant cases. These provide a good guide to the changing way in which the court decided other cases. Sir James Balfour, whose reports were influential, showed no sign of uneasiness at heritable tacks. He quoted decisions of 1561 and 1562 concerning tacks to a husband, a wife, and their heirs and assignees *seriatim*, in which the only debatable points concerned their rights to constitute assignees.[11] Sir Richard Maitland also collected several legal decisions in favour of tacksmen, usually against their landlords, between 1551 and 1571.[12]

Heritable rentals and other heritable tacks, however, came under sustained attack in the early seventeenth century. In 1615, a perpetual tack was found null, even though the granter's heir wished to sustain it.[13] In 1626, a landlord's written obligation to receive the tenants' heirs as long as they paid rent was found to be a perpetual obligation and thus null.[14] Rentals were treated somewhat more favourably, in that a heritability clause did not nullify them outright – but heritability itself was on the way out. Four cases between 1625 and 1631 found that a rental *from* the granter and his heirs was valid only during the lifetimes of the initial granter and initial tenant.[15] An undated case from the 1630s found that a tack with no time limit should be treated as 'ane rentall for his lyfetyme'.[16] Two decisions in 1627 and 1630 found heritable rentals, granted to a tenant and his heirs,

---

10   Goodare, *Government of Scotland*, p. 250.

11   Sir James Balfour of Pittendreich, *Practicks*, 1, ed. P. G. B. McNeill (Stair Society, 1962), p. 201.

12   Sir Richard Maitland of Lethington, *Practiques*, ed. Robert Sutherland (Scottish Record Society, 2007), nos. 27, 71, 304, 327.

13   William M. Morison, ed., *Dictionary of the Decisions of the Court of Session*, 2nd edn (Edinburgh, 1811–15), no. 15187.

14   Morison, *Dictionary*, no. 15188.

15   Morison, *Dictionary*, nos. 7191, 7193, 15190, 15191.

16   Sir Thomas Hope, *Major Practicks*, ed. James A. Clyde (Stair Society, 1937–8), III.19.52.

valid only during the lifetimes of the initial tenant and his eldest son.[17] A few cases raised the issue of local custom. In 1627, concerning a rental to a tenant and his heirs, the tenant's son acknowledged the emerging general rule that such rentals were valid only during the initial tenant's lifetime, but argued that the custom of the burgh of Wigtown allowed the first heir to succeed. The court accepted his proof of this custom, having specified that custom required probation 'by writ or oath of party'.[18] The local custom in question was usually the custom of the barony. In 1593 and 1619, heritable rentals were actually found null because the tenants failed to prove that such rentals were the custom, either of their own barony or of adjacent baronies.[19] In 1632, after heritable rentals had repeatedly come into question, the court made a general declaration on the subject: 'It being questionable how long a rental given to a man and his heirs should last, the Lords [of session] having decided it sometimes this way, sometimes that', they decided in one case 'that it should last for the lifetime of the first heir of him to whom the rental was given . . . which they declared they would keep and follow in all time thereafter'.[20] This was thought to be a compromise, but it spelled the end for heritable rentals. By 1681, this had not only been confirmed by subsequent decisions, but unwritten or customary 'kindness' had also been lost from sight.[21]

In a wide-ranging survey of 'custom' in England and Scotland, Rab Houston has recently called for 'an analysis of court cases where such rights [of customary inheritance] were disputed' in Scotland, to test his hypothesis that 'custom' was legally more restricted there than in England.[22] The foregoing outline analysis substantiates Houston's view that kindly tenancy proved unenforceable at law once landlords ceased to concur with it. However, Houston's doubts about whether Scottish local customs were legally valid seem unfounded, at least for this period. Some local inheritance customs, established by oral testimony and upheld in local courts, were recognised nationally as late as the 1620s. The cases from which we can deduce this also show that the customary aspects of tenure were becoming more restricted, but this restrictive process can also be found in England, and more attention should perhaps be paid to the similarity of these developments.

---

17   Morison, *Dictionary*, nos. 15189, 15191.
18   Morison, *Dictionary*, no. 7194. This last stipulation seems to have been standard; cf. Winifred Coutts, *The Business of the College of Justice in 1600* (Stair Society, 2003), p. 173.
19   Morison, *Dictionary*, no. 15187.
20   Morison, *Dictionary*, no. 15192.
21   Lord Stair, *Institutions of the Law of Scotland*, ed. David M. Walker (Edinburgh, 1981), II.9.15–19.
22   Rab Houston, 'Custom in Context: Medieval and Early Modern Scotland and England', *Past & Present* 211 (2011), 50.

IV

The preceding discussion has, in principle, embraced all types of landlords – certainly both churchmen and secular lords – and their tenants.[23] Let us return to the feued Church lands and to the majority of the peasant tenants therein who found their lands feued over their heads. What of the rights of incoming feuars over their tenants? This was the single most pressing agrarian question to exercise Scottish 'statesmen' in the third quarter of the sixteenth century. The issue was often presented in stark form: did an incoming feuar have the right to evict his tenants?

In considering evictions, and even government policy on evictions, it is important to bear in mind that evictions, for landlords, were usually a last resort. In the context of applying Tawney's ideas, it should also be noted that subsequent scholars have placed less emphasis on evictions than he did. And in the context of applying Tawney's ideas to Scotland, it may be necessary to consider that Tawney regarded evictions as a consequence of enclosure, especially for sheep. Scotland, like England, exported wool, but it seems unlikely that enclosure was common in sixteenth-century Scotland. An English visitor to Scotland wrote in 1629 that 'they have little or nothing enclosed', though he added that the Moray region was 'most part enclosure'.[24] Scottish policy makers and social commentators – Tawney's 'statesmen' – nevertheless thought that evictions were occurring or might occur. This was not because of enclosure, but because of the intrusion of new landlords over most of the feued Church land. Contemporaries sometimes thought that these landlords would want to clear off the existing tenants in order to introduce their own friends and relations. A different idea surfaces in other contemporary comments: landlords wanted to evict tenants in order to bring in replacements willing to pay higher rents. Both of these arguments may have been made through *a priori* moralising rather than detailed knowledge, and should be treated with care. Today, an *a priori* economic argument should also be considered: in our recognition that population was rising, we may hypothesise that landlords were experiencing increased demand for holdings, and thus might be tempted to raise rents. A landlord who had taken a feu, investing a large cash sum in an estate to whose tenants he had no prior obligations, might feel this temptation particularly strongly.

How, then, did government policy develop on feuars' powers over their

23 No court cases have so far been found that are explicitly about tenants of Crown estates. Such cases might have been heard in the Court of Exchequer rather than the Court of Session.

24 [Christopher Lowther,] *Our Journall Into Scotland, Anno Domini 1629, 5th of November, From Lowther*, ed. W[illiam] D[ouglas] (Edinburgh, 1894), p. 13. For scattered evidence of enclosure see Sanderson, *Scottish Rural Society*, pp. 9–10.

tenants? This was a component of policy on feuing generally.[25] Just before
the Reformation, in 1559, the last general council of the Scottish Church
issued a statute that no churchmen were to set feus 'to others than the
ancient native tenants, occupiers, and tillers of the lands', for the next five
years.[26] The statute did not specify the nature of its objections to such
feus, but considering it in the context of subsequent policies makes it reasonable to infer that evictions were among its concerns. The Reformation
Parliament of 1560 used concern over feuing as a weapon against its opponents, banning further feuing by some named Catholic churchmen and
cancelling any feus they had set since 6 March 1559 (the nominal legal date
for the beginning of the uprising that led to the Reformation).[27] In 1561,
there were acts of council against feuing by churchmen, and against feuars
seeking papal confirmation of feus.[28] Explicit concern for tenants emerged
in December 1561, along with an explicit acknowledgement of the uncertainty of the current legal position. It was unclear whether feuars, the new
landlords of the Church lands, had the legal right to evict their tenants. A
convention of the nobility thus ordered that no removals of feuars' tenants should occur before Whitsun 1563, to allow time for Parliament to
pass a definitive act on the subject. By February 1563, no parliament had
yet been summoned, so the moratorium was extended to Whitsun 1564.[29]
Parliament met in June 1563 and issued yet another temporary compromise, this time revealing more of the policy makers' concerns. The act cited
'grevous complaintis . . . be [by] the lauchfull possessouris, occupyaris and
tennentis of the kirk landis', because feuars were evicting them. It was thus
enacted that 'na kyndlie, lauchfull possessour, tennent or occupyar of ony
of the saidis kirk landis be removit fra thair kyndelie rowme, steiding or
possessioun' by any feuar, or holder of a long tack granted since 6 March
1559, until Whitsun 1566. No further feus of Church lands were to be set
before Whitsun 1566, without the queen's licence.[30]

   This series of temporary measures evidently arose because different interests were in contention, with none able to predominate. The two principal interests were those of existing tenants and new landlords – bearing in

---

25   On this see R. K. Hannay, 'On the Church Lands at the Reformation', *Scottish
Historical Review* 16 (1919), an article to which all subsequent studies are indebted.
26   *Statutes of the Scottish Church, 1225–1559*, ed. David Patrick (Scottish History
Society, 1907), pp. 179–81.
27   *Records of the Parliaments of Scotland, to 1707*, ed. Keith M. Brown *et al.* (2007),
www.rps.ac.uk, accessed 9 April 2011 (hereafter *RPS*), A1560/8/8; Julian Goodare, 'The
Scottish Parliamentary Records, 1560–1603', *Historical Research* 72 (1999), 250.
28   *Accounts of the Lord High Treasurer of Scotland*, 11, ed. Sir James Balfour Paul
(Edinburgh, 1916), pp. 55–6, 71–4; *Register of the Privy Council of Scotland*, 1, ed. J. H.
Burton (Edinburgh, 1877), pp. 162–3.
29   *Register of the Privy Council of Scotland*, 1:192, 234–5.
30   *RPS*, A1563/6/13.

mind that some of the existing tenants were members of the elite, threatened by feus granted to rivals. A third interest was the fledgling Protestant Church, trying to establish itself financially and frustrated at being denied access to 'Church' lands. The final interest was the Crown itself, beginning to realise that its recently announced power to grant licences, together with the recent prohibition on confirmation of feus by the pope, presented a fiscal opportunity. The Crown's interest was uppermost when a resolution of the problem was reached, in the parliament of December 1564. This parliament enacted that feus of Church lands granted since 8 March 1559 should be confirmed by the Crown in order to validate them, such confirmations being as effective as those previously granted by the pope.[31] Machinery was established to collect 'compositions' for confirmations, and large sums flowed into the treasury from feuars.[32] What did the tenants think? All we know is that no further government action addressed their problems.

There was one further government effort at *discussing* the tenants' problems. This occurred in December 1567 in an advisory commission preparing legislation for a forthcoming parliament. The commissioners, excited by the recent overthrow of Mary Queen of Scots and the advent of an unambiguously godly regime, were in a reforming mood. One of the many 'articles' that they considered was on evictions. Many people, it complained, were being removed from their 'native and kyndlie' holdings although they were willing to pay their rent, generating an increased number of beggars. Evictions were particularly common when rents had been 'hichtit' (raised). The article proposed a moratorium on evictions of tenants paying their rent, to enable a long-term settlement of the matter to be reached.[33] However, Parliament took no action. The new feuars, from now on, were simply landlords, with the usual legal powers over their tenants.

V

The Scottish agrarian problem had several dimensions. One can certainly agree with Tawney that these were 'economic, legal, and political'. The present study has focused more closely on legal and political aspects. Some issues have had to be sidelined, and before drawing overall conclusions, it is worth outlining four such issues here.

First, one legal issue deserving further consideration is that of teinds (*anglicè* tithes). In early sixteenth-century Scotland, most teinds pertained

---

31 *RPS*, A1564/12/13. The change of date from 6 to 8 March appears to be an error.
32 Hannay, 'Church Lands', 59–65.
33 *RPS*, 1567/12/103.

to monasteries and bishops, who had 'appropriated' the parish benefices during the Middle Ages, leaving stipendiary curates in the parishes. Monasteries and bishops in turn usually leased the teinds out to lay 'tacksmen' in arrangements that were increasingly seen as irreversible, especially once the monasteries were secularised. Teinds, a nominal tenth of the gross crop, were still collected in the fields at harvest time, but gradually came to be seen and assessed as a form of rent – often a quarter or a fifth of the rent. The late sixteenth and early seventeenth centuries saw government efforts to combine teinds and rent in the hands of a single landlord, creating machinery for commutation of teinds and establishment of ministers' stipends therefrom. This was largely successful by the 1630s – much earlier than in England.[34] The present study has left teinds on one side because peasants themselves were mainly bystanders in a complex struggle over the allocation of their surpluses. But teind reform surely eased the emergence of a commercial regime in the countryside.

Second, this study has perforce remained at a national level rather than investigating regional variations. The biggest 'variation', though not the only one, was the division between Lowlands and Highlands. The legal and political developments discussed here affected the Highlands less; the 'national' government of Scotland impinged little there until the 1580s. When government policies did begin to be developed systematically for the Highlands, these were at first so coercive as to bear little resemblance to Lowland government.[35] The main agrarian documents for the sixteenth-century Highlands are a handful of rentals from Kintyre and Islay, compiled when these estates were temporarily in Crown hands; their relationship to normal Highland conditions remains obscure.[36] More could be done to analyse these and other sources. Indeed, it is in Highland Perthshire that we find the only document from sixteenth-century Scotland that approximates to a peasant's diary.[37]

Third, the issue of contemporary social comment is one that Tawney himself would have been disappointed to see ignored. Scotland did not have a Sir Thomas More, nor even a Sir Thomas Smith or a Sir Thomas Wilson. But it did have several commentators on the oppression of poor tenants. A leading example is Sir David Lindsay, whose play 'Ane Satyre of the Thrie Estaitis' appeared in 1554 at a time of rapid feuing and febrile

---

34   Alexander A. Cormack, *Teinds and Agriculture: An Historical Survey* (Oxford, 1930).
35   Michael Lynch, 'James VI and the "Highland Problem" ', in *The Reign of James VI*, ed. Julian Goodare and Michael Lynch (East Linton, 2000); Goodare, *Government of Scotland*, chapter 10.
36   Robert A. Dodgshon, *From Chiefs to Landlords: Social and Economic Change in the Western Highlands and Islands, c.1493–1820* (Edinburgh, 1998), pp. 56–63, 71–2, 103–4.
37   'The Chronicle of Fortirgall', in *The Black Book of Taymouth*, ed. Cosmo Innes (Bannatyne Club, 1855), pp. 107–48.

reforming ferment. He castigated rack-renting, rigorous exaction of teinds, and evictions, and especially the feuing of Church lands over tenants' heads. He demanded that the lands be feued to the occupants:

Divine Correction:

Mairover my Lord Spiritualitie,
In gudlie haist I will that ye
Set into few your temporall lands,   [set in feu]
To men that labours with thair hands,
Bot nocht to ane gearking gentill man,   [term of abuse]
That nether will he wirk, nor can.[38]

The 'gearking gentill man' seems to have been the main beneficiary of sixteenth-century agrarian changes, perhaps because few attacked him as vigorously as Lindsay. But Lindsay was not alone, and he and the other Scottish agrarian commentators should receive further attention.

Fourth, it would be highly desirable to incorporate the agrarian 'problem' into a detailed analysis of the agrarian economy itself. The discussion above has indicated some assumptions, based on existing economic studies, that appear to be cognate with my findings and with contemporary social commentary.[39] These assumptions can be summed up as follows. Population was rising, possibly from a low level, but was pressing against resources by the second half of the century, with repeated famines, a vagrancy problem and large-scale emigration. Diets were declining in value, with peasants eating less meat and relying increasingly on oatmeal. There was inflation, especially in the later years of the century, when the coinage was depreciated. Rents were probably rising in real terms, though existing evidence is impressionistic. Despite population growth, holdings do not seem to have been subdivided; some marginal land was probably ploughed up, and the number of cottars may well have grown – though these points are speculative in the current state of research.[40] There are

---

38   Sir David Lindsay of the Mount, *Works*, 2, ed. Douglas Hamer (Scottish Text Society, 1931), p. 255.

39   In addition to works cited above, see Ian D. Whyte, *Agriculture and Society in Seventeenth-Century Scotland* (Edinburgh, 1979); Ian D. Whyte, *Scotland before the Industrial Revolution: An Economic and Social History, c.1050–c.1750* (London, 1995), chapters 5–9; A. J. S. Gibson and T. C. Smout, *Prices, Food and Wages in Scotland, 1550–1780* (Cambridge, 1995); T. C. Smout, *A History of the Scottish People, 1560–1830* (London, 1969), chapters 5–6.

40   Evidence on ploughed acreages is scanty, but see Martin L. Parry, 'The Abandonment of Upland Settlement in Southern Scotland', *Scottish Geographical Magazine* 92 (1976); Joseph Donnelly, 'In the Territory of Auchenross: Long Continuity or Late Development in Early Scottish Field Systems?', *Proceedings of the Society of Antiquaries of Scotland* 130 (2000). Much of the latter article is a critique of Robert A. Dodgshon, *Land and Society*

several indicators of economic buoyancy, especially in the early seventeenth century; starvation cannot be ignored, but at a time when starvation was occurring, it is important that not everyone in the countryside was being immiserated.[41] The agrarian economy eventually lifted itself out of crisis, with the run of famines largely ceasing in the 1620s and with grain, for the first time, becoming a regular net export. A number of these trends, at least at a broad level, were found in England too, strengthening the case for further Anglo-Scottish comparisons.

One way of developing some of these issues, and broadening them beyond the present study's focus on inheritance and landlord–tenant relations, would be to follow Jane Whittle. She has provided an important reinterpretation of the issue of peasant inheritance, which she summarises as follows:

> Inheritance patterns, fascinating as they are in their own right, are only an indirect indication of economic development and change; rather, we should define peasant societies according to their *degree* of market involvement. And here the sale of home-produced goods, agricultural and otherwise, the purchase of goods from outside the household and the use of hired labour are far more significant than the market in land.[42]

This is persuasive, and could well be taken as a research agenda for the next generation of Scottish agrarian historians. We need more research on the destinations of farm produce – how much was marketed, as opposed to being consumed directly, either by peasants themselves or by their lords' households. Was the marketing done by lords, or by entrepreneurial tenants? What use did such tenants make of hired labour? There are certainly indications of government concern to regulate agricultural labour in the early seventeenth century.[43] Sanderson has shown that the archives can be made to yield quite a few details of the property transactions of humble folk. There is much that we will never know, but the right questions, directed to the right sources, could produce valuable results.

---

in Early Scotland (Oxford, 1981). Further research is needed here, and also on the related topic of yields per acre.

41   Ian D. Whyte, 'Poverty or Prosperity? Rural Society in Lowland Scotland in the Late Sixteenth and Early Seventeenth Centuries', *Scottish Economic and Social History* 18 (1998).

42   Jane Whittle, 'Individualism and the Family-land Bond: A Reassessment of Land Transfer Patterns among the English Peasantry, c.1270–1580', *Past & Present* 160 (1998), 62–3 (emphasis in original).

43   Goodare, *Government of Scotland*, pp. 270–1.

VI

This chapter has aimed to show that Tawney's research questions can profitably be asked in Scotland, and produce some preliminary answers not too different from their equivalents in England. The apparent shift in inheritance patterns in Scotland between about 1550 and 1630 should not be expected to tell us much about peasant choices, but it does reveal – indirectly, to be sure – a pattern of landlord assertiveness that is likely to have been felt also in levels of rent.[44] Along with the indirectness of these findings comes chronological imprecision. There appear to have been two phases to the 'problem', with one generation of landlords assertively feuing Church land, and assertively evicting tenants, in the 1560s, and another generation challenging heritable tenancies in the 1620s. These developments were probably linked, but as yet the links are unclear. One could speculate about cohorts of tenants – rentals for lives that had been set during the 1560s might fall in during the 1620s – but this merely indicates a possible answer to another question that needs more research.

However, the late sixteenth century was not necessarily a bad time to be a farmer in Scotland. It was a bad time to be a small tenant farmer, certainly; these were the people who were abandoning their holdings in famine years, becoming vagrants, enlisting in continental armies, or dying of starvation. But the larger farmers may have done better. No explicit Scottish parallel has yet been found to the rise of English yeomen, but this may be because of difficulties of evidence. Sanderson's small feuars are relevant here – after all, some of them did survive, and inflation was on their side in the long run – but one would also, and perhaps primarily, be looking at larger tenants.[45] The period in which one might find equivalents of yeomen, the late sixteenth and early seventeenth centuries, is poorly documented, as Ian Whyte has observed; but his fragmentary evidence does indicate consolidation of holdings, and this may at least be the same sort of trend that created England's yeomen.[46]

One Anglo-Scottish difference is the absence of Scottish peasant revolts. Here the difference may be one of degree; after all, not all areas of England saw peasant revolts. There may be a difference between a broad-brush analysis of revolts, seeking common factors, and a detailed

44 Scattered suggestions of rack-renting are gathered in Keith M. Brown, *Noble Society in Scotland: Wealth, Family and Culture, from Reformation to Revolution* (Edinburgh, 2000), p. 42.

45 Equivalence between small feuars and yeomen has been denied by Ian D. Whyte, 'The Emergence of the New Estate Structure', *Making of the Scottish Countryside*, ed. Parry and Slater, p. 117.

46 Whyte, 'Poverty or Prosperity?', 25–9.

analysis of specific combinations of local grievances and political circumstances without which, it may well be argued, revolts such as Kett's
Rebellion would not have occurred.[47] A common trigger for continental
revolts was royal taxation, but Scotland did not tax peasants directly
until the introduction of an excise in 1644, and its fiscal regime was generally lighter than England's. However, popular assertiveness on other
issues was certainly known in Scotland, and it was credibly reported in
1599 that a proposed tax on sales of grain, cattle and sheep would lead
to revolt.[48] In principle, of course, there could be more than one explanation for the absence of revolt. One possibility is that Scottish peasants
were too downtrodden, or too insecure, or both. This has sometimes
been assumed, but rarely on the basis of much evidence. Neil Davidson,
who has pursued the question further than some, argues that change
could not occur before the eighteenth century because Scottish baronies
and regalities exercised direct, coercive control over their tenants, preventing them from doing anything capitalist.[49] This probably overesti-
mates these institutions' power and single-mindedness, but the subject
would benefit from further research. A contrasting possibility is that
early modern Scottish peasants did not *need* to revolt because landlords
did not place them under pressure, or at least not under that much pressure. The foregoing analysis of legal cases has suggested that pressure on
customary inheritance is a barometer of wider landlord assertiveness,
but only further research could reveal how peasant tenants experienced
this pressure. Removal of inheritance rights did not threaten people's
immediate livelihoods; only other accompanying demands would have
been likely to provoke open revolt. We should certainly not assume that
early modern Scottish peasants had a tradition of passivity. They were,
after all, the descendants of those peasants who, in the fourteenth and
fifteenth centuries, had been so aggressive that their landlords had not
dared to attempt the kind of seigneurial reaction that led to the English
revolt of 1381.[50] They were also the ancestors of the eighteenth-century
Scottish common people, who were far from 'tame' in their attitudes
to authority.[51] The popular assertiveness of this latter period has been

---

47 Whittle, 'Lords and Tenants'.
48 Julian Goodare, *State and Society in Early Modern Scotland* (Oxford, 1999), pp. 116–
17, 318–21.
49 Neil Davidson, 'The Scottish Path to Capitalist Agriculture 1: From the Crisis of
Feudalism to the Origins of Agrarian Transformation (1688–1746)', *Journal of Agrarian
Change* 4 (2004).
50 Alexander Grant, *Independence and Nationhood: Scotland, 1306–1469* (London,
1984), pp. 87–8.
51 Christopher A. Whatley, 'How Tame were the Scottish Lowlanders during the
Eighteenth Century?', in *Conflict and Stability in Scottish Society, 1700–1850*, ed. T. M.
Devine (Edinburgh, 1990).

argued to be a product of the revolutionary disturbances of the 1640s.[52] However, a longer-term perspective would suggest that ordinary Scots were not passive in the sixteenth or any other century. In the present state of knowledge it would be hard to argue that Scottish governmental and legal structures were more repressive than English ones. One suggestive point is that sixteenth-century England still had a few serfs, but Scotland did not. Scottish rentallers by inheritance lost their inheritance rights, while English copyholders of inheritance had theirs entrenched, becoming effectively freeholders.[53] To some extent this represents an Anglo-Scottish difference, but it was also an alternative solution to a common problem: the wish to convert these tenures to a more commercial form.

The Scottish dimension, then, can shed important light on Tawney's 'agrarian problem' – even for England. Scotland's economy was broadly similar, as Keith Wrightson pointed out some while ago. He concluded that 'the case for Scottish exceptionalism, backwardness and stasis seems fatally flawed' and that Scotland should be integrated into the patterns of regional diversity familiar to English agrarian historians: 'there were many Englands and many Scotlands in the early modern period.'[54] This also, of course, undermines any case for *English* exceptionalism. Theories linked to England's early industrialisation must certainly take Scotland into account, as Scotland's industrialisation was equally early.

Sixteenth-century Scotland, however, still had a separate legal and political system. This search for the Scottish agrarian problem cannot claim to have been comprehensive, but it has pointed to several ways in which processes comparable to those found in England were at work in Scotland. Different structures existed, but similar processes occurred. The legal and political entry point to the question has perhaps been particularly significant here. If we find similar legal and political trends in these two still-separate countries, these surely represent similar responses to a common economic problem, rather than a phenomenon originating in the law

---

52   David Stevenson, 'The Effects of Revolution and Conquest on Scotland', in *Economy and Society in Scotland and Ireland, 1500–1939*, ed. Rosalind Mitchison and Peter Roebuck (Edinburgh, 1988).

53   French and Hoyle, *Character of English Rural Society*, pp. 8–9, 124.

54   Keith Wrightson, 'Kindred Adjoining Kingdoms: An English Perspective on the Social and Economic History of Early Modern Scotland', in *Scottish Society, 1500–1800*, ed. R. A. Houston and Ian D. Whyte (Cambridge, 1989), pp. 256, 258. Numerous such insights are to be found in Wrighton's *Earthly Necessities*, although his statement that 'Scotland and Wales were far less variegated' than England (p. 88) arguably reflects either the paucity of Scottish regional research, or a need for regional criteria that take more account of Scottish conditions, or both. See also: Ian D. Whyte, 'Is a British Socio-economic History Possible?', in *The New British History: Founding a Modern State, 1603–1715*, ed. Glenn Burgess (London, 1999).

or politics of either country separately. This in turn tends to confirm not only that the agrarian problem was real in both countries, but that it had economic roots.

7

The Transfer to Leasehold
on Durham Cathedral Estate, 1541–1626

JEAN MORRIN

R. H. Tawney identified the insecurity of leasehold tenure and increasingly commercial landlord policies as part of the agrarian problem of the sixteenth century. He suggested that landlords converted their estates from customary to leasehold tenure so that the 'fruits of economic progress' would no longer be retained by the peasant cultivators but would instead enrich the great landowners.[1] This chapter discusses one dispute over the conversion of customary tenures to leasehold which suggests a greater variety of outcomes than Tawney anticipated. Most importantly, perhaps, it stresses that leasehold tenures came in a variety of forms, some of which benefited tenants more than others. The dispute developed on Durham Cathedral estate during the Reformation when the newly created Dean and Chapter of Durham tried to grant commercial leases to the tenants they had inherited from the suppressed Durham Priory.

The Crown instructed the new Chapter to impose a 21-year lease on each agricultural property at the same fixed annual rent previously charged by Durham Priory. Two problems rapidly arose. First, many tenants refused to accept the new leases, believing that they held their farms by the customary tenure of tenant right as a result of their duty to perform military service on the Scottish border. To the tenants, tenant right meant low rents, security of tenure and the inheritability of their farms. In contrast, the Chapter argued that tenants who refused to take leases were mere tenants at will who held 'without a documentary title'.[2] The statutes of the Cathedral specified that the new leases must contain no agreement to renew after the term. Such a lease was completely at variance with tenants' belief in their tenant right. While refusing to accept a lease, each tenant

---

1 Tawney, *Agrarian Problem* (1912 edn), pp. 6, 283, 301–4, 404.
2 Dean and Chapter of Durham (hereafter DCD) Chapter Acts 13 June 1581. Tawney, *Agrarian Problem* (1912 edn), pp. 34, 47.

continued to pay the annual fixed rent which was recorded in the receivers' books under the tenant's name.[3]

The second problem was that the Chapter faced an increasingly difficult financial situation: inflation reduced their real incomes at a time when they needed more revenue to run the cathedral. As a consequence, soon after 1541 they began charging multiples of the fixed rents as entry and renewal fines.[4] The levels of these were only incidentally recorded, but by 1575 the Chapter charged four times the fixed rent as a fine on a 21-year lease.[5] Durham Chapter embraced this option because they lacked the flexibility of private landlords or the Crown, being forbidden to sell, alienate, demise at fee farm or exchange any manor, land, rents or tenements: this was a consequence of the Crown's desire that the Church 'should grow fat not thin'.[6] Faced with tenant resistance, the Chapter resorted to a number of devices to enforce leases and the payment of entry and renewal fines. The dispute climaxed in the 1570s when some one hundred tenants appealed to the Crown to protect them from abuses of their landlord. Similar disputes arose on the Crown estate in Durham in the 1580s and 1590s,[7] while tenants of Crown lands in Cumbria also refused the offer of leases in the 1560s and sought confirmation of their tenant right.[8]

The tensions between the Durham Chapter and their tenants were heightened by religious differences intensified by the appointments of Bishop James Pilkington and Dean William Whittingham, both Puritans, in 1561. Dean Whittingham sought to maximise revenues and constructed a new Exchequer over the old abbey gatehouse as a symbol of these ambitions.[9] Oates has argued for the strength of Catholicism in this area of south-east County Durham.[10] Certainly the region was involved in two large-scale popular rebellions in the sixteenth century, the Pilgrimage of

---

3   The dean delegated to the receiver responsibility for property, land and rents. Virtually all the receivers' books survive for the sixteenth and seventeenth centuries.

4   See Tawney, *Agrarian Problem* (1912 edn), pp. 304–5.

5   Chapter Act 26 September 1575 in DCD York Book, fol. 40.

6   A. H. Thompson, ed., *Statutes of the Cathedral Church of Durham* (Surtees Society, 143, Durham, 1929), 95–7, 119; R. W. Hoyle, 'Shearing the Hog: The Reform of the Estates, c.1598–1640', in *Estates of the English Crown,* ed. Hoyle, p. 232.

7   R. W. Hoyle, 'Customary Tenure on the Elizabethan Estates', in *Estates of the English Crown,* ed. Hoyle, p.196. C. Kitching, 'The Durham Palatinate and the Courts of Westminster under the Tudors', in *The Last Principality: Politics, Religion and Society in the Bishopric of Durham, 1494–1660,* ed. D. Marcombe (Nottingham, 1987), p.60.

8   Hoyle, 'Customary Tenure', p. 199.

9   This followed the deprivation of the Catholic Bishop Tunstall and a number of prebendaries following the royal visitation of 1559. See: D. Marcombe, 'A Rude and Heady People: The Local Community and the Rebellion of the Northern Earls', in *Last Principality*, ed. Marcombe, pp. 120–6.

10   R. Oates, 'Catholicism, Conformity and the Community in the Elizabethan Diocese of Durham', *Northern History* 43:1 (2006), 53–76.

Grace of 1536 and the Northern Rebellion of 1569, both of which aimed to reverse Protestant reforms to traditional religious practices.[11] In the 1560s Durham tenants regarded Charles Neville, the Catholic sixth earl of Northumberland, as their leader. Traditionally the Nevilles had been paid £10 a year by the Cathedral for leading the Chapter tenants in war, but on the accession of the sixth earl in 1564 the Chapter refused to pay. Charles Neville was one of the leaders of the Northern Rebellion of 1569. It has been argued by Marcombe that the loss of the tenants' traditional leader and the Chapter's use of new types of leases led directly to the tenants' participation in the rebellion.[12]

I

At the heart of the dispute between the Durham Chapter and their tenants was the tenants' claim that they held their lands by tenant right as a result of military service. In his research on the Durham Cathedral estate, Marcombe considered the tenants' claims in this respect to be 'largely fictitious'. This view is disputed here; instead it is argued that the tenants genuinely believed in their tenant right, and that their convictions were reinforced both by the confirmation of their duty to perform border service in their new leases and by their landlords' actions.[13] Border service required the tenants to equip themselves with horse and armour for fifteen days' service a year.[14] In return, all tenants demanded the privileges of tenant right, effectively the right to rent their lands at reasonable cost and to freely bequeath, assign and sell their properties.[15] From 1541 onwards, for many years, some Durham Cathedral tenants refused to take leases because they believed their lands were held by tenant right.

Tenant right tenures existed across Durham, Northumberland, Cumberland, Westmoreland and parts of Yorkshire, with military service as one of its chief features.[16] Tawney described one form of this tenure on the Northumbrian border, where copyhold for life with tenant right of renewal to the heir could be granted if a constant custom of renewal was

---

11 R. W. Hoyle, *The Pilgrimage of Grace and the Politics of the 1530s* (Oxford, 2001); Kesselring, *Northern Rebellion*.

12 Marcombe, 'A Rude and Heady People', pp. 128–30.

13 D. Marcombe, 'The Dean and Chapter of Durham, 1558–1603' (unpublished PhD thesis, 1973), p.141; Marcombe, 'A Rude and Heady People', p.125.

14 For example DCD/B/BA5, fol. 297v.

15 E. J. Morrin, 'Merrington: Land, Landlord and Tenants 1541–1840' (unpublished PhD thesis, 1997), p.40.

16 M. Campbell, *The English Yeoman in the Tudor and Early Stuart Age* (Yale, 1942), pp. 148–9.

proved.[17] Tenant right emerged as an important agrarian grievance in the
Pilgrimage of Grace of 1536 when rebels accused landlords of charging
large gressums or entry fines contrary to tenant right.[18] Bush notes that
although tenant right was regarded in law as a customary tenure at the will
of the lord, in practice the custom of the country caused it to be considered
a hereditary tenure.[19] Drury, discussing tenant right in Weardale, usefully
summarises the key features of the tenure: the right of a tenant to pass his
holding on to his heir with little or no landlordly interference, or to sell it;
and the duty to do border service.[20] Hoyle's study of North Yorkshire confirms and extends these observations: such tenancies could, on payment of
a fine, descend to the tenant's heir, or the tenant during his life was able
to assign his interest to another as if the land were freehold or copyhold
but often without the formality of the surrender characteristic of copyhold tenures. A lord who wished to increase his profits was forced to do so
through the exploitation of fines or gressums.[21] Hoyle found that during
the sixteenth century pressure from landlords had often turned gressums
into an arbitrary fine which nonetheless could not be 'unreasonable'. This
led to conflict if the lord wanted to increase the rate or the frequency of
the fine beyond what the tenants considered to be customary.[22] Durham
tenants argued that fines were contrary to custom and the landlord should
only charge the fixed rent.

To permit in-depth study of the dispute, an area of the Dean and
Chapter estate comprising six linked townships has been selected: Kirk
Merrington, Ferryhill, Hett and Great Chilton in Kirk Merrington parish; and Middlestone and Westerton, in St Andrew Auckland parish. For
convenience, this area will be referred to as Merrington. It contained six
thousand acres divided into forty-eight farms, each of 100–160 acres, and
two mills. This amounts to ten per cent of the whole of the Chapter's agricultural estate.[23] The Chapter Acts suggests that the estate management

17   Tawney, *Agrarian Problem* (1912 edn), p. 299.
18   M. L. Bush, 'Tenant Right and the Peasantries of Europe under the Old Regime', in
Social Orders and Social Classes in Europe since 1500: Studies in Social Stratification, ed.
M. L. Bush (London, 1992), p. 137; M. L. Bush, *The Pilgrimage of Grace: A Study of the
Rebel Armies of October 1536* (Manchester, 1996), p. 257.
19   Campbell, *English Yeoman*, p. 148; Bush, *Pilgrimage*, chapter 17.
20   J. L. Drury, 'More Stout than Wise: Tenant Right in Weardale in the Tudor Period', in
Last Principality, ed. Marcombe, p.71.
21   R. W. Hoyle, 'Lords, Tenants, and Tenant Right in the Sixteenth Century: Four
Studies', *Northern History* 20 (1984), 38–84.
22   Hoyle, 'Lords, Tenants, and Tenant Right', p. 39. See also Kerridge, *Agrarian Problems*,
pp. 44–5; C. B. Phillips, 'The Gentry in Cumberland and Westmoreland 1660–1665' (unpublished PhD thesis, 1973), pp. 128, 177.
23   Chapter leasehold land in Kirk Merrington comprised some 4,600 acres. In addition, about 1,500 acres in St Andrew Auckland parish were included in the study, as this
comprised the two townships of Middlestone and Westerton which were satellites of Kirk

problems encountered in Merrington were typical of those on the whole Cathedral estate.[24] Merrington tenants were also typical of the larger estate in being mainly yeomen or husbandmen, who occupied and cultivated their farms, and bequeathed them if possible to their eldest son. If the son was underage, the farm was bequeathed to the widow or the widow and son jointly. In the absence of a son, tenants passed their land to their widow, daughter(s), son(s)-in-law, or more distant relatives. In the second half of the sixteenth century twelve per cent of lessees were described as gentlemen. These were mainly in Westerton and Middlestone where the Pilkington family, relatives of Bishop Pilkington, gained two farms in the 1580s, which were re-granted in the names of four Pilkington brothers and sisters. During the period of the dispute, seven per cent of the leases were granted to bishop or dean's servants in the form of lottery or concurrent leases, as is discussed below. Of the 177 tenants named in leases in the sixteenth century, in only eight cases was the status of the tenant not given.[25] The average value of tenant inventories from 1541 to 1600 was £69.70 and the range of values was from £23.60 to £164.66.[26] The vast majority of tenants, over eighty per cent, had only one farm and in the last sixty years of the sixteenth century ninety-nine per cent of the tenants lived in the township where their landholding was located.[27]

II

Across the whole estate the sitting tenants were suspicious of their new landlords and resisted the new leases.[28] In Merrington the occupiers of the two mills in Hett and Kirk Merrington were the first to accept leases. Perhaps they were motivated by the fact that the Dean and Chapter could force tenants, as required by custom, to repair the mills and to grind their corn at them. Eight out of forty-eight farm tenants accepted leases in the 1550s, but the acceptance rate decreased in the 1560s with only three tenants accepting leases.[29] By 1570, of the fifty properties, only twenty-six

---

Merrington. Within Merrington there were a few cottage leases which are not included in this study.

24   For example, DCD Chapter Acts, 7 April 1636.

25   DCD/B/BA1–6. All the chapter lease registers survive for this period.

26   Durham Diocesan Records, Durham Probate 1541–1660.

27   Eighteen Merrington farm tenants' inventories survive from 1562–98. Only sitting tenants have been included in this analysis.

28   Sitting tenants were defined as those recorded in the DCD receivers' books as paying rent.

29   DCD/B/BA1, fols 25, 120, 162. For an example of the dean and chapter manorial court commanding a tenant to grind at Merrington mill see DCD, MAN/4/35/5.

per cent of the sitting tenants had accepted leases.[30] The Durham Chapter could not afford this slow pace of change. It resorted to a number of devices to persuade tenants either to give up their claims of tenant right or to leave their farms altogether. First, from 1548 they offered leases of properties occupied by sitting tenants to third parties who were linked to the Chapter. These were either concurrent leases to begin after the existing lease, or leases in reversion commencing after the death of the existing tenant. None of the recipients of the concurrent leases were named as tenant in the receivers' books. To retain their farm, existing tenants had to pay a cash sum to the person granted the lease of their farm.[31]

These practices became more ruthless after the appointments of Bishop Pilkington and Dean Whittingham in 1561. The combination of this pressure and Catholic religious beliefs led some Merrington tenants to join the Northern Rebellion in November and December 1569. Merrington was in the Darlington ward of the diocese of Durham in which there were more rebels (481) than in the other three wards combined.[32] John Lilborn, for example, tore the Protestant Bible into pieces and 'took the boards of the communion table' in St Andrew Auckland church.[33] The vicar of Kirk Merrington, William Metmarbie alias Mellerbye, was pardoned for his part in the rebellion.[34] For forty out of the fifty properties studied, either the tenant or his son received a pardon.[35] Whether any from the study area were executed for their part in the rebellion is not known.[36]

Within Merrington, of the first leases for each property granted to Chapter friends over the tenants' heads, eleven were the first lease on the property and nine followed a previous lease to the sitting tenant; in the latter cases the Chapters' motives were clearly to extort cash.[37] For example, a concurrent lease was granted in Kirk Merrington to John Lever in 1564,[38] which started from the point when the lease, also granted in 1564,

30   DCD/B/BA1–3.

31   W. H. D. Longstaffe, ed., *Durham Halmote Rolls*, 1 (Surtees Society, 82, 1889), pp. 232–88.

32   C. Sharp, ed., *Memorials of the Rebellion of the Earls of Northumberland and Westmoreland* (London, 1840; repr. Durham, 1975), p.140. Durham rebels comprised: Darlington ward 481, Easington 66, Stockton 212, Chester 35.

33   Sharp, *Memorials*, p. 262.

34   *Calendar of the Patent Rolls 1569–72*, p. 94.

35   CPR 1569–72, pp. 89, 99, 100, 101, 102, 103.

36   Sharp, *Memorials*, p. 251. Names of the five in Ferryhill, one each in Westerton, Middlestone, Great Chilton and Hett who were executed, are not given. There is a ten-year gap between receiver's book 9, 1564–65, and book 10, 1574–75. In Ferryhill for example, the Christian names of two of the fifteen tenants have changed but it may be due to natural causes.

37   DCD/B/BA1–4.

38   DCD/B/BA2, fols 193–4. John Lever was a relative of Canon Ralph Lever (prebendary in Durham Cathedral 1567–85).

to Richard Heighington, the sitting tenant, expired. The property was leased again to Richard Heighington in 1568.[39] In 1564 the Chapter for the first time used a device deemed a 'lottery' by their tenants: leases of farms occupied by tenants who claimed tenant right were auctioned to the Dean and Prebendaries. In order to retain their farms, sitting tenants each had to pay a large sum of money to whoever had purchased their lease.[40]

Despite the Northern Rebellion of 1569, Durham Chapter continued to auction leases in 1572, 1575 and 1576. The effect of this policy is recorded in a survey of the Cathedral estate in 1580.[41] Within the study area, twelve tenants suffered the consequences of these leases.[42] To secure their family farms, the twelve paid a total of £272 13s 4d, or £22 14s per farm. The average fixed rent was £2 10s. Thus the fines on average amounted to nine times the fixed rents. In total twenty-seven grants of lease, concurrent or lottery, were made in Merrington to people who were not sitting tenants. One hundred years later, Durham Chapter admitted that during this period tenants often had to spend ten times the fixed annual rent or occasionally as much as fifty times the fixed rent, to pay off lottery victors. Similar abuses occurred on the lands of other cathedrals and colleges. For example, between 1559 and 1576, St John's College, Cambridge, granted both long leases of up to fifty years and reversionary leases contrary to college statutes. [43]

III

Durham tenants, like others elsewhere in England, appealed to the government to preserve their traditional rights in the face of landlord oppression.[44] They petitioned the Privy Council against concurrent leases and lotteries,

---

39   DCD/B/BA2, fols 238–9.
40   Marcombe, 'Dean and Chapter', pp. 141–2; Roland Seamer, tenant in Coatsay Moor, was the author of the lottery descriptor.
41   Longstaffe, *Durham Halmote Rolls*, pp. 189–250.
42   In Kirk Merrington, George Taylor paid Mr Stephenson £30; Giles Gowland paid Mr Halliday £26; Richard Binley paid Dean Whittingham £24; William Middleton paid Thomas Darby £16; John Heighington paid Magister Swift £30; and Thomas Hixon, Senior, paid Mr Stephenson £30. In Middlestone, John Laxe paid £30 to Philip Parkinson and William Pearson paid John Dixon £13 6s 8d. In Ferryhill, Robert Willy paid £30 to retrieve his farm from Mr Cliffe; Widow Willy paid £20 to regain hers from Mr Stephenson and Robert Darnton paid £13 6s 8d to Mr Swift for his farm. In Hett, Ralph Corby paid £10 to Mr Swift to recover his farm. See: Longstaffe, *Durham Halmote Rolls*, pp. 232–8.
43   BL, Tanner MSS. 144, fol. 106. H. F. Howard, *An Account of the Finances of St John the Evangelist in the University of Cambridge 1511 to 1935* (Cambridge, 1935), pp. 28–9. Howard found leases granted from 1559 to 1576 for thirty, forty and fifty years contrary to the statute of 13 Elizabeth c.10 enforcing 21-year leases or leases for three lives.
44   Tawney, *Agrarian Problem* (1912 edn), pp. 125, 325, 333.

pleading that their lands were held by tenant right. The case at the heart
of the petition occurred outside the study area but was supported by some
Merrington tenants. Francis Pilkington, a relative of Bishop Pilkington, acquired a reversion of the lease due in 1572 for a property in Coatsay Moor,
just south-west of the study area.[45] In 1572, instead of demanding a cash
sum, Pilkington commenced action in the Council of the North against
the sitting tenants, Roland Seamer and Roland and Agnes Denham, to obtain possession of the property. It is possible the antagonism was increased
by religious differences as Seamer was a Roman Catholic.[46] Pilkington's
action was dismissed by the Council of the North who accepted the tenants' proof of their tenant right. Pilkington then brought and won an
eviction case in 1574 in the Court of Common Pleas at Durham against
Seamer.[47] Seamer and one hundred tenants replied with a petition to the
Privy Council alleging bias in the Durham courts and protesting against
the practices of Dean Whittingham and the prebendaries, particularly the
lotteries and the high level of fines paid to recover properties. This action
was supported by six Merrington tenants: Christopher Woodifield, Robert
Rose, John Gray, William Pearson, Martin Smith from Ferryhill and John
Robinson of Middlestone. All these men had also received pardons for
their parts in 1569 Northern Rebellion.[48]

The case was a sensitive one for the Privy Council to determine as they
feared provoking further unrest only six years after the Rebellion. The
Council referred the case to the President of the Council of the North,
Francis Hastings, earl of Huntingdon. Huntingdon sought a compromise:
he gave some recognition of hereditary rights to the tenants because of
their duty to do border service and his desire to avoid further rebellion,
but he also supported the Chapter's right to impose leases. Huntingdon ordered all the tenants except Seamer (who was deemed to have complained
'untruely' to the Privy Council), to be restored to their lands. However, in
return the tenants had to admit the restoration was 'of favour not of right'
and renounce claims of tenant right.[49] The tenants appealed again in 1576,
this time to the queen, but the case was again referred to the Council of the
North who restated Huntingdon's opinion. The final definitive order, involving a compromise designed to regulate relations between the Chapter

---

45   The Pilkington family dominated the Durham Chapter in the 1580s. Leonard and
John Pilkington were brothers of the bishop and were both prebendaries. Leonard, receiver
four times during the 1580s, assisted his family to gain leases. Jacob was one of his sons.
Francis, who provoked the dispute led by Seamer in 1574, was a member of the family.

46   Marcombe, 'Dean and Chapter', p. 157.

47   Marcombe, 'Dean and Chapter', p. 146.

48   CPR 1569–72, p. 99; Longstaffe, Durham Halmote Rolls, pp. 233, 237–8, 246; Morrin,
'Merrington', p. 59.

49   Acts of the Privy Council 1571–75, p. 337.

and those of its tenants who had not accepted leases, was promulgated by Huntingdon on 17 August 1577. It aimed to placate the tenants by offering an alternative lease recognising limited hereditary rights for which a fixed and lower fine was to be paid.[50]

Huntingdon instructed Durham Chapter to offer tenants a choice of leases. In addition to the simple leases granted since 1541, tenants would have the option of a 21-year lease under his order (*sub ordinem*) for which they would pay a fixed fine amounting to three times the fixed annual rent, rather than the four times charged for simple leases. In return, each tenant's right to bequeath his lease would be restricted, and as a result leases would fall in more frequently enabling the landlords to offer a new simple lease for a higher fine.[51] Huntingdon stated that the Chapter could grant *sub ordinem* leases to tenants who claimed to be tenants at will or by tenant right but not to tenants who already held by lease for years or lives.[52] To receive a lease under the order a tenant had to give up all claims of tenant right while still accepting the obligation to do border service. Descent was restricted to sons and grandsons of the previous tenant or brothers and nephews, but with no provision for women except widows, who were to remain in possession throughout their widowhood without paying fines. If a widow remarried, the new husband was, on payment of two years' rent, entitled to retain the farm during his wife's life only.[53] Failing such heirs, the property reverted to the Chapter. Lands could not be forfeited except for treason, rebellion, murder or felony. If a tenant did not pay his rent on time or within forty days of the due date, he had to pay double rent, whereas holders of simple leases who defaulted were evicted. The Chapter offered these *sub ordinem* leases to their tenants from 1577 alongside the original simple leases.[54]

Initially some tenants accepted leases under Huntingdon's order, presumably as the financial cost was less than for simple leases. Thirty-two Merrington tenants opted for *sub ordinem* leases between 1577 and 1608, almost twenty-one per cent of Merrington lease renewals.[55] Tenants taking these *sub ordinem* leases were concentrated in eighteen properties in Ferryhill, Hett and Middlestone. The thirty-two leases granted to Merrington tenants comprised one third of the ninety-six leases granted

---

50 APC 1575–77, p. 90; Marcombe, 'Dean and Chapter', pp. 148–9.
51 DCD Chapter Acts, 26 September 1575.
52 DCD/B/BA3, fols 140–1.
53 DCD/B/BA3, fols 140–1. This provision for inheritance by family was reminiscent of medieval patterns recorded in the Halmote court rolls of the late fourteenth century. See: R. A. Lomas, 'Durham Cathedral Priory as a Landowner and a Landlord 1290–1540' (unpublished PhD thesis, 1973), pp. 25–6.
54 Longstaffe, *Durham Halmote Rolls*, pp. 232–8.
55 DCD/B/BA3–4.

under the order across the whole cathedral estate. Furthermore, Merrington tenants continued to opt for *sub ordinem* leases for a longer time period than tenants elsewhere on the estate. The last three leases *sub ordinem* granted by the Chapter, all in 1608, were to tenants in Merrington. Thus this area, comprising one tenth of the estate, accounted for one third of the grants of these alternative leases.[56] The intervention of Huntingdon largely resolved the dispute. The tenants had to accept that the Crown intended them to lease their land from the Durham Chapter. The acceptance of leases, whether simple from 1574–77 and *sub ordinem* from 1577, increased dramatically. By 1610 all tenants of the fifty Merrington properties had taken out either a *sub ordinem* or a simple lease.

The Durham Chapter did not always observe the rules set out under Huntingdon's order. For instance, they failed to restrict *sub ordinem* leases in Merrington to those who had never been granted leases by the Dean and Chapter. In the period 1578–1601, eleven tenants took out leases *sub ordinem* when they renewed existing simple leases. However, in all these cases the original lease had been issued after 1575–76 when Seamer was evicted, so perhaps the tenants argued that they were obliged to take leases by the decision of the Court of Common Pleas in Durham which Huntingdon's order had since superseded. This is suggested in an 1580 estate survey where three entries relating to Robert Mebourne and John Hobson of Hett and John Trotter of Middlestone, who had all taken simple leases for the first time in 1575–76, stated that leases *sub ordinem* were to be granted to the tenants.[57] Similarly, Durham Chapter found it impossible to enforce reversion of property to themselves where there were no descendants, as specified under the 1577 order. John Robinson in Middlestone refused a lease but was still listed as the tenant in the receivers' books. His farm was leased to Philip Parkinson in 1568, but Robinson continued to be listed as tenant. John Robinson joined with Seamer in 1575–77 objecting to lotteries and protesting his tenant right. In 1580 Robinson had neither child, uncle, nor brother's child to whom he could leave the farm, so it should have reverted to the Dean and Chapter according to Huntingdon's order, but instead Robinson sold all his claim and interest to Dr Pilkington for £120.[58]

Huntingdon's new leases had only short-lived popularity. Between 1575 and 1627 the Merrington tenants who had opted for *sub-ordinem* leases converted them to simple leases which they could bequeath to whom they

---

56   DCD/B/BA3, fols 145, 155, 156–84; BA5, fols 114–15, 149, 188–90, 194–5, 199, 226, 231, 235–7, 264–73, 289, 297–9, 317, 324–5, 334–5, 367–8, 411–13, 441, 446–7; BA6, fols 3, 13, 15, 17–18, 27, 39, 44–5, 60, 64–6, 79, 84–5, 130, 143, 163, 270–72, 300–1; BA7, fols 64–5, 77–9.
57   Longstaffe, *Durham Halmote Rolls*, p. 234, DCD/B/BA3–5.
58   Longstaffe, *Durham Halmote Rolls*, p. 237.

wished or sell freely – rights which they regarded as fundamental to their tenure.[59] The Chapter Acts of 1622 recorded one Merrington tenant's decision to give up a *sub ordinem* lease stating:

> Thomas Trotter disclaiming the Lord's [Huntingdon's] order a Lease of a Tenement in Middlestone late his brother John's who died without issue for 21 years.
> Fine £60.[60]

Importantly, the use of concurrent and lottery leases had surprisingly little impact on the sitting tenants' continued tenure. Only three out of fifty tenant families permanently lost their farms during the lotteries. One was the John Robinson discussed above, whose line expired.[61] One farm in Westerton was also gained by Pilkington and another in Kirk Merrington was lost to the sitting tenant but no evidence survives as to why this happened.[62] Over the period 1550–1600, surname and probate evidence shows that forty-one out of fifty tenant families occupied their property continuously. Further properties could well have been inherited by relatives with different surnames.[63]

IV

The Chapter continued to deny that their tenants enjoyed tenant right but their own actions contradicted these denials. They did not evict tenants who refused to take out leases. The 1580 survey and the receivers' books still recorded as the tenants those who refused to take leases but paid rent, a tacit admission of right to the land. Beyond Merrington, the 1580 survey records John Wheatley, tenant in Shincliffe, and Raiph Harle, tenant in Nether Heworth, who are both described as holding by tenant right.[64] There are also examples of the Chapter upholding tenants' hereditary rights within Merrington.[65] From 1541–1601 one Ferryhill tenant, John Gray, consistently refused to take a lease but was not evicted.[66] After Gray's death, his widow remarried to Francis Crawe of Ferryhill, who accepted a lease for the property in 1601. The Chapter's lease to Crawe gave John

59 Marcombe, 'Dean and Chapter', p. 155.
60 DCD Chapter Acts, 21 November 1622.
61 DCD/B/BA2, fol. 237; BA5, fols 18–19; Longstaffe, *Durham Halmote Rolls*, p. 237.
62 DCD/B/BA3, fol. 102; BA5, fols 51–2, 175; BA6, fol. 70; BA7, fol. 130.
63 DCD Receivers Books 1–24.
64 Longstaffe, *Durham Halmote Rolls*, pp. 216, 223.
65 DCD/B/BA3, fols 111–12.
66 Longstaffe, *Durham Halmote Rolls*, pp. 237–8.

Gray, son of the deceased tenant, the option of taking the lease once he reached twenty-one years of age. Gray was duly granted the lease in 1616 and the lease was accompanied by an order to Thomas King, a lawyer, to take possession of the farm and deliver it to John Gray.[67] Similarly the Chapter granted a concurrent lease to Philip Parkinson of the Downes family's farm at Middlestone which was inhabited at the time by William Baynes who had married Downes' widow. The 1580 survey acknowledged the lease to Parkinson, but described William Baynes as the tenant and stated that he would pay neither for his wife's widow right nor for tenant right *sub ordinem* for himself. Despite this the Dean and Chapter continued to recognise him as the tenant and the farm was eventually leased to Anthony Downes, the last *sub ordinem* lease to be granted, in 1608.[68]

The Dean and Chapter supported their tenants' hereditary interest by endorsing bequests of leases in tenants' wills. One of the most important examples of this involved the will of Joseph Pilkington in 1623. Pilkington, a man of Middlestone, held farms in Kirk Merrington, Middlestone and Westerton which he left to his wife for life, instructing her to renew the leases in her own name for the unexpired period of the lease and on expiry to renew them again, provided that she secured the 'interest and tenant right to their children' after her decease. In his will he asked his good friends the Dean and Chapter to renew the leases according to the meaning of his will.[69] The Chapter granted Anne a lease in Kirk Merrington, inserting a clause in the lease which recognised tenant right despite the fact that this will was made after James I had ordered the abolition of tenant right:[70]

> Provided always that the said Anne Pilkington shall not at any time during her life, alienate her interest, estate or terme of years hereby granted her of the premises or any part thereof or forfeit do or commit any other act or thing whereby to make void or extinguish the same, but that according to the true intent and meaning of the last will and testament of Joseph Pilkington, her late husband, Tobie Pilkington his son shall and may enter into have and enjoy the remainder of the terme of years in the premises unexpired in this present lease together with the tenant right thereof presently after her death anything heretofore contained in this present grant to the contrary in any way not withstanding.[71]

---

67   DCD/B/BA6, fols 134–5; BA8, fols 472, 486.
68   DCD/B/BA1, fols 141–2, 204–5; BA2, fols 176–7, 196–7, 197–8, 220, 237; BA3, fols 42, 56, 72, 89–90, 92, 106; BA5, fols 2, 28–9, 290, 317; BA7, fol. 64; Longstaffe, *Durham Halmote Rolls*, p. 237.
69   Durham Probate (hereafter DP), Joseph Pilkington 1623.
70   P. L. Hughes and J. F. Larkin, ed., *Stuart Royal Proclamations*, I (Oxford, 1983), pp. 488–90.
71   DCD/B/BA9, fol. 790, 26 June 1623.

The Westerton and Middlestone leases were similarly renewed, protecting Thomas Pilkington and Leonard Pilkington.[72] The bishop's consistory court where tenants' wills were proved similarly endorsed tenant right. Wills reflected tenants' right to bequeath their leasehold land and for their heirs to enjoy the lease until it was time to renew it.[73] For instance, the 1614 will of Michael Harrison of Middlestone provided that his farm should be sold by his father and brother and the proceeds shared among his wife and five children. The will was overturned in the bishop's consistory court at the request of his widow 'for the good of the children and saving of the farm to the eldest son'.[74]

Gradually the Chapter became more aware of the need to be, and to be perceived to be, good landlords. The Chapter Act of 1584 decreed that fines should be shared amongst residentiaries rather than given arbitrarily to the dean or individual prebendaries. In the Chapter's response to Archbishop Sheldon in the 1660s they stated that lotteries were not used again after 1577.[75] However, distrust amongst tenants lingered on, with some justification. There were allegations of theft by receivers and treasurers in the 1570s and 1580s.[76] There is some evidence that favouring of Chapter and royal friends continued during the last years of Elizabeth's reign. George Freville, a friend of the queen who served as clerk of the ordinance during the Northern Rebellion, was offered as a reward in 1580 at the request of the queen the whole town of Westerton, all of which was already tenanted.[77] Freville refused because the farms were leased to sitting tenants who claimed tenant right and he knew that it would be virtually impossible to evict them.[78] However, in the main, after 1577 Durham Chapter worked very hard to create a viable, fair and profitable system of estate management while observing tenants' rights of inheritance.

V

Durham tenants' belief in their tenant right survived its abolition by James I, whose accession in 1603 made border service redundant. James abolished tenant right and border service on his own estates, and in 1620

---

72 DCD/B/BA10, fol. 420 (1628).
73 For example, DP, Richard Liddell, 1605.
74 DP, Michael Harrison 1614 Will and Award of the Arbitrators.
75 Tanner MSS 144, fol. 106.
76 Marcombe, 'Dean and Chapter', p. 98.
77 DCD/B/BA4, fol. 22. The lease in reversion became the main way of rewarding members of the Queen's household. See Thomas, 'Leases of Crown Lands', p. 184.
78 Marcombe, 'Dean and Chapter', p. 140

issued a proclamation ordering others to follow suit.[79] The proclamation
stated that lawsuits over tenant right or customary rights of inheritance
were incurring great cost, and the combination of tenants could lead to
seditious acts. It ordered that no entry was to be made in any court roll
either on Crown estate, princes or any other estate mentioning tenant right
or customary service pretended for border service. Thus James urged that
the memory of tenant right should be forgotten: 'That tenant rights . . .
are utterly extinguished and abolished, being but dependences of former
separation and hostility'.[80]

Durham Chapter found it impossible to abolish tenant right. Instead
they finally resolved the dispute of 1626 in a manner which was mutually
beneficial to themselves and to their tenants. They renounced the practice
of imposing arbitrary renewal fines in favour of charging one year's real
value of any agricultural property as a fine to renew a 21-year lease when
seven years had elapsed. By so doing they renounced the power to take
leases in hand and alter tenancies when the lease expired, one of the chief
advantages of leasehold identified by Tawney, and instead gave their tenants the security of tenure they sought.[81] Tenants gained rights which far
exceeded those expected from a commercial lease: they always had fourteen years left in their leases which they could leave or sell to whomsoever
they wished with no interference from the landlord provided the rents and
fines were paid. Thus Durham Dean and Chapter converted the 'feeling
and custom' of their tenants into estate policy.[82]

As landlords they profited by gaining regular income that was linked
to the real value of their estate. To achieve this they had to embrace more
active estate management, moving away from multiple values of ancient
fixed rent as fines to estimating the real value of each of their properties. These valuations were recorded in a receiver's book of c.1628. All
the farms of Kirk Merrington, Westerton and Middlestone were valued
at £18, Ferryhill at £20 and Hett at £12. The receiver's book was a working document, recording revaluations until the 1670s.[83] Durham Chapter's
implementation of the new policy is apparent from the grants of leases for
Merrington properties. The fine of a farm in Kirk Merrington after seven
years was £18, or around seven times the fixed rent of 49s. For the fifty
properties, lease renewals in the first decade of the seventeenth century
were undertaken on average every 15.4 years. By contrast, in the ten-year
period up to 1642, leases were renewed on average every 8.3 years. In an

79   S. J. Watts, 'Tenant Right in Early Seventeenth-Century Northumberland', *Northern
History* 6 (1971), 74–5.
80   Kerridge, *Agrarian Problems*, pp. 59–60.
81   Tawney, *Agrarian Problem* (1912 edn), p. 286.
82   Tawney, *Agrarian Problem* (1912 edn), p. 246.
83   DCD RB 34 and 34A; Renewals Book 2.

Act of 26 June 1639 the Chapter decreed that tenants were to be warned to renew their leases after seven years at most or else to expect no such indulgence or favour as they had heretofore obtained.[84] As a result, from 1626 onwards fine income was very significant.[85] The system had in effect developed into a form of beneficial leasehold.

The Chapter's *de facto* recognition of tenant right did not solve all its tenurial problems. Some tenants still resented inflation-linked fines and occasional protests continued.[86] Contrary to Marcombe's view, Durham tenants did not give up their claim of tenant right. This claim re-emerged during the Interregnum land sales of cathedral land, at the Restoration and in the nineteenth-century parliamentary committees which preceded the sales of cathedral estates.[87] Surtees in his *History of Durham* commented that the Committee for the Sale of Church Lands reduced sale prices to Durham Chapter tenants to allow for their tenant right.[88] Most tenants, however, accepted the secure tenurial system after 1626. Their leases became a source of strength allowing them to make agricultural improvements such as enclosure. Within Merrington, the whole township of Ferryhill, including open fields and wastes, was enclosed in 1637 at the initiative of the tenants and largely for their benefit. The freeholders of Ferryhill had enclosed in 1599, and in 1639 leaseholders throughout the wider estate successfully petitioned the Chapter for permission to enclose to profit from the demand for food arising from the increasing numbers of coal miners.[89] The enclosures of Hett, Middleston and Kirk Merrington followed just after the Restoration.[90] Contrary to Tawney's assumptions, these enclosures were undertaken by leaseholding tenants with hereditary rights, not by commercialising landlords.[91]

Tenant resistance to the abolition of customary tenures, in this case tenant right, was not futile. The tenants of Merrington ended up with leases, but those leases took a beneficial form which retained many of the advantages of their old tenures, despite allowing increased fines and income for the landlord. By the time of the Civil War, Durham Chapter

84 DCD/B/BA6–13.
85 Unfortunately fines were not recorded in chapter accounts before 1660 so progress towards fines reflecting real values before 1626 cannot be analysed. For new leases or renewals after different terms of years, tables were used such as *Sir Isaac Newton's Tables for Renewing Cathedral Leases*, 6th edn (London, 1742).
86 For a full discussion see Morrin, 'Merrington'.
87 Morrin, 'Merrington', pp. 130–50, 170–2, 321–4.
88 R. Surtees, *The History and Antiquities of the County Palatine of Durham*, 1 (Durham, 1816), p. 112.
89 Morrin, 'Merrington', pp. 101–2.
90 DCD/B/BA12, fols 473–8; Register 20, fols 519–20. DCD First Renewals Book 1669, fol. 412.
91 Tawney, *Agrarian Problem* (1912 edn), pp. 9, 405.

had secured adequate estate income through a tenurial compromise which also benefited their tenants who enjoyed security of tenure, provided they paid the fixed rents and agreed fines. This encouraged tenants to improve their farms in the knowledge that they would share the proceeds with their landlords, and also gave them the right to bequeath, sell or mortgage their lease to whomsoever they wished.[92] This chapter has shown that a more nuanced approach is needed towards the nature of early modern leases, as they existed in a much greater variety of forms than Tawney suggested.[93]

92   A small fee had also to be paid for a licence to alienate the property. To encourage improvements, the Chapter allowed at least one renewal to take place after any innovations were made before increasing the fine.
93   Tawney, *Agrarian Problem* (1912 edn), p. 283.

8

The Financial Rewards of Winning the Battle for Secure Customary Tenure

JENNIFER S. HOLT

In *The Agrarian Problem in the Sixteenth Century*, R. H. Tawney described a wide range of possible constraints that customary tenure might impose upon lords and tenants.[1] He noted that customary rents were normally fixed, and that during a period of rising land values lords could seek to increase their share of income from the land in a limited number of ways. They might overturn custom and persuade the tenantry to convert to lease-hold, or retrieve the situation through increased fines 'so as to get in a lump sum what he could not get by yearly instalments'.[2] This last statement suggests that it was possible to increase fines to keep pace with the rise in market rents and that such increases could allow transfers from tenant to lord which would equate to the 'lost' rents.[3] This chapter uses a detailed study of a tenant right estate in north-west England to demonstrate a number of points which have a more general application for other forms of customary tenure. It examines two aspects of the power struggle between lords and customary tenants on the Hornby Castle estates in north Lancashire.[4] First, it identifies the potential income from the customary lands and quantifies the relative shares accruing to lord and tenants. This demonstrates how substantial the benefits were for manorial tenants who defeated their lords' attempts to raise rents and fines, and retained their tenures on customary terms. Secondly, it briefly explores the level of organisation and legal costs among the tenants that were necessary to win this battle.

The nature of tenant right tenure has already been discussed in chapter 7. Here two important features of the tenure need to be stressed. A

---

1 Tawney, *Agrarian Problem*.
2 Ibid., p. 305.
3 Tawney limited his discussions to copyhold where fines only fell due upon the death or change of tenant: *Agrarian Problem*, p. 301.
4 For a wider discussion of these estates, see Jennifer S. Holt, *The Hornby Castle Estates: Agrarian Change from the 1582 Survey to the 1751 Sederunt* (Chetham Society, forthcoming). It partly rests upon evidence from the uncatalogued archives of the Hornby Castle estates, referred to hereafter as HHC.

characteristic of tenant right, which set it apart from other customary tenures, was that a general fine (gressom or gressum) was payable on the change of lord in addition to the casual fine payable on the admittance of a new tenant. This increased the monetary burden of fines relative to rent in comparison to other customary tenures. Secondly, it was a flexible and poorly defined type of tenure. There were probably as many forms of tenant right as there were manors which held by it.[5] Even within particular manors, tenant right never really seems to have settled into one form, although it could be described in intricate detail in the documents generated by a particular dispute. Such descriptions should be taken as a statement of future intent rather than previous practice. The fluid nature of tenant right led to many disputes between lords and tenants. Although lords would have been delighted to overturn their tenants' strong customary rights, it has also been pointed out that some tenant right cases brought by lords were not serious attempts to overturn tenure but an exercise in extracting additional fines from the tenantry.[6] Some of the disputes described below could be categorised as money-raising opportunities.

I

In 1500 the Hornby Castle estates comprised the honour of Hornby together with a diverse range of lands spread across north Lancashire, Yorkshire and Westmorland. The majority of these lands were brought to Sir Edward Stanley in the late fifteenth century by his first wife, Anne Harrington, and were then combined with his own inheritance in the area. Sir Edward was well connected, although a younger son. His father, Thomas Stanley, first earl of Derby, took Margaret Beaufort as his second wife, making Sir Edward the stepbrother of Henry VII. Edward's heir, Thomas, married Mary Brandon, daughter of the Duke of Suffolk and stepdaughter to Mary Tudor, the French queen.[7] In 1514 Sir Edward was given a peerage and created Lord Mounteagle. After his death in 1523, this title was borne by his son Thomas (1507–60) and grandson William (1528–81). The sole heir of William Stanley, the third Lord Mounteagle, was his daughter Elizabeth (c.1558–85) who married Edward Parker, the twelfth Lord Morley. The couple's eldest son, William Parker (1575–1622), was given his grandfather's title, as Lord Mounteagle, and when Edward

5   A. Bagot, 'Mr Gilpin and Manorial Customs', *Cumberland and Westmorland Antiquarian and Archaeological Society* new series 62 (1962), 228.
6   For the experiences upon manors adjacent to the Hornby Castle estates, see: Hoyle, 'Lords, Tenants and Tenant Right'.
7   R. W. Hoyle and H. R. T. Summerson, 'The Earl of Derby and Deposition of the Abbot of Furness in 1514', *Northern History* 30 (1994), 184–92.

Parker, Lord Morley, died in 1618, William Parker became Lord Morley and Mounteagle.

Sir Edward Stanley failed to maximise the opportunities offered by his kinship links and was content to remain in the north-west. His son and grandson seem to have lacked any obvious talents which could have generated extra income or power. After the death of William, Lord Mounteagle, in 1581, the family's focus was their lands in Essex, and the Hornby Castle estates were subsequently leased to a younger brother of William Parker, the first Lord Morley and Mounteagle. The second Lord Morley and Mounteagle, Henry Parker, is only visible in the Hornby Castle records when he got into trouble and needed to raise money; whilst his only son, Thomas, had the misfortune to inherit in 1656. He raised loans to buy back his paternal inheritances in Essex and Lancashire only to find that the income generated by the lands was insufficient to service his debts. Thomas died without heirs in 1697. By 1670, the Essex lands were sold and the remains of the Hornby Castle estates had passed into the hands of Thomas Parker's cousin, Robert Brudenell, earl of Cardigan. Cardigan's grandson sold the Hornby Castle estates to Colonel Francis Charteris in 1712 whose grandson, Francis Charteris, later earl of March and Wemyss, inherited them in 1732. The earl's lands were mainly in Scotland and the Hornby Castle estates must always have been of only peripheral interest. They were put up for sale in the 1780s.

Key to the discussion here are three valuations of the Hornby Castle estates which were all generated by a change, or proposed change, of owner. These valuations state the real value, or market value, of the lands that theoretically could have been raised if rack rents had been charged; these can be compared with the actual value of customary rents paid to the lord. The first is the 1582 survey ordered by Edward Parker, Lord Morley, who had married the Mounteagle heiress. The other two are valuations undertaken prior to the enfranchisement of customary holdings and subsequent sale of the Hornby Castle estates: in 1711 the sale from George Brudenell, earl of Cardigan to Colonel Francis Charteris, and in 1774 the sale from Charteris's grandson to John Marsden. The eighteenth-century documents are essential in revealing how land values rose across the seventeenth century and into the eighteenth, offering a long-term perspective on the gains accruing to tenants from their secure tenure of customary lands.

When the last Lord Mounteagle died in November 1581, management of the estate was taken over by Edward Parker, the husband of his heiress and only daughter. Edward Parker ordered the making of the first survey in May 1582. It was not completed until 1584, and was linked to a period of turmoil on the Hornby Castle estates.[8] Alongside the survey, and as

---

8 In comparison, some ten years earlier Nathaniel Bacon had considered that a month

part of the same strategy to increase income, Parker granted leases of four tenant right farmholdings to one of the chief estate officers. When the customary tenants refused to hand over their holdings, the lessee made a complaint of *ejectio firmae* in the common law courts on the grounds that tenant right did not exist.[9] In response, the tenants took the case to equity, a court which did recognise custom. In 1584 the Privy Council handed down a decree that confirmed the tenant right tenants in possession of their lands, with general fines of eight times the customary rent.[10] The general fines were those paid at the change of lord; the casual or dropping fines payable on change of tenant were not covered by the decree but were later agreed at twice the annual market value, less charges such as parish assessments.[11]

In coming to their conclusion, the Privy Council took into account one critical factor to which close consideration should be given. In 1565 William, Lord Mounteagle, was in dire financial straits and made a grant which was to control the outcome of a number of later disputes with the tenants, including that of 1584. The 1565 grant does not survive, but it was quoted, apparently in its entirety, in a dispute of 1698. Under the terms of the grant Lord Mounteagle confirmed the rights of inheritance, fixed rents and fixed fines to all his customary tenants across his whole estate in exchange for an additional general fine of four times the customary rents. Only desperate financial need could have triggered this grant in exchange for such a very modest return.

The survey of 1582 was a thoroughly professional job, listing all the tenants by township with a complete description of their holdings and the customary rents payable. This was followed by a valuation of each component so that different grades of land can be distinguished and gives useful insights into the uneven quality found across such a varied landscape. A fair copy of the working documents was made, but by about 1670 it had become damaged through regular use and a new copy was made.[12] Where possible, the figures below are taken from the 1582 working papers. Failing that, the figures from the copy made c.1670 are used.

The valuations made in 1711 are at least as detailed as those of 1582 but part of the entries for some townships have been lost. These losses served to limit the potential area analysed here. The 1774 valuations are

---

would suffice for a full survey of his manor of Stiffkey, Norfolk: A. H. Smith, G. M. Baker and R. W. Kenny, eds, *The Papers of Nathaniel Bacon of Stiffkey* (Norwich, 1979), p. 72.

9   TNA DL1/123.

10   HHC-27, item 3.

11   Where figures are available, the amounts actually paid seem to be calculated using a multiplier of 1.5 times the annual value.

12   The original fair copy is now lost but the 1670 copy is still held in Hornby Castle: HHC-23.

the most detailed of all and some of the original maps linked to those schedules are extant. However, working with this third set of figures was a little more complex as lands enfranchised in 1711 were not included. In order to produce comparable totals for the later date, the 1774 values were adjusted upwards on a township basis to take into account the changes in customary rents.[13] The values of the customary rents enfranchised in 1711, and the township to which they related, could be cross-checked using the lists of customary, fee farm (that is ex-customary rents) and freehold rents given in the *sederunt* of 1751.[14]

The three sets of valuations describe estates which experienced substantial change over time. For instance, significant sales of land took place in the 1590s after the coming of age of William Parker, later Lord Morley and Mounteagle. This analysis focuses on the core lands of the honour of Hornby, comprising the townships of Arkholme with Cawood, Farleton in Lonsdale, Hornby, Melling with Wrayton, Roeburndale and Wray with Botton, but excludes Wennington which was entirely held by free tenants. These are the only parts of the estate for which we have good sets of valuations for all three dates: they represent more than nine thousand hectares of diverse topography and economic potential. It should be noted that some of the townships within the Hornby Castle estates had very little demesne land,[15] so that the ability of the lord to access the income potential of those townships was already severely limited. Hornby itself, which was a significant seigneurial market town in the 1580s, was seriously damaged during the Civil War. It declined throughout the period under discussion.[16]

II

The real annual value of the tenant right land, or market-determined rent at rack-rent level as recorded in the surveys, can be divided into two parts: the rent paid to the landlord and the potential income stream accruing to

---

13 For instance, if the customary rents were reduced by ten per cent due to the 1711 enfranchisement, the valuation for that township in 1774 would be divided by 0.9 to give a value that would compensate for the absence of the enfranchised lands from the 1774 valuation.

14 A *sederunt* was originally a term used by Scottish Law Courts to indicate the written records of their proceedings. Here it refers to an estate document which was a combination of survey, rental, discussion of management strategy and five-year plan, created by officers working for Hon. Francis Charteris. See: Holt, *Hornby Castle*.

15 On average, demesne accounted for a little over ten per cent of the core lands in these townships.

16 Jennifer S. Holt, 'Hornby Town and the Textiles of Melling Parish in the Early-Modern Period', *Transactions of the Lancashire and Cheshire Antiquarian Society* 101 (2005), 39–70.

the tenant. There was also, potentially, a third party: the actual farmer of the lands who in this case would be a subtenant of the customary tenant. Such subtenancies seem to have been relatively rare on the Hornby Castle estates in the sixteenth century but were common by the eighteenth century. For the purposes of this discussion, such subtenants are largely ignored, but it is nevertheless important to remember they existed.

The total customary rents for the whole Hornby Castle estate in 1582 were £261 11s 9d, which represented just over twenty per cent of the potential rack rent. In the light of that ratio, the attempt by Edward, Lord Morley, to overturn tenant right at Hornby was a worthwhile risk. In the core lands of the honour of Hornby analysed in table 8.1, the lord's share was an even lower proportion: £112 13s 10½d or eighteen per cent. Table 8.1 shows the valuations (or market values) of the tenant right lands in each of the seven townships. These are compared with the customary rents, which are used to calculate the percentage of the annual values that was actually being paid to the lord by the tenants. The remainder of the lands' value accrued to tenants: in the core townships the percentage rose

Figure 8.1: Gross income per annum for customary lands in the honour of Hornby, 1582–1774

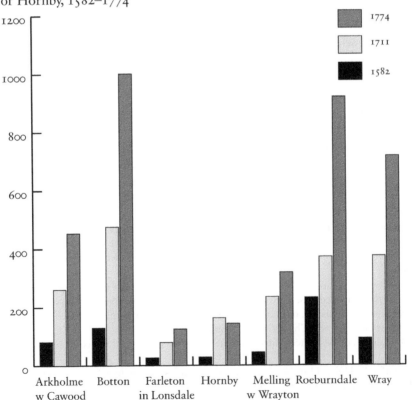

Table 8.1: The potential income from tenant right lands and its division between lord and tenants, 1582–1774

Township	Total annual value of market rents (£)			Customary rents paid to lord (share of market value received by lord) (£)			Annual value accruing to tenants (market rents minus customary rents) (£)		
	1582	1711	1774	1582	1711	1774	1582	1711	1774
Arkholme with Cawood	81.68	261.00	454.00	18.02	16.00	16.00	63.66	245.00	438.00
Botton	128.91	475.95	1001.40	20.22	18.40	18.40	108.69	457.55	983.00
Farleton in Lonsdale	26.47	78.60	124.70	9.62	9.70	9.70	16.85	68.90	115.00
Hornby	28.14	162.40	143.45	13.01	13.45	13.45	15.13	148.95	130.00
Melling with Wrayton	44.38	235.17	319.10	8.66	9.01	9.01	35.72	226.16	310.00
Roeburndale	232.07	371.97	921.18	24.19	25.18	25.18	207.88	346.79	896.00
Wray	92.14	374.97	719.13	18.97	19.13	19.13	73.17	355.84	700.00
Total	633.79	1960.06	3682.96	112.69	110.87	110.87	521.10	1849.19	3572.00
Percentage	100	100	100	18	6	3	82	94	97

Table 8.2: Calculated increases in annual values per annum

Township	1582 value (£)	Inc in AV p.a. (£)	1711 value (£)	Inc. in AV p.a. (£)	1774 (£)
Arkholme with Cawood	82	1.39	261	3.06	454
Botton	129	2.69	476	8.34	1001
Farleton in Lonsdale	26	0.40	79	0.73	125
Hornby	28	1.04	162	0.30	143
Melling with Wrayton	44	1.48	235	1.33	319
Roeburndale	232	1.08	372	8.72	921
Wray	92	2.19	375	5.46	719
Totals (£)	634	10.28	1960	27.35	3683
Annual percentage increase		1.62		1.40	

from an already high eighty-two per cent of the value in 1582, to an even higher ninety-four per cent in 1711 and ninety-seven per cent by 1774.

The lands included in the 1582 and 1711 surveys correspond very closely; those in 1774 relate to a slightly more limited area, being only those lands which had not been enfranchised in 1711. Table 8.1 demonstrates the growth in market land values for each township over time, also shown graphically in figure 8.1. These range from Hornby, which declined in value, to the woodland townships of Botton, Roeburndale and Wray which experienced significant increases over time. The woodland townships were also those where there was least demesne. Evidently it was the customary tenants who received most benefit from the rise in land values.

The data shown in table 8.1 are also the basis for calculating a theoretical accumulated income. The starting point was an assumption that between the dates of each survey values increased in a linear fashion, that is, the increase year on year was constant with no sudden rises and subsequent falls. While this clearly does not reflect the actual situation there was no practical alternative and, as we shall see, a more sophisticated approach would not have significantly altered the overall picture. The results shown in table 8.2 demonstrate that on average the total value of the seven townships rose by £10.28 per annum between 1582 and 1711, and by £27.35 per annum between 1711 and 1774. The averaged annual rate of change stood at 1.62 per cent for the first period, falling slightly to 1.40 per cent in the second. The cumulative effect of these year-on-year increases in income are given in table 8.3. For the period 1582–1711, the lords received an aver-

Table 8.3: Potential accumulated income for the periods 1582–1711 and 1712–1774

Township	1582-1711 (£)	1712-1774 (£)	Totals (£)
Arkholme with Cawood			
Lord	2,210 (12%)	1,008 (4%)	3,219 (7%)
Customary tenants	16,594 (88%)	24,370 (96%)	40,964 (93%)
Botton			
Lord	2,544 (6%)	1,191 (2%)	3,735 (4%)
Customary tenants	36,806 (94%)	47,180 (98%)	93,986 (96%)
Farleton in Lonsdale			
Lord	1,256 (18%)	611 (9%)	1,868 (14%)
Customary tenants	5,574 (82%)	5,830 (91%)	11,403 (86%)
Hornby			
Lord	1,721 (14%)	848 (8%)	2,569 (11%)
Customary tenants	10,666 (86%)	9,303 (92%)	19,970 (89%)
Melling with Wrayton			
Lord	1,154 (6%)	573 (3%)	1,727 (5%)
Customary tenants	17,015 (94%)	18,400 (97%)	35,415 (95%)
Roeburndale			
Lord	3,209 (8%)	1,587 (4%)	4,796 (6%)
Customary tenants	36,033 (92%)	40,744 (96%)	76,777 (94%)
Wray			
Lord	2,995 (10%)	1,457 (4%)	4,451 (7%)
Customary tenants	27,769 (90%)	34,710 (96%)	62,478 (93%)
Totals			
Lord	15,090 (9%)	7,275 (4%)	22,635 (6%)
Customary tenants	150,456 (91%)	180,538 (96%)	330,994 (94%)

age of nine per cent of the potential income, falling to four per cent in 1711–74. The average over the full period 1582–1774 was six per cent. In cash terms, the total sum received by the lords was £22,635, compared to the tenants' £330,994. However, the customary rents were not the only monies passing from tenants to lords: fines payable on change of lord or tenant also amounted to a significant sum.

The general fines payable on a change of lord are clearly noted in the estate records, and are given in table 8.4. In contrast, calculation of the casual fines payable on the admission of a new tenant, or when the lord's

Table 8.4: General fines levied, 1581–1744

Year	Occasion	Multi-plier*	Fine
1581	Death of William, Lord Mounteagle	8	£902
1585	Death of Elizabeth, Lady Morley (first payment)	2	£225
1592/3	Death of Elizabeth, Lady Morley (second payment)	4	£451
1596	Death of Elizabeth, Lady Morley (third payment)	2	£225
1622	Death of William, Lord Morley and Mounteagle	8	£902
1622	Confirmation of custom by Henry, Lord Morley and Mounteagle	4.25	£479
1660	Death of Phillippa, Lady Morley and Mounteagle	8	£902
1662	General admittance by Thomas, Lord Morley and Mounteagle, Messrs Charleton and Sheldon	8	£902
1706	Deaths of Thomas, Lord Morley and Mounteagle and others (not levied until the heir came of age)	8	£902
1744	Death of Col. Francis Charteris (not levied until the heir came of age)	8	£902
		Total	£6790

* The customary rents are £112.69 in all cases.

permission was needed on the granting of a mortgage or lease lasting more than one year, are less easy to track as only a handful of firm annual totals could be identified.[17] Values for the fines in the missing years were calculated based on the assumption that increases in the intervening periods were linear, and that land values changed in a simple step mode which drove the increase in casual fines accordingly. This led to the rough estimate that the casual fines paid by tenants between 1582 and 1774 amounted to a total of £10,000. Together, the £6,790 received in general fines and the £10,000 in casual fines increase the lords' share of profits recorded in table 8.4 as £22,365 to £39,425. Similarly they reduce the tenants' share from £330,994 to £314,204. In percentage terms, this means that while the lords received only six per cent of the lands' value in rents, with fines factored in they

17   The majority of manor court books do not survive for this period.

received eleven per cent of the value of the lands, and the tenants eighty-nine per cent on average over the whole period 1582–1774.

Tawney distinguished between fixed and variable fines.[18] The two types of fine borne by the tenant right lands on the Hornby Castle estate gives one of each category: the fixed fine on a change of lord and the variable fines on change of tenant. Compared to copyhold lands with their single fine, the lord of a tenant right manor had greater opportunities to recover the shortfall in his rental income by the use of entry fines. Yet even with this double opportunity, the great majority of the market value of the lands still accrued to the tenants and not the lord. Fines allowed a slight adjustment of the balance, but it cannot be argued that they allowed the lord to claw back the whole difference between customary rents and real rental values, as Tawney implied.

Although some fairly large assumptions have had to be made in generating the figures given above, they do not necessarily result in a bias towards either lord or tenant. If a substantial error has been created so that the total for casual fines is erroneous, for instance if the lord received double the amount shown, the effect would be to change the ratios by three per cent: it would have little impact upon the general picture. These figures demonstrate that there was a lot of money at stake. However, in order to contest or defend the status quo, money also had to be spent by the tenants on legal fees and other costs, and they too could amount to a substantial sum.

III

Two tenant right disputes on the Hornby Castle estate provide insight into how the tenants organised their legal cases and paid the related costs. In the dispute of the 1580s, the records that throw most light on the tenants' organisation were generated by some of the claims and counterclaims which ran alongside the central case. In particular, a plea brought in May 1583 by Thomas Marsh highlights a number of important aspects. Thomas Marsh alias Mort was a senior officer to Lord Morley, and the man to whom the four leases had been granted in connection with which the plea of *ejectio firmae* had been entered, as described above. Marsh claimed that in January 1582, that is only two months after the death of William Stanley and before the survey had begun in May 1582, he had been the subject of a vicious attack by a tenant during which he had feared for his life. In his supporting testimony Marsh claimed that there was a confederacy

---

18   Tawney refers to 'fines of two years' rent' (i.e. the current potential rack rent): *Agrarian Problem*, p. 306.

amongst Lord Morley's tenants which included not only those townships discussed here, but extended across all the adjacent lands held of the honour of Hornby: a substantial part of the Lune valley and beyond. Marsh's statement continued with the accusation that this confederacy was seeking to levy money in order to fund the tenants' legal charges.[19]

The effect of Thomas Marsh's newly made charges, which suggested civil disorder and conspiracy, was that the hearings in the case which had formerly been held at Hornby or Lancaster were moved to London. The defendants, the Hornby Castle estate tenants, were thus imprisoned in London until the case was heard – a traumatic experience, although they were later freed once the case came to court and they were found not guilty. Given the time delay between the alleged assault and Thomas Marsh's accusation it seems reasonable to assume this strand of the case was brought precisely to have this effect: to change the nature of the offences from those which would be heard locally, where the defendants could carry on with their normal lives, to one which automatically meant imprisonment in London whilst awaiting trial.[20]

The meeting at which Marsh said the tenants had planned the 'maintenance of their suit against the lord' was the annual parish meeting held on the Tuesday of Easter week at which the Twenty Four (the extended parish vestry) were selected and the parish rate set for the forthcoming year. The defendants claimed they knew nothing about the amounts involved, but said that most of the tenants had contributed to the costs and this extended to all the towns, villages and hamlets in the lordship.[21] This matches the greater detail that comes from another set of cases brought more than fifty years later.

In the late 1630s, Henry Parker, Lord Morley and Mounteagle, was in dire financial straits, a situation largely of his own making. In 1634, fines of £11,000 had been imposed on him for a fracas in the king's presence and this, together with his other debts, encouraged Parker to look for financial resources to exploit.[22] Parker's own view of the profitability of the honour of Hornby is helpful. In 1643 Parker was to put this part of his estates in trust with his brother-in-law, William Habbington of Henlipp, Worcestershire, and one John Harris of the Inner Temple, to pay debts of £3,900. At that time Parker stated that the clear value of the manor and lordship of Hornby was £800 per year. To this may be added the Melling in Lonsdale tithes which were owned by the lord of Hornby: the tithes of

---

19 TNA DL4/25/65.

20 Marsh's plea combined the statement that the attack took place sixteen months earlier with the accusation that the meetings about levies to raise legal costs had occurred in Easter week 1583 – that is, the month prior to his plea: TNA DL1/130.

21 TNA DL4/25/65.

22 There is also evidence of various opportunities he pursued on his Essex estates.

wool and lambs generated £47 17s 5d in 1636 and £51 3s 5d in 1637;[23] in 1654 the tithes of grain with the tithe barns were leased for a total of £140 per year.[24] However, there were other possibilities in a parish which was well endowed with natural resources, particularly timber and iron ore.

There were iron works in the Honour of Hornby by 1560,[25] but these may have been affected by Elizabeth I's ban on iron-working in Furness.[26] Surviving estate documents provide little evidence beyond a passing reference to 'the iron works' in 1613.[27] There was certainly a forge operating in Hornby by 1626 when the lord of Hornby received £3 6s 8d for 'Forge Rent'.[28] In the 1630s, one Alexander Rigby was lessee of Hornby Forge, employing Alexander Worthington as his surveyor of the ironworks. However, for the lord of Hornby, the charcoal they needed was more profitable than the ironworks themselves. Estate accounts for the half-year to Pentecost 1640 record that £172 9s 4d was received for 'wood sold in Tatham Park and Hornby Park cordwood to Mr. Rigby'.[29] These timber sales from the lord's deerparks were not problematic, as he could do as he wished with these lands. But similar sales from lands held by the customary tenants were open to challenge as tenants claimed extensive timber rights to the trees that grew there.

The resulting timber dispute was one of a number of interlocking cases brought by Lord Morley and Mounteagle and his customary tenants. The Duchy of Lancaster court ordered Lord Morley and Mounteagle to stop felling all timber whilst a commissioner appointed by the court came to review the situation. Then the Duchy's commissioner settled the timber case in favour of the tenants in all respects, a victory which seems to have resulted in a certain degree of humiliation for the lord and to the closure of the ironworks. The Russell brothers, employed as hammermen at Hornby Forge, moved away from Hornby at about this time whilst the receivers' accounts for the half-year to Pentecost 1642 state that '[f]orge implements sold to Mr Spachers £32 at the least'.[30]

The loss of this income stream was a blow to the lord's standing locally and to his pocket. But the customary tenants' victory also came at significant financial cost. The main record for the methods the customary

23 HHC-28, item 66.
24 Northamptonshire Record Office, H.vii.19.
25 Lancashire Archives (LA), DDHC Box 12.
26 The bloom smithies in Furness were closed by royal decree in 1564 to preserve the woodlands there: Mark Bowden, ed., *Furness Iron* (London, 2000), p. 6.
27 The context could mean the works were proposed rather than actual: Huntington Library, EL 710.
28 HHC-1, fol. 22.
29 HHC-1, fol. 34.
30 HHC-1, fol. 84v.

tenants used to prosecute their cases and fund their legal fees comes via a later dispute. The starting point for the relevant cases was Lord Morley and Mounteagle's attempts around 1634–35 to interfere with the timber allowances due to the customary tenants and he

> also did sell great quantity of woods to divers foreigners and did set up iron works with in the said lordship and in such sort fell, sell and burn and waste the woods growing within the lordship contrary to the custom of the said manor and contrary to a decree conceived in the reign . . . [of] Queen Elizabeth . . .[31]

As a result of the lord's actions, a meeting was called of all the customary tenants within the lordship of Hornby and the adjoining manors of Tatham and Gressingham which were also owned by the lord of Hornby. This meeting took place at the house of one Thomas Marshall who lived in Wray.[32] The tenants appointed two of their fellows, Thomas Ewan of Melling and John Procter, to act as their solicitors in a group action whilst William Winder, probably of Winder in Roeburndale, and another John Procter, of Lower Salter, also in Roeburndale, were authorised to collect money from all the customary tenants within the honour of Hornby. It should be noted that according to Procter of Lower Salter, the solicitors were asked at this meeting to disburse money on the promise that, the requisite sums having been collected, they would then be reimbursed. The legal proceedings dragged on for at least six or seven years and involved much work by Ewan and Procter which included 'many journeys' to London.

At the successful conclusion of the suit in the early 1640s another meeting was called, this time at the house of Francis Maddison in Melling, where all or the most part of the tenants attended and Procter and Ewan

> made accounts before them, both of their receipts and disbursements and did calculate how much money was borrowed about the said suit and of whom and how much was unpaid and to whom and the said tenants then and there present allowing their accounts and perceiving great sums of money to be owing.[33]

The tenants agreed to the financial arrangements which included an assessment levied on

---

31   TNA C10/39/123.
32   This is probably the same man who paid a £10 fine in 1631 in order to avoid being knighted: William Farrer, and J. Brownbill, eds, *Victoria History of the County of Lancashire*, 8 (London, 1908), p. 210.
33   TNA C10/39/12.

every tenant within the said lordship as well new tenants or tenants of the New Improvements[34] as old tenants should forthwith be levied and gathered up for making good the disbursements and satisfying the debts and ingagements aforesaid. And the said sessment of three years rent a piece of every tenant within the said lordship [c. £500] was then and there, thereupon made and reduced into a roll or rental. And he John Procter and one John Procter of Salter the other defendant and one William Winder now sithence deceased were appointed attorneys or bailiffs for the collection of the same (as by a Power of Attorney under the hands of several of the said tenants may appear).[35]

Procter continued by saying that

now lately vizt upon the 20th day of June last past [1650] most part of the tenants within the said lordship . . . have agreed upon a new levy or assessment of one years rent through out the whole lordship [c. £166] . . . did retain Master Overend in the bill named to be an attorney for the tenants against the said Lord Morley . . . Howbeit this defendant doth confess that the said Master Overend was retained by him <and> the said Thomas Ewin for the purpose aforesaid[36] and received of them the sum of £80 or thereabouts for fees and disbursement as may appear by his bills and acquittances in that behalf towards which said sum and towards all other sums expended in and about the aforesaid suit and towards all use money paid and to be paid for moneys borrowed for the purpose aforesaid (amounting in all to the sum of £800 or thereabouts) . . . 18 January 1650 at Lancaster by Domini Lawrence Dowbikin of Fowgill in the county of York before us Stephen Husband and Lancelott Dowbiggin.[37]

There are indications that Ewan and Procter suffered real financial difficulties during the case; their customary estates were subsequently sold and at least one of the men, John Procter of Salter, left the area. As Procter sought to finalise his accounts and took legal means to pursue the few tenants whose levies were still unpaid, seven customary tenants brought a counterclaim against him. It is only in Procter's statement in his defence

34   Land newly enclosed in the 1620s and which had been granted by tenant right.
35   TNA C10/39/12.
36   The implications of this reference to Overend (who was probably a member of the local family of that name) are confusing but serves to emphasise the number of lawyers employed.
37   TNA C10/39/12. Husband was a lawyer and a member of a Roman Catholic family, he later became steward to the last Lord Morley and Mounteagle. Lancelott Dowbiggin held a large customary holding in Roeburndale through his marriage to Elizabeth Winder.

against the counterclaim that the evidence of how the defence was organised and funded emerges.[38]

The most obvious point here is that these men knew exactly what to do and how to go about it. This should not cause any surprise, for they were a large and diverse group in terms of wealth, education and social status, and were used to fulfilling the many roles to be found within any parish or township and of acting upon a wider stage. It is worthwhile to note in passing that Edward Parker, Lord Morley, Philip Lord Wharton and Sir James Leyburne, all of whom were involved in tenant right conflicts on their own estates, were all also tenant right tenants to other lords within Cotterdale in 1613.[39] The customary tenants represented a cross-section of the local community, a point which directly contradicts Tawney's simplistic distinction between freeholders on one hand and the 'humble figures' of the customary tenants who stood 'in awe' of the social superiors on the other.[40]

As with any court case, it would be unwise to take all aspects of Procter's statement at face value. For instance, if all the customary tenants of the manors named had met in the house of Thomas Marshall they would not have got in the building, or even fitted in Wray High Street where he lived, as they numbered more than four hundred people. It seems much more likely that each township sent representatives so that a level of rational discussion could take place. On the other hand, perhaps it was possible to have a forum at which several hundred people could grasp the issues, formulate solutions and agree upon a course of actions. In either case, it gives a strong impression of local democracy in this part of the Lune valley. We have already seen that during the disputes of the early 1580s all the manors then comprising the Hornby Castle estates, and apparently some that were not part but where the tenants claimed to hold their lands 'by the custom of Hornby', cooperated in collecting funds. It seems that there was a clear tradition of decision-making which bound all the customary tenants.

IV

The tenants on the Hornby Castle estates won and won again in their power struggles with their lords. On every occasion the grant of 1565 was

---

38   Additional documents traced which relate to the tenant right cases of the 1630s may be found in TNA DL 1/356 (1638), DL 1/357 (1640), DL 4/92/30 (1638) and DL 4/93/30 (1638/9).

39   T. S. Willan and E. W. Crossley, eds, 'Three Seventeenth-Century Yorkshire Surveys', *Yorkshire Archaeological Society* 104 (1941), 53–4, 73; W. H. Chippindall, 'A Sixteenth-Century Survey and Year's Account of the Estates of Hornby Castle Lancashire' (Chetham Society, series 3, 1939), 113, 118–20, 126.

40   Tawney, *Agrarian Problem*, pp. 122, 252.

critical and the tenants knew it. In 1698, when there was one final case which related to it, the lady of Hornby had to borrow a copy from the tenants as the lord's copy had been lost.[41] The critical reason behind the grant was the lord's desperate need for cash in order to maintain the life-style which justified his title. However, William, Lord Mounteagle, had sold the family birthright for a very modest recompense, which is itself a sign of a fundamental imbalance in the distribution of power between lord and tenantry. The impact of this imbalance in 1565 served to consolidate the tenants' advantages over a much longer period of time. The tenants' profits from their tenant right land continued to grow over time relative to that of the lords, and enabled them to bear the costs of disputes to an extent that the lords might well have envied. The reality is that these tenants were not powerless victims but a diverse group who, even in the sixteenth century, held their lands by a range of tenures. Between them, they had the status, skills and knowledge sufficient to use the legal system for their own advantage. Tawney contended that it was possible for lords to exploit the variable fines to a level which would recompense them for the uneconomic customary rents. The calculations made here demonstrate how far the lords were from achieving this, even on a tenant right estate with its two sets of fines. If this was true of the Hornby Castle estate, it is surely impossible to envisage for a copyhold manor. In other words, the history of the Hornby Castles estates demonstrates that customary ten-ants had more powers of resistance, and more economic advantages than Tawney predicted.

---

41   The document was probably lost when Hornby Castle was effectively destroyed by the Parliamentarian Army in 1643. The representatives of the tenantry required receipts and bonds before they would release their copy of the 1565 grant.

9

Risks and Rewards in Wasteland Enclosure

Lowland Lancashire c.1500–1650

WILLIAM D. SHANNON

In his *Agrarian Problems*, Eric Kerridge accused R. H. Tawney of conjuring up a sixteenth century characterised by 'a relentless and remorseless capitalism which impiously rode down a wretched peasantry'.[1] Certainly no one could accuse Tawney of equivocation in terms of his Christian Socialist views: and it is not too hard to find forthright quotations in *The Agrarian Problem*, such as his dismissal of the Edwardian Riot Act as 'a straightforward attempt to prevent the poor from protesting when their possessions were taken from them by the rich'.[2] Yet Tawney's views were perhaps more nuanced than he is sometimes given credit for. Thus he distinguished piecemeal enclosure from 'the great enclosures made by lords of manors from which the peasants obviously lost' – the 'obviously' being a typical Tawneian touch – while he made it clear that, when talking of enclosure, he meant converting open arable fields to pasture, which he claimed 'the word would have suggested to nine men out of ten in our period'.[3]

Yet depopulating enclosure was a regional phenomenon: and it is with the tenth man's interpretation that this chapter is concerned. Although far from Tawney's main focus, there are in fact numerous references in the *Problem* to wasteland enclosure. Perhaps unusually, he seems to have seen piecemeal enclosure as a win–win situation – 'the lord gained by leasing part of it [the waste] to be broken up and cultivated while, so long as sufficient land was left for grazing, the tenants gained by getting land which they could add to their holdings and on which a growing population could settle'.[4] He also remarked, without developing the point, that whereas eighteenth-century landlords invested in enclosure *and* improvement, in

---

1 Kerridge, *Agrarian Problems*, p. 15.
2 Tawney, *Agrarian Problem* (1912 edn), p. 372. *Statutes of the Realm*, 3 and 4 Edward VI c.5.
3 Tawney, *Agrarian Problem* (1912 edn), pp. 9, 150.
4 Ibid., p. 88.

the sixteenth century 'there is very little trace of any movement of this kind. What improving is done, is done by the peasants themselves.'[5] It is this observation – that *enclosing* was done by the lord but *improving* was done by the tenant – which this chapter seeks further to explore, using as case studies two extensive early seventeenth-century wasteland enclosure events, and building upon earlier work by this author which concluded that, in enclosing the early modern wastes of lowland Lancashire, 'local landlords [had] settled for a modest reward for no risk rather than undertaking a high risk project'.[6]

I

The literature of early modern enclosure has tended to assume that the answer to the question *cui bono?* (to whose benefit?) is always the landlord. However, this comes back to Tawney's nine-out-of-ten rule, the assumption that the norm was Midland-style arable-to-pasture enclosure. As to who should benefit from reclaiming the waste, Norden in *The Surveiors Dialogue* warned his landlord readers to be particularly vigilant in case their tenants took the initiative, for

> this kinde of incroachment is not rare, especially where great wastes and mountainous grounds are, where the Lord nor his officers walke not often, and where Tennants, for favour or affection will winke at evill doers, or for their owne private lucre, commit the same errour themselves, with hedges, ditches, pales, wals, shedds etc.[7]

From Norden's perspective if there was any 'lucre' to be had from wasteland enclosure, it belonged to the lord. Yet not all wasteland enclosure was piecemeal, let alone illicitly undertaken by tenants and squatters.

Unfortunately the contemporary language of enclosure is not precise, with words such as 'intake' or 'encroachment' used casually: it is therefore useful to rehearse the terminology.[8] First there is *approvement*, enclosure by a lord of part of his waste under the terms of the Statute of Merton (1236) which allowed a lord to enclose common waste as long as sufficient

---

5   Ibid., p. 183.
6   William D. Shannon, 'Approvement and Improvement in the Lowland Wastes of Early Modern Lancashire', in *Custom, Improvement and the Landscape*, ed. Hoyle, pp. 175–202. See also William D. Shannon, 'Approvement and Improvement in Early-Modern England: Enclosure in the Lowland Wastes of Lancashire c.1500–1700' (unpublished PhD thesis, 2009).
7   John Norden, *The Surveiors Dialogue* (London, 1618), p. 101.
8   Shannon, 'Approvement and Improvement in the Lowland Wastes', p. 189.

unenclosed commons remained for his tenants' needs. *Intake* is a special form of approvement, involving enclosure of a parcel of waste by the tenant, under the lord's licence. Enclosure without such licence is *encroachment*, which might subsequently be regularised and thus become an intake. Next, if the lord or his tenants wished to enclose more of the waste than could be achieved under Merton, then an *agreement* was required between the lord and his tenants. Finally, there was *partition*, the division of an intercommon between neighbouring proprietors or manors into separately owned wastes, often the essential prelude to a wider enclosure of the waste, for a lord could only approve that which he exclusively owned.

Where approvement, partition and, in most cases, agreement was concerned, the initiative lay with the lord or lords, and would inevitably require some initial investment on their part. Heal and Holmes have claimed that in the sixteenth century 'those with money to invest in land sought to acquire estates either that were already largely enclosed and turned to pasture, or that could be so converted'.[9] Some investment in wasteland improvement was clearly going on, however, and examples can be found of individual lords such as Sir Thomas Culpepper, who spent £1,000 on the 'inning' of two hundred acres of his waste of Dengemarsh in Kent.[10] Yet historians have tended to focus more on large-scale, capital-intensive projects, notably Vermuyden's work on the Great Level in the fens.[11] The sort of return generated can be seen in the increase in Crown income from West Fen in Lincolnshire which, after the enclosure of 4,798 acres in the 1630s, increased from £18 to £600 per year.[12]

Turning to less capital-intensive schemes, Porter's work on the early modern Forest of Bowland, where the Crown owned large tracts of upland waste intercommoned by a number of surrounding townships, reveals a history of small-scale encroachments by the inhabitants, prior to the Crown taking the initiative in the 1620s to partition and then apportion the waste.[13] The resultant compounding with the copyholders to make their fines certain and their holdings secure, for the agreed sum of forty years' rent, was a satisfactory outcome for the Crown, for very little outlay. Rossendale in Lancashire was similar in many ways, again an upland

9 Felicity Heal and Clive Holmes, *The Gentry in England and Wales 1500–1700* (Basingstoke, 1994; repr. Basingstoke and New York, 2002), p. 108.

10 Clay, *Economic Expansion and Social Change*, 1:110.

11 Margaret Albright Knittl, 'The Design for the Initial Drainage of the Great Level of the Fens: An Historical Whodunit in Two Parts', *Agricultural History Review* 55:1 (2007), 23–50.

12 Clive Holmes, *Seventeenth-Century Lincolnshire*, History of Lincolnshire 3 (Lincoln, 1980), p. 129.

13 J. Porter, 'Waste Land Reclamation in the Sixteenth and Seventeenth Centuries: The Case of South-Eastern Bowland 1550–1630', *Transactions of the Historic Society of Lancashire and Cheshire* 127 (1977), 1–23.

district characterised by disafforested land and royal demesne manors,[14] whose occupiers were nearly all copyholders, with virtually no lords apart from the Crown. Tupling, writing in 1927, and conscious of Tawney, contrasted what he described as 'enclosure by little men' in this district with 'the enclosures by great men' which comprised 'the agrarian problem of the sixteenth century'.[15] His key point was 'the great bulk of the changes that took place [in Rossendale] were brought about by the tenants and by settlers in search of land and not by great landowners'.[16] He did not enquire too closely into the relative benefits accruing to the respective parties: yet nevertheless, like Tawney, he implied a win–win situation between Crown and copyholder. However, Tupling and Porter's work amongst the Crown manors of the uplands are not necessarily a good guide to what was happening in manors where the lords were locally based, and potentially more 'hands on'.

The records of the Stanleys, as the leading Lancashire aristocratic family, might be expected to be particularly instructive on the subject of improvement.[17] However, like the Crown, the family were slow to adopt new ideas, and it was only early in the seventeenth century that they began acquiring estates which 'might be improved and inclosed and turned to tillage' – which could then be let 'for reasonable fynes and yerelie rents'.[18] Gritt has similarly shown how the Molyneux family in the second half of the seventeenth century began enclosing their lowland wastes in southwest Lancashire to help tackle their debt problems, raising perhaps £1,100 in entry fines together with new rents adding to between £30 and £35 a year by the end of the century.[19]

Although the benefits seem clear, it still remains difficult to quantify the costs associated with wasteland reclamation, or the risks of failure, nor do we see any evidence for return on capital invested by either landlord or tenant. Certainly we have no equivalent to that late eighteenth-century analysis, noted by Overton, which suggested that conversion of 'commons, heaths and moors' to arable would result in profits (that is, return to the tenant) increasing six-fold, while rents (that is, return to the landlord)

14   Disafforested land was land that had formerly been subject to forest law. Forests were not necessarily covered in trees, but rather were subject to particular legal controls; see Charles R. Young, *The Royal Forests of Medieval England* (Leicester, 1979).

15   G. H. Tupling, *The Economic History of Rossendale* (Manchester, 1927), pp. 42–69.

16   Tupling, *Economic History of Rossendale*, p. 48.

17   Barry Coward, *The Stanleys: Lords Stanley and Earls of Derby 1385–1672: The Origins, Wealth and Power of a Land-owning Family* (Chetham Society, 30, third series, 1983); R. W. Hoyle, 'The Management of the Estates of the Earls of Derby 1575–1640: Some New Sources', *Northern History* 39:1 (2002), 25–36.

18   Coward, *The Stanleys*, p. 59.

19   Andrew John Gritt, 'Aspects of Agrarian Change in South-West Lancashire c.1650–1850' (unpublished PhD thesis, 2000), p. 164.

would increase eight-fold.[20] It is therefore necessary to turn to other sources for information regarding investment and return in wasteland enclosure.

II

Some indirect light may be shed on these matters by evidence given in land cases before the Chancery Court of the Duchy of Lancaster.[21] We should however be wary of preconceptions: in *Tudor Economic Documents*, Tawney headed two cases from the Star Chamber respectively 'Enclosures, evictions and other oppressions . . .' and 'Enclosure of commons and oppression of copy-holders'.[22] Those headlines are certainly justified if one reads only the plaintiff's bill: but in both cases the defendants' answers are at least as credible, leading to the conclusion that the two cases could just as well have been headed 'Copyholders break enclosure agreement' and 'Lord encloses his waste in accordance with the Statute of Merton'.

The cases analysed here were initially consulted in connection with a general study of wasteland enclosure in lowland Lancashire. In c.1500 those wastes covered perhaps a third of the land in lowland Lancashire, with about a quarter of this waste being enclosed between 1500 and c.1650.[23] However, it was not the prime purpose of that study to examine the economics of enclosure; and of over ninety cases reviewed, there were in fact very few that provided any financial detail. While annual rents were frequently mentioned, there was seldom a need from the perspective of plaintiff, defendant or deponent to raise in court the subject of the entry fines that had been paid, while even more rare was any account of the investment by either side in the actual process of enclosure and improvement. Nevertheless, enough information could be gleaned to allow the conclusion that, while licensing an intake was the least risky method of enclosure, significant rewards were only likely to flow from larger-scale approvements or agreements, when the ratio of lordly reward to risk was dramatically increased.

However, quantifying the initial outlay is not easy, especially as it obviously varied according to circumstances. For example partitioning an intercommon could perhaps require no more than the placing of merestones,

20   Overton, *Agricultural Revolution*, p. 161.

21   Shannon, 'Approvement and Improvement in Early Modern England'; Shannon, 'Approvement and Improvement in the Lowland Wastes'; William D. Shannon, 'On the Left Hand above the Staire: Accessing, Understanding and Using the Archives of the Early-Modern Court of Duchy Chamber', *Archives* 35:123 (2010), 19–36.

22   R. H. Tawney and Eileen Power, *Tudor Economic Documents, 1: Agriculture and Industry* (London, 1924), pp. 19–39.

23   Shannon, 'Approvement and Improvement in Early Modern England'.

but would more normally involve more permanent, although more costly, fences and ditches. Thus the boundary between Heysham and Oxcliffe through 'the deepe of the mosse', initially marked out c.1610 with 'a sheete on twoe powles', by c.1630 was made certain by digging a ditch.[24] Some crude costing may be attempted from a case concerning the boundary between Hindley and Ince in 1638, which resulted in a ditch almost a mile long ('tenn score roodes acomptinge eight yardes to the Roode'), dug by five men, while a second 40 roods long was said to have taken four days to dig with a rather larger team of diggers.[25] Taking the two together, at 6d per man-day, the cost cannot have been much less than £6 or so to divide the two townships. Simply dividing up a manorial waste would not need such partition, but the area to be improved would still require measurement and allotment which, as the sixteenth century wore on, would increasingly have involved professional surveyors. Thus in 1617 the Duchy paid Roger Kenyon £5 10s for '[s]urveying of the manor of West Derby and admeasuring the several commons and wastes there by the space of vi daies', plus a further £3 'for surveying the manor of Tottington and admeasuring the Comons there', together with the sum of £2 16s 8d for 'surveying the Common Moss and Wasts yet unenclosed in Rachdale'.[26]

Modest legal costs might be incurred where an agreement was proposed, lawyers being employed in drawing up the documents. However, significant legal costs would only have been encountered where a neighbouring lord, or the tenants themselves, sued in the Westminster courts. Details are rare, but in a case concerning a disputed enclosure in Huyton-with-Roby, near Liverpool, the Chancellor ordered that the defendants must pay 6s 'being the half charge of this Commission', before an examination of defence witnesses would take place.[27] Whether a cost of 12s for a hearing was exceptional is impossible to say, and Somerville is silent on the question of costs of actions. However, some data exists for the analogous Queen's Court, set up on the model of the Duchy Chamber, which shows that legal fees were anything but excessive: in 1641 the fee for a subpoena was 2s, and that for a Commission was 4s 6d.[28]

Where a case was won, the winner might be awarded costs, such as in a dispute over a parcel of marshland in Widnes when the farmer of the royal manor was ordered to pay £5 towards the tenants' costs and charges.[29] Generally, though, it would seem litigation was not a punitively expensive

---

24 TNA DL 4/86/10.
25 TNA DL 4/92/33.
26 LA Kenyon Papers, DDKe 5/46.
27 TNA DL 4/111/11.
28 N. R. R. Fisher, 'The Queenes Courte in Her Councell Chamber at Westminster', *English Historical Review* 108:427 (1993), 314–37.
29 TNA DL 5/13, pp. 47–8.

exercise – hence its popularity.[30] However, one reference in the cases studied mentions the sum of £20 spent on travel and court costs in attending a
hearing at Westminster, so perhaps for the Lancastrian gentry the greatest
cost, particularly where the case dragged on from term to term, may well
have been that of travel to and from London.[31] All in all, a landlord, finding himself involved in a drawn-out suit, and so faced with heavy legal
costs on top of his surveying and boundary-making expenses, might have
to pay out tens or even hundreds of pounds. Yet spread over potentially
hundreds of acres, such an outlay cannot be regarded as significant.

Turning from the cost of the investment to the return on that investment, Manning asserted with regard to the Duchy that 'much of the waste
enclosed and improved for cultivation was divided into tenancies created
primarily to produce rents.'[32] In fact, such evidence as we have suggests
that the Lancashire landlord was motivated more by the desire for an immediate lump sum. Entry fines, set at anything up to £12 an acre, were
a major consideration, if not *the* major consideration, as can be seen in
an enclosure episode carried out in Audenshaw in c.1608–11 on behalf of
Lady Elizabeth Booth, an elderly widow whose interest in the land would
die with her.[33] Although the total acreage allotted is not altogether clear,
it seems to have involved more than a hundred acres, generating something between £400 and £600 in fines from land which before enclosure
was yielding her a mere £2 a year gross from the sale of peat. A windfall
on this scale should be seen in the context of the more general incomes of
Lancashire gentry, which appear usually to have been less than £250 a year
as late as the civil war period.[34]

Rents on the new wasteland enclosures, on the other hand, seem generally to have been set at low levels in lowland Lancashire, perhaps in recognition of the heavy initial investment required by the tenant. Although
rents of up to 6s 8d an acre are occasionally encountered, the normal
level certainly seems to have been less than that prevailing for newly let
old established farmland in the vicinity. Annual rents of 1s or 2s an acre
are common, and the ratio of 1s rent to £2 fine (forty years' rent) found
in Nether Wyresdale and the Clifton leases, to be discussed later, appears
far more typical for new enclosures than, for example, the modal value
of ten years found by Hoyle across a wide range of leases on the Earl

30   Shannon, 'On the Left Hand above the Staire'.
31   TNA DL 4/95/10.
32   Manning, *Village Revolts*, p. 113.
33   TNA DL 4/71/26; Shannon, 'Approvement and Improvement in the Lowland Wastes',
pp. 198–9.
34   B. G. Blackwood, 'The Catholic and Protestant Gentry of Lancashire during the Civil
War Period', *Transactions of the Historic Society of Lancashire and Cheshire* 126 (1976),
1–29.

of Derby's estates in 1573.[35] Even more modest rents were settled on for cottages, 2d to 4d a year, or for small-scale licensed intakes 1d to 8d per acre per year. Those whose illicit encroachments had been exposed could not necessarily rely upon such generous treatment, encroachments on Angerton Moss in 1546, for example, being assessed by the commissioners at 1s 4d an acre, while a retrospectively licensed intake in Penwortham in 1547 was rated at 2s.[36]

Individually, such rents were not significant to manorial income, but collectively even a small rent from each new intake could over time add considerably to the income of an estate, as can be seen from the Penwortham rental of 1570, where encroachment around the moss edge had been going on for a long time.[37] Although the information in the survey is not adequate to distinguish rents on new enclosures from those of other copyholds/ lands at will, entries distinguished by the words *intacke*, *incroachment* or *new close* are listed under the names of 117 individuals, and these intakes appear to have made up a significant proportion of all rents at will; while rents at will together brought in more income in total to the manor than did freehold rents. At an average of around 1s an acre, those 117 enclosures would have accounted for fifteen to twenty per cent of Penwortham's estimated total combined manorial income from freehold, copyhold and at-will tenancies at this date, although this may well be an underestimate of their true contribution.

As regards the leases themselves, although the Crown in Rossendale had opted for the creation of new copyholds and long leases, Lancashire landlords seem more generally to have agreed with James Bankes, Lord of Winstanley, who in 1600 advised his son:

> I strait lye charge you in gods most holye holye name that you never make ane longer leais tow ane of youere tanant for ane longer tyme then for twente and on yeare for so shall you find theare in great profit and gane tord the advancement of yor Estaitt.[38]

Leases for years rather than lives, and 21-year leases in particular, seem to have been the norm, although three-life leases were certainly not uncommon, while the occasional lord could still conclude an anachronistic deal, such as that struck for four acres of newly enclosed land in Upper Rawcliffe in 1657, leased for one hundred years for an £8 fine and a yearly

35 Hoyle, 'Estates of the Earls of Derby'.
36 TNA DL 3/48/R5; TNA DL 3/50/P2.
37 Charles W. Sutton, 'Survey of the Manor of Penwortham in the Year 1570', *Chetham Miscellanies, 3* (Chetham Society, 73, new series, 1915), pp. 1–43.
38 Joyce Bankes, ed., *The Memoranda Book of James Bankes 1586–1617* (Inverness, 1935), p. 10.

rent of 7s, plus boon hens, one day's work, tithes of corn, grain, pulse and straw, and grinding at the lord's mill.[39] Similarly, in return for a lease for the shorter of one hundred years or three lives, one lessee in Lytham in 1611 had to provide not just his £2-an-acre fine and 1s-an-acre annual rent, but also two days 'shearinge' at harvest time, one capon and six eggs on 20 December, twelve eggs at Easter, and one and a half days' 'delvinge of turfe yearlye'.[40] However, even where such services were not called for, there were other long-term benefits accruing to the lord. For example, once enclosed, the now-several land, unlike common land, could be sold off in parcels. If the lord was also the lay impropriator he was, under the provisions of the Statute of Tithes, entitled after seven years to tithes from the new enclosures.[41] Finally, and most importantly, at the end of the leasehold period the now-improved land reverted to the lord, to be re-let at a commercial rate.

III

Balancing all the actual and potential returns against the outlay, it seems clear that, for the lord, enclosing the waste by whatever process involved low risk and high reward. The balance of risk and reward was very different for the tenant. Throughout England, leases that required the tenant to leave the tenement in good repair were the norm.[42] Similarly, for a new holding won from the waste, physically enclosing it and making the land productive appears to have been the responsibility of the incoming tenant. Such costs varied according to the original state of the land and the use for which it was intended. A small parcel of waste taken in and added to the tenant's adjacent enclosed pasture would not have cost a great deal in terms of investment. However, where the aim was to create a new holding of arable land, as applied in around a third of the cases studied, and where the waste was poorly drained moss or former turbary, the costs could be very significant indeed.

Once the land had been physically enclosed with fence, hedge or ditch, the scrub would have to be removed, to be followed by paring and burning, and then marling, before ploughing and sowing could take place. Marling was expensive but widely used, as Camden noted with respect to the Lancashire mosses:

---

39   TNA DL 4/106/9.
40   LA DDCL 2173.
41   2 and 3 Edward VI, c.13, *An Act for payment of Tithes* (1549).
42   J. P. Cooper, 'In Search of Agrarian Capitalism', in *The Brenner Debate*, ed. Aston and Philpin, pp. 138–91.

Underneath also in divers places they affourd abundance of marle, which serveth instead of mucke to enrich their grounds. Whereby, the soile that in mans opinion was held most unapt to bear Corne, beginneth now to be so kinde and arable, that it may be justly thought, mens idlenesse in times past was greater than any naturall barrainesse of the soile.[43]

In Chadderton c.1624 the initial improvement phase involved stubbing and ridding four acres at a cost of twenty marks, or £3 6s 8d an acre, followed by marling at £5 1s 8d an acre, adding to an initial investment of £8 8s 4d an acre.[44] Such detail is rare, but we also learn of an enclosure in Stalmine where the combined cost of fencing, ditching, ridding, levelling and manuring c.1628 was between £2 10s and £4 10s an acre, while in Knowsley c.1636, fencing, ditching and levelling part of a seven- or eight-acre parcel of barren heath came to £9 in total.[45] However, this was just the start, as £33 was then spent on marling and improving the land, equating in all to something over £4 an acre.

Altogether, improvement costs of, let us say, £4 to £8 an acre, added to entry fines perhaps averaging another £2 to £4 an acre, plus the initial outlay in ploughing, seed and sowing, not to mention in some cases the provision of buildings, collectively meant that the incoming tenant could be faced with start-up costs amounting to £10 an acre or more, significantly more than the costs falling to the owner of the waste. How did the new leaseholder raise such sums? The cases studied are silent on this question: nevertheless, there must have been those to whom one could turn for the necessary money, such as Tawney's 'village financiers' who 'might be the local corn-dealer, brewer or maltster'.[46] Gritt's work suggests that the 'third life' on many leases for lives in Lancashire may have been such an individual.[47] The evidence of the Clifton leases, to be discussed later, however, does not back this up, as the second and third lives named on these leases are without exception close family of the first named individual, such as his wife, sons or daughters.

Having raised the capital, the tenant now faced the risk that the land might never repay the investment. In the Knowsley case quoted above, for example, it was claimed that the crop from the seven or eight acres enclosed was so poor that it was sold for a total of three shillings, a very poor

43   William Camden, *Britain, or A Chorographical Description of the Most Flourishing Kingdomes . . . etc.,* trans. Philemon Holland (London, 1637), p. 745.
44   TNA DL 4/85/35.
45   TNA DL 4/95/10, DL 4/107/7.
46   Tawney, *Agrarian Problem* (1912 edn), p. 108.
47   Andrew John Gritt, 'The Operation of Lifeleasehold in South-West Lancashire 1649–97', *Agricultural History Review* 53:1 (2005), 1–23.

return indeed for such a heavy outlay.[48] Elsewhere, it seems likely that some parcels never paid back the investment and reverted to rough grazing. Thus the White Moss alongside Theyle Moor, the site of a long-running dispute, is today the ill-drained Blackley Golf Course; while the last part of Brentlache, the scene of a disputed enclosure event in the 1540s, remains open to this day as Brindle Heath and Bolton Road Playing Fields in Salford.[49] Yet there were also reports of bumper crops valued at £4 an acre with 'yeeldes as good as most in Salford hundreth'.[50] Such a return would have allowed a rapid payback on the investment, in perhaps as little as four years.

Rather than being given details of the price obtained for the crop, we more often hear that the land is now 'worth' so much per acre, without it always being clear what is meant by that phrase. Thus land in Eccleston which had not been worth £1 a year was, after enclosure, worth £5 a year.[51] Other increases in 'worth' are even more spectacular, such as the land in Knowsley which when it 'lay open and unenclosed . . . was not then worth twelve pence per annum' (4d per acre) but which was now (1663) worth 15s an acre.[52] These figures probably relate to the value to the tenant. Elsewhere, 'worth' is seen from the landlord's perspective, such as the land enclosed from the wastes of Stalmine (1640) said to be worth 8s 'with the green syde up, and better if it be tilled' – green side up being the common term for unploughed land.[53] However measured, though, it seems that where the improvement resulted in arable land of reasonable-to-good quality, payback could be rapid, and after the first few years an annual net income of several pounds per acre might be anticipated. A relatively small number of such acres could thus provide a respectable living for a husbandman, of the order of £10–20 a year, although of course only for the lifetime of the lease.

IV

Two early seventeenth-century enclosure agreements provide useful case studies of the relative benefits of enclosure to the two sides. The first of these was possibly the largest enclosure in Lancashire in this period, and has been touched upon by Hoyle, as well as treated in some depth by Manning, who saw it purely in Tawneian terms of 'agrarian conflict'

48   TNA DL 4/107/7.
49   TNA DL 1/58/C1: DL 3/49/F1h.
50   TNA DL 4/85/35.
51   TNA DL 4/113/8.
52   TNA DL 4/107/7.
53   TNA DL 4/95/10.

and 'seigneurial oppression'.[54] Thomas, Baron Gerard, had inherited the Crown moiety of Nether Wyresdale in 1574, and bought the other moiety in 1602. In doing so he was not just acquiring a manor, but a superior lordship too. This is important, as Manning confused the two, suggesting that Gerard was lying when he claimed to own eight thousand statute acres of waste, as the whole manor only amounted to 4,215 acres.[55] However, the waste to which Gerard laid claim extended over eleven townships, and included not just the upland moors of Nether Wyresdale itself but extensive tracts of lowland moss in Winmarleigh, Nateby, Cabus and Rawcliffe. The total acreage of the townships was 22,570 acres, and there is certainly nothing inherently improbable in assuming about a third of this, or eight thousand acres, was waste at this date.[56]

There was, however, some doubt as to whether Gerard really was superior lord, or whether in Nateby for example the right to enclose belonged to the leading resident of that township, who claimed to be a manorial lord owning parts of Garstang and Pilling Mosses, a claim subsequently rejected by the Duchy court.[57] Nevertheless, despite challenges from both outside and within, Gerard was intent upon enclosing a thousand acres by the local measure (say two thousand statute acres) of the potentially valuable lowland wastes. Following an initial meeting with tenants, a manorial court held at New Hall in Nether Wyresdale, agreed 'with the general applause and good likeing of all the tenants' (according to Gerard's version of events, that is) that the enclosure should proceed. Allotments were let for twenty-one years or three lives, in parcels *pro rata* to the tenants' holdings, for a £2 fine and 1s per acre per year rent. Manning comments that these rates 'might seem extortionate yet they were apparently attractive' to the tenants.[58] However, he was comparing rents with the levels Tupling found in the Rossendale moors of 4d to 6d per acre, and fines for established copyholds of two and a half year's rent. Neither comparison is appropriate here, and for the tenants those rates would have seemed fair, providing the land was all of equal quality. Inevitably, though, it was not, giving rise to opposition from dissenting tenants, probably concerned more about the equity of the allotments than enclosure *per se*.

54   R. W. Hoyle, 'Introduction', in *Custom, Improvement and the Landscape*, ed. Hoyle, pp. 14–16; Manning, *Village Revolts*, p. 114; TNA STAC 8/153/2 and 3, DL 5/23, fols 851 and 979, DL 43/5/26, DL 4/49/38, 71 and75, DL 4/55/35, DL 4/111/9, DL 1/237/7.
55   Manning, *Village Revolts*, p. 116.
56   Acreages are from William Farrer and J. Brownbill, eds, *Victoria History of the County of Lancashire* 2 (London, 1908), p. 334, referring to the townships of Holleth, Cleveley, Nether Wyresdale, Cabus, Winmarleigh, Nateby, Garstang, Barnacre with Bonds, Kirkland, Catterall and Upper Rawcliffe.
57   TNA DL 1/237/7, DL 5/26, fols 40–2
58   Manning, *Village Revolts*, p. 115.

Some enclosures were thrown down in protest, but a Duchy decree of 1604 accepted that eight thousand acres (at the rate of the statute *de terris mensurandis*) was 'much more than was sufficient for the tenants and commoners', and therefore acknowledged that Gerard could, had he wished, have approved 'soe much thereof as he pleased without consent of the tenants or commoners . . . which nevertheless he hath forborne to doe'.[59] Yet despite this gloss by the court, it seems fairly clear that, however Gerard dressed it up, the initiative was clearly his; and there remain doubts, to put it no more strongly, about the extent to which this really was a freely negotiated agreement. The allotment schedule which survives in the Duchy archive shows not everyone was prepared to take up their allotments immediately, or indeed at all: and some seventy-two names are listed as tenants who by April 1605 had 'refused their porcons of the said common to them allotted', amounting to over four hundred acres.[60] However, on the other hand more than one hundred tenants had accepted allotments adding over five hundred customary acres, paying their £2-an-acre fines. Whilst this fell short of Gerard's hopes of £2,000, it should be remembered that there were probably fewer than a dozen families in the whole of Lancashire enjoying an annual income of more than £1,000 at the time.[61]

A later case before the Duchy court allows us some insight into what happened next, at least as far as one tenant was concerned.[62] Richard Greene of Garstang is said to have been allotted fifty acres out of the original thousand-acre enclosure, having probably taken up some of the refused allotments, as his three-life lease only dated from between 1617 and 1623. The case involved a small parcel of this, comprising four acres which he had sublet in 1637 for seven years initially, and subsequently for twenty-one. It is probable that it was only at this stage that *improvement* actually took place, a generation after the original enclosure. It is noteworthy too that while Greene held his lease for three lives, his subtenants were given leases for years: and that when this four-acre parcel was sublet, it was done in a way that mimicked fines, in that half the rent of £9 for twenty-one years was to be paid up front, the other half to be paid subsequently.[63] At

59   TNA DL 43/5/23, fols 851 and 979. The reference in the decree to the statute *de terris mensurandis* relates to the statute of 1304 which defined the acre in terms of a five-and-a-half-foot perch, as opposed to the customary acres generally in use in Lancashire, which varied between seven and eight acres to the perch, and were thus much larger. See E. H. Smith, 'Lancashire Long Measure', *Transactions of the Historic Society of Lancashire and Cheshire* 110 (1959), 1–14.

60   TNA DL 43/5/26; see also partial transcription in Henry Fishwick, *The History of the Parish of Garstang in the County of Lancashire* 1 (Chetham Society, 104, 1878), pp. 47–54.

61   Blackwood, 'Catholic and Protestant Gentry'.

62   TNA DL 4/111/9.

63   TNA DL 4/111/9.

an average of 2s 2d per acre per year, this was more than twice what Greene was paying his lord.

V

At almost the same time as Gerard began enclosing, another local lord took a similar initiative. Cuthbert Clifton of Westby had not long reached his majority when he acquired the neighbouring manor of Lytham in February 1606 for £4,300 from his cousin Sir Richard Molyneux.[64] The township comprised some five thousand statutory acres, of which probably a thousand or so were taken up by the open fields and enclosures of Lytham and its outlying hamlets. The rest was made up of mossland, sand dunes, marsh and other low-lying rough grazing. Molyneux had acquired the estate in the late 1590s, and had possibly already licensed some enclosure in the south-east of the township, but it was left to young Clifton to carry more ambitious plans into action. A dispute with the neighbouring lord to the north, which had begun under Molyneux, plus an extensive collection of leases ('the Clifton leases') provide the evidence.[65]

By September 1607, just eighteen months after his acquisition, Clifton had created new leases for lives in thirty customary acres (probably around sixty-three statutory acres in total) of recently enclosed and improved land to the east of Lytham, at an entry fine of £2 and 1s per acre annual rent.[66] In October he leased a further thirty customary acres to the north of the village to Molyneux's former bailiff, again at 1s per acre rent, but with no fine, 'in consideracon of [his] good & ffaithful dealing . . . in procuringe a purchaise of the lordshippe of Lithame . . . from Sir Richarde Molyneux, his master, to the said Cuthbert Clifton'. [67] It is clear from these leases that the land concerned had already been 'measured and meared forth from the rest' of the waste, and that the tenant was required thereafter to keep and maintain all the relevant ditches and hedges. Then in March 1608, by mediation of the Attorney of the County Palatine, Clifton concluded an agreement with thirty-two of his tenants whereby, providing he left unenclosed as much common and waste as 'all the severall lands of all the said tenants and Inhabitantes of Lythame', plus a further one hundred acres,

64   Alan Crosby, 'An Historical Account of the Cliftons of Lytham from the Twelfth to the Eighteenth Centuries', *The Clifton Chronicle*, ed. John Kennedy (Preston, 1990), pp. 13–28; *VCH Lancashire*, 7:213–9.
65   TNA DL 4/53/39, DL 4/54/40, DL 5/24; LA DDCL 2161–2178, DDCL 1660, 1661, DDCL 686–691, DDCL 1113.
66   LA DDCL 2160, 2161.
67   LA DDCL 2160, 2161.

then he was free to enclose the rest, giving first refusal to the Lytham tenants, but thereafter leasing them off to whomsoever he pleased.[68]

At a conservative estimate, this allowed Clifton to enclose at least a thousand customary acres. However, the intractable nature of the mosslands and the sand dunes meant that much was to remain open well into the eighteenth century: indeed the dunes remain open to this day. The agreement did not spell out the fines or rents but it is clear from the leases that survive that they were the same as we have seen for Nether Wyresdale, namely a £2 fine and 1s per acre per year rent. Between March 1610 and September 1611, Clifton made leases covering more than 115 customary acres, all of which had already been 'devided meared ditched & severed' from the waste, and/or 'composed aboute with hedge and ditche', and by implication it was the incoming tenant who had done this work *prior to* signing his lease.[69] All the leases were for three lives (in some cases expressed as the shorter of the three lives or one hundred years): and while the earlier leases are silent on the subject of service, at a manorial court held in 1611 it was ordered that the new tenants should 'paye halfe boones and services and to have halfe libertie in the common'.[70] Thereafter the leases refer to this order, although in the one case already mentioned above, more onerous boons and services are specified.

After several years with little or no further enclosure, on 10 June 1616, another thirty-one leases were signed, amounting to 185 customary acres, under similar terms and conditions. Of these, sixteen were for less than five acres, ten between five and ten, and five for ten or more acres. After 1616, new leases for land enclosed and improved from the waste continued to be signed, with five in 1617, one in 1618, eight during the 1620s, and one in 1630, adding nearly another hundred acres. All in all, prior to Clifton's death in 1634, leases for over 460 customary acres, or almost one thousand statutory acres, were created amounting to around twenty per cent of the whole township, or about half of the notionally available waste. Fines would have totalled some £800, thus giving back to Clifton nearly a fifth of the purchase price he had paid, while his annual rent roll would have grown by £20 a year. The benefits were by no means one-sided, however, and it is noticeable that several of the tenants of 1610–11 featured again in 1616, taking on additional holdings, obviously satisfied with their earlier deal. Thus George Fletcher added two and a half acres to his earlier lease of ten acres, while George Saltoes added two and a half to his fourteen, and John Galter added five to his twelve and a half acres.

68   LA DDCL 2162.
69   LA DDCL 2163–2175.
70   LA DDCL 1113.

VI

In Lytham as in Nether Wyresdale, the initiative lay with the lords. Thus Tupling's model of 'enclosure by little men' does not apply to the lowlands of Lancashire; but Tawney's generalisation that *enclosing* was done by the lord while *improving* was done by the tenant certainly holds good. There was nothing comparable to the seventeenth-century large-scale capital-intensive projects of the Lincolnshire fens until the very end of the century when a group of neighbouring landlords made abortive attempts to drain Martin Mere, a shallow but extensive lake in the south-west of the county. This scheme never generated any return on the capital spent on their 'foolishly ambitious and financially imprudent' project.[71]

Tawney's other conclusion, that wasteland enclosure benefited both landlord and tenant, in other words, that it was not part of the agrarian problem of the sixteenth century at all, also holds true, although it does not go far enough. The lord had little to lose and much to gain from wasteland enclosure, under virtually any scenario. In the right circumstances, the tenant also had much to gain, but his gains were much less certain. A small intake added on to a tenant's existing holding carried little in the way of risk or reward for either landlord or tenant: the big benefits for both came from a successful large-scale approvement or agreement, creating profitable new arable holdings from the waste. The benefit for the lord, indeed, was so great compared with the risk that the question has to be asked as to why only a quarter of the Lancashire lowland waste was enclosed at this time: why not all? The answer must lie with the potential tenants: however anxious lords might have been to enclose waste and gather in entry fines, without willing tenants prepared to take on the risks of improvement, there was no reward for the lords. The Tawneian scenario of rapacious landlords and depopulating enclosure was never more than a regional phenomenon. In lowland Lancashire – and no doubt in many other parts of the country too – the relationship was symbiotic: lords needed tenants.

---

71 Tupling, *Economic History of Rossendale*, p. 47; Tawney, *Agrarian Problem* (1912 edn), p. 183; W. G. Hale and Audrey Coney, *Martin Mere: Lancashire's Lost Lake* (Liverpool, 2005), p. 125ff; Andrew John Gritt, 'Making Good Land from Bad: The Drainage of West Lancashire c.1650–1850', *Rural History* 19:1 (2008), 1–27.

10

Improving Landlords or Villains of the Piece?

A Case Study of Early Seventeenth-Century Norfolk

ELIZABETH GRIFFITHS

This chapter turns attention to Tawney's villains of the piece: the improving landlords and their role in the transition to a fully commercial and capitalist agriculture. The period covers the first half of the seventeenth century, the end of Tawney's long sixteenth century which ran from 1485 to 1642, and focuses on the activities of three Norfolk gentry families engaged in raising rental incomes and modernising their estates. These families, the Windhams of Felbrigg, Hobarts of Blickling and Le Stranges of Hunstanton, commended in the eighteenth century for the excellence of their estate management, faced a range of difficult issues in the early seventeenth century and responded in distinctive ways.[1] The Windhams, having acquired a notorious reputation for litigation with their tenants in the late sixteenth century, simplified their methods and concentrated on demesne farming, while the newly enriched Hobarts, in their purchase of a great estate, avoided complicated holdings and the potential for disputes as far as possible. The Le Stranges, embedded on their ancient estate in north-west Norfolk, faced the most complex task, needing to implement far-reaching reforms within existing constraints. The Hobarts and Le Stranges, the newcomers and the financially embarrassed, have been identified as the most likely to behave badly, but in reality how did they fare?[2] Do they deserve Tawney's description of a 'blind, selfish, indomitable, aristocracy of county families which made the British Empire and ruined a considerable proportion of the English nation'?[3]

This is not the first time that Tawney has been confronted on this issue. His protégé Eric Kerridge denounced him in a blistering attack for 'his wholly untrue picture of early capitalism as cruel and greedy, destructive alike of social welfare and true spiritual values'.[4] For this he blamed

---

1   W. Marshall, *The Rural Economy of Norfolk*, 2 (1787), pp. 365–71; N. Kent, *General View of the Agriculture of Norfolk* (1794), pp. 18, 28.
2   Heal and Holmes, *Gentry in England and Wales* (1994 edn), pp. 114–16.
3   Tawney, *Agrarian Problem* (1912 edn), p. 316.
4   Kerridge, *Agrarian Problems*, p. 15.

Tawney the politician for viewing the world past and present through the prism of socialist dogma: 'No one would wish to deny that Tawney was a great man, but this greatness caused him to lead whole generations of history students into grievous error.' While we might not wish to align ourselves with Kerridge, other less controversial figures similarly question the sweeping portrayal of a rising and rapacious gentry and offer a more moderate assessment rooted in the circumstances of the time. A few may have behaved badly, but the majority respected custom and quietly improved their estates without impinging too drastically on the lives of their tenants.[5] More recently, Richard Hoyle reminded us that *The Agrarian Problem* was an intensely political book, while Andy Wood called for a social history of paternalism and deference to balance the history of defiance.[6] The time is clearly ripe for a reappraisal of early modern landlordism.

A significant omission in Tawney's book was his failure to recognise the demographic crisis of the late sixteenth and early seventeenth century and the pressures this placed on resources, consumers and food producers. Turner, Becket and Afton, in their work on sustainability in English agriculture, identify the first decade of the seventeenth century as a fundamental turning point, when the open-field system, designed for subsistence, could no longer meet the demands of a steeply rising population.[7] Against a background of dearth, with escalating prices threatening social stability, more productive and sustainable systems had to be devised. This perspective, raising fundamental issues about sustainability, has moved the argument away from the villainous nature of the gentry to the practical needs of an expanding population. In this context there was bound to be a struggle to secure and improve resources. The question is how far did landowners overstep the bounds of reasonable behaviour as they exploited and modernised their estates?

I

At the root of the dramatic changes outlined by Tawney was the modernisation of land tenures from customary arrangements governed by the manorial courts to commercial leaseholds based on market valuations. The

5   C. Clay, *Economic Expansion and Social Change*, 1:81–91; Heal and Holmes, *Gentry in England and Wales* (1994 edn), pp. 97–116.
6   A. Wood, 'The View from Mousehold Heath: Kett's demands and popular politics', a paper given at the conference Tawney's Agrarian Problem 100 Years On: Landlords and Tenants in Rural England c.1400–c.1750, held at Exeter University, 11–12 July 2011.
7   M. Turner, J. Beckett and B. Afton, 'Agricultural Sustainability and Open-Field Farming in England, c.1650–1830', in *Sustainable Agriculture and Food, 1: History of Agriculture and Food*, ed. J. Pretty (Oxford, 2008).

argument turns on how this came about.[8] One view, advanced by Tawney, sees it as an illegal process whereby landlords manipulated customary payments to their advantage, forcibly evicted tenants and replaced them with leaseholders on rack rents, and often turned common open fields into sheepwalks, thereby depriving small men not only of their holdings but common rights to graze their animals. Another view is that customary tenants received the full support of the law against illegal activity and that the transition to leaseholds was an equitable process dictated more by the economics of farming than landlord coercion. In reality, as Mark Overton explains, landlords had plenty of opportunity to establish leasehold farms without much controversy: they could lease their demesne lands, buy out copyholders, or re-let these holdings as leaseholds when the line of succession failed. At Felbrigg, Thomas Windham systematically pursued this policy from the 1620s, buying out smallholders and then leasing the holdings back to them with additional land and buildings. In this way, the tenants gained a capital sum to stock the new farm and benefited from landlord investment in fixed capital, while Windham increased his already large and mainly enclosed demesne.[9] From this transaction both parties built up their resources and profited from economies of scale. In 1608 when Windham's father, Sir John Wyndham of Orchard, Somerset, inherited the Felbrigg estate from his cousin he sent his steward John Blinham to Norfolk to carry out a survey and keep the accounts before his son Thomas took up residence in 1616; from this document we can see the new policy taking shape.[10]

The Felbrigg estate had suffered miserably from the 1570s to the 1590s at the hands of Sir John's cousin, Roger Windham. Conforming to the Tawney model, he was 'litigious to the point of mania', persecuting clergymen about their tithes and small copyholders about their tenures. In the course of sixteen years he brought actions against more than a hundred of his poorer neighbours who in desperation appealed to the Privy Council and obtained some redress. Windham seldom met with success at law and suffered humiliating reverses, indicating the futility of his approach.[11] R. W. Ketton-Cremer argues that on Roger Windham's death in 1598 his younger brother Thomas sought to rectify the situation, declaring his intention to return to the manorial customs of his father's time and invalidating the alterations made by his brother. Unfortunately, it is difficult to check this

8   Overton, *Agricultural Revolution*, pp. 154–6.

9   Elizabeth Griffiths, 'The Management of Two East Norfolk Estates in the Seventeenth Century: Blickling and Felbrigg, 1597–1717' (unpublished PhD thesis, 1987), pp. 223–33.

10   R. W. Ketton-Cremer, *Felbrigg: The Story of a House* (Woodbridge, 1962), pp. 26–33. Thomas Windham adopted this spelling of the family name, which henceforth distinguished the Felbrigg Windhams from other branches of the family.

11   Ketton-Cremer, *Felbrigg*, pp. 26–7; Griffiths, 'Two East Norfolk Estates', p. 34.

statement as Ketton-Cremer's book on Felbrigg was neither referenced nor indexed, and the documents do not appear in the current catalogue of the estate.[12] However, we can be sure that Sir John and his steward, like Ketton-Cremer, were acutely aware of this legacy.

In his survey and account of 1608–15, John Blinham, Sir John's steward, indicated their priorities by differentiating between the 'Demeanes' in the lord's hands, the 'Manorlands' which seem to be former demesne lands which had been granted by copy of the court rolls, and the assize rents paid by copyholders for customary tenures.[13] In the Felbrigg area, the demesne lands amounted to 646 acres with just ninety acres of field ground left unenclosed. In 1611 these lands were let for £265, averaging just over 8s per acre. By 1615, Blinham had raised the rent to £318 or nearly 10s per acre. The 'Manorlands' consisted of 176 acres divided into forty-two holdings. In 1608 the rent was £8 18s 4d, averaging 1s per acre. In 1609, Blinham notes that these lands were 'seized of the lord's mannor and devised to farm this year'; and against each tenant's holding, 'late in possession by copie'. Thus the copyholds of these lands were extinguished and transformed into leaseholds, which allowed the rents to be raised to £33 11s 2d in 1609 and to £37 2s 9d by 1615, achieving a more than fourfold increase.[14] Perhaps most significant were the copyholds on fixed rents, where 231 tenants paid £36 7s 5d, which at 4d per acre accounted for about 2,200 acres; entry fines were fixed at 4s per acre. At the outset, Blinham listed every tenant and the rent paid, but by 1615 he provided only the totals for the rents of assize and fines; in effect these holdings, amounting to over two thirds of the estate, had been written off.

The pattern was repeated at Tuttington, Colby and Banningham, and at Wicklewood and Crownthorpe. For these properties, rents for leasehold farms survive from the 1590s. The rent for Hegge Piece, Tuttington, let in 1591 for £3 6s 8d, was raised in 1614 to £20, a six-fold increase, while that for Colby Hall Close was raised from £1 6s 8d to £5 18s 0d. The assize rents of £39 18s 5d, fixed at 4d and 8d per acre, accounted for about two thousand acres. At Wicklewood, the rent for the manor site with 160 acres, let on a 21-year lease in 1591 for £28, was raised in 1615 on seven-year leases to £95 13s 8d, or from 3s 6d per acre to nearly 12s per acre. The rent included eleven holdings of arable land which sustained the largest increase from £10 to £52 10s 8d; this indicates the increased value of arable strips

12 Report on family and estate papers of the Ketton-Cremer family of Felbrigg Hall, thirteenth–twentieth century, reproduced for the Norfolk Record Office (hereafter NRO) by the Royal Commission of Historical Manuscripts, 1978. Several documents referred to by Ketton-Cremer in his book do not appear in the catalogue.
13 Griffiths, 'Two East Norfolk Estates', pp. 52–62.
14 Blinham's survey for 1609, NRO, WKC 5/419 464 X, under Manorlands. My thanks to R. W. Hoyle for raising this point.

when they were incorporated or engrossed into large farms. Crownthorpe Manor with two hundred acres was leased for twenty-one years in 1599 at £55 or 5s 6d per acre; in 1655 it was let for £127 6s 8d or 12s 6d per acre. The assize rents for these two properties, fixed at 4d and 8d per acre, amounted to £25 indicating an area 'lost' to the landlord of between 850 and 1,500 acres. From these examples, we can see that fixed copyhold rents effectively deprived landlords of control over much of their estates. Significantly, Sir John Wyndham made no attempt to challenge these tenures. Instead, he focused on modernising and improving the demesne and manorial lands on unfixed rents by restructuring holdings, raising rents and introducing leases to promote good husbandry. By this method, the rental value of the estate rose from £566 to £798, an increase of forty-one per cent between 1608 and 1615. In the 1620s and 1630s Thomas Windham developed the policy by specifying in his leases the requirements for a sustainable system of up-and-down husbandry, alternating grass and corn. In addition, he built up a highly profitable enterprise fattening bullocks in the park operated through grazing agreements with local butchers. Thus, he increased not only his income and capital assets but the productive capacity of the estate, the physical resources of the neighbourhood and economic opportunities for the local community. After 1616, in this developing commercial environment, the distinction between 'Demeanes' and 'Manorlands' disappeared from the documents.

II

Sir Henry Hobart was in a very different position to Sir John Wyndham. The younger son of a cadet branch of a leading gentry family, he received no inheritance in land and was left to make his fortune.[15] He built up his estate in Norfolk from scratch, selecting properties for their scope for improvement and avoiding properties with problematic tenurial structures. Trained in the law, he brought an acute understanding to the process of estate building. Where possible he chose substantial properties already enclosed and operating as large commercial farms as at Intwood and Keswick Halls (purchased in 1596 and 1601, respectively), Langley Abbey and Grange (1608) and the two parks at Wymondham (1619); these holdings consistently performed well and were retained by the Hobarts until the eighteenth century. Sir Henry's attention turned to the Blickling area in about 1608 as his career progressed and his resources increased.[16] He had

15   Elizabeth Griffiths, 'Sir Henry Hobart: A New Hero of Norfolk Agriculture?', *Agricultural History Review* 46:1 (1998), 15–34.
16   Sir Henry, prominent in Norfolk legal and political scene since 1588, was appointed

long been involved in the legal affairs of its owner, Lady Agnes Clere, and would have been fully aware of the possibility of acquiring the remnants of the ancient and prestigious Blickling estate. The property had a long and illustrious pedigree before passing into the hands of the Boleyn family, who built themselves a fine brick house in the 1450s.[17] By the early 1600s it had fallen into decay, offering Sir Henry the opportunity of restoring it and making Blickling his family seat, but the plan was not without risk.

On the death of Sir James Bullen in 1561, the Boleyns' estate had been divided between the descendants of his sister Alice, married to Sir Robert Clere of Ormesby, and the daughter of his niece Anne, namely Queen Elizabeth I. All parts of the estate had suffered, either from the extravagance and mismanagement of the Cleres or the negligence of the Crown, so by the early seventeenth century it consisted of a mixed bag of unreformed, fragmented and degraded properties. As early as 1602, Sir Henry Hobart received a Royal Grant of Sir Edward Clere's substantial estate in Martham and Somerton, situated in the most fertile parts of the Broadland region. However, the area was divided into tiny family holdings offering little scope for landlord intervention and capital improvements.[18] In 1610, he received another Royal Grant of Sir James Bullen's estate in Cawston, Marsham and Hevingham Park, lying to the west and south of Blickling on the Northern Heathlands which stretch from Norwich to Cromer. At Cawston the extensive grazing rights of the lord had been seriously eroded by manorial tenants enclosing portions of Cawston Heath and open field. In 1573, a survey commissioned by the Crown noted that 'the use and feeding of the Comon pasture and bruery [heath] of the Queen's Maj. Towne of Cawston in Norfolk, hath bene for long in controversy'.[19] The disputes engendered much litigation and a unique set of maps showing parcels 'anciently' and more 'recently' enclosed. In the absence of any restraining influence, copyholders had been able to pursue and successfully establish their claims to the detriment of the Crown estate. Given its proximity to Blickling, the Hobarts retained this property until the 1630s and 1640s when Sir John sold out to Erasmus Earle of Heydon and bought a more attractive estate at Wood Dalling. The lands in nearby Marsham consisted of a foldcourse and a close of sixty acres. These holdings were earmarked for improvement and later attached to the principal holding of the Hevingham estate which Sir Henry purchased from Thomas Thetford in 1608; Hevingham Park was sold to the Marshams of Stratton Strawless.

Attorney-General in 1606 and Lord Chief Justice to the Court of Common Pleas in 1613. See Griffiths, 'Sir Henry Hobart'.

17   Elizabeth Griffiths, 'The Boleyns of Blickling, 1450–1561', *Norfolk Archaeology* 45:4 (2009), 453–68.

18   Griffiths, 'Two East Norfolk Estates', p. 108.

19   Ibid., pp. 151–6.

In this way, the Hobarts cherrypicked worthwhile parts of these properties and disposed of the rest to neighbouring landowners – an early modern version of asset stripping – but as with the Windhams, they did not attempt to challenge the status quo.[20]

When it came to making purchases in this area, Sir Henry engaged professionals to carry out surveys and obtain a true market value. For Thomas Thetford's estate at Hevingham, Marsham and Saxthorpe he enlisted his cousin, John Hobart of Spitalfields, and for the adjoining properties at Horsham St Faith's and Horsford he used a local man, Leonard Mapes. With the exception of Horsford, they were acquired at competitive prices and retained until 1685 when they were sold to repay debt.[21] Sir Henry's rejection of Horsford, against the advice of Mapes, provides further insights into his methods. The attraction of Horsford lay in the vast grazing rights it shared with Horsham St Faith's over Horsford Park. The origins of this arrangement dated back to the twelfth century when the lords of the principal manor of Horsford established a Benedictine Priory in Horsham St Faith's. Ownership had been divided at the dissolution, leaving the issue of grazing rights unresolved. In 1614, Sir Henry brought a legal case against Lord Dacre of the South asserting his rights to grazing in Horsford Park. He won the case and was compensated with four closes in Horsford and a further sixty acres in Drayton; he then tried to buy the Horsford estate. In 1617, he commissioned a survey from Mapes which listed the lands, heath and warren extending to nearly three thousand acres, the lord's rights and the status of the manorial tenants; these amounted to 107 tenants holding several hundred acres by knight's service and copyhold paying 'certaine' rents. Despite the obvious advantage of reuniting the two properties, Sir Henry did not proceed with the sale. He recognised the risks associated with this property, but judged he was 'fitt' to deal with them.[22] However, in the survey he underlined '16 years purchase' indicating the price was too high at sixteen times the rental income. Sir Henry's dealings show that even a man with his expertise in the land market was wary and took the greatest care in assessing the value of properties. Despite his cautious approach, the Hobarts were not immune to disputes with their tenants and became involved in a costly legal battle with the tenants of the manor of Aylsham Lancaster which lasted from 1625 to 1647.[23]

One of the drawbacks of Blickling, which Sir Henry finally acquired in 1616, was its close proximity to the prosperous market town of Aylsham. In the absence of effective control by the Cleres at Blickling, the area to the

20   Ibid., pp. 149–56.
21   Griffiths, 'Sir Henry Hobart', 33–4.
22   Ibid., 27.
23   Griffiths, 'Two East Norfolk Estates', pp. 259–64.

east of the Hall was in the hands of manorial tenants operating a vigorous trade in open-field strips, which made consolidation and emparking extremely difficult.[24] In 1622, the king granted Sir Henry a 23-year lease of the manor of Aylsham Lancaster for his services as chancellor to the Prince of Wales; it was to commence at the expiry of a 21-year lease granted to the tenants in 1609. In 1625, Sir Henry petitioned the king to purchase the freehold of the manor; he knew the fines were certain and there was no prospect of improvement, but given its location so close to his new seat at Blickling, he wanted it 'not for proffytt, but for ornament and conveynancye'.

The project was complicated by the fact that the king had granted a 99-year lease of the manor to the commonalty of the City of London, for the payment of £1,000, with the right to dispose of the property to recover the sum. Despite concerted efforts, Sir Henry died before the sale was fully resolved. When his heir, Sir John Hobart, revived the claim in 1629 the tenants had been forewarned by a member of the commonalty of his intentions. A bidding war ensued with the tenants finally securing the sale at £1,200. Sir John then used every means at his disposal to reverse the decision. In 1631 he approached the Lord High Treasurer and the Chancellor of the Court of the Exchequer to put pressure on the Mayor of London, but without success. He then petitioned the king, reminding him of the commitments to his father and explaining the purpose of the tenants, of which there were over one hundred, to manumise the copyholds and break up the manor. In the meantime, the tenants submitted a bill of complaint to Chancery and petitioned the king for protection and justice, pointing out that they were the 'antient tenants', not Sir John. Despite their protests, the king directed that the sale should be overturned in Sir John's favour, on the grounds that 'his Majestie will not have such a manor dismembered'. But the tenants were not finished; they extracted considerable concessions from the ensuing agreement, including fixed fines and fixed rates for market stalls, messuage and mortgages. In 1641 they sought, amongst other things, a reduction in their fines, permission to grant 21-year leases without licence, the right to appoint the heyward to collect the market dues, thereby facilitating evasion. Sir John refused their demands, so they brought another bill of complaint; this time judgement found in their favour and Sir John was forced to comply shortly before his death in 1647.

With this notorious example before them, we begin to see why Norfolk landowners were reluctant to take on their manorial tenants; only in the most extreme cases was it worth pursuing these claims, but even with

---

24 For the involvement of Blickling tenants in Kett's Rebellion, see Whittle, 'Lords and Tenants', 7, 11, 16–17, 20, 25, 30–4.

contacts in the highest places, Sir John secured only partial satisfaction and at great cost. It seems, as Overton says, that by the seventeenth century the law increasingly took the side of tenants in dispute with their lords.[25] This might explain why families long established on their estates, like the Le Stranges, became almost obsessive in researching their archives and keeping meticulous records. Even so, they did not avoid an embarrassing conflict with equally strident tenants.

III

The Le Stranges of Hunstanton provide a classic example of an ancient family, steeped in their own culture and traditions, having to radically reform the management of their estate. Figure 10.1 shows the problems facing Sir Hamon when he came of age and inherited his estate in 1604. In real terms, his income was a fraction of that enjoyed by his great grandfather, Sir Thomas Le Strange.[26] If Sir Hamon was to secure the future of his family and counter the effect of inflation, he needed to put the estate on a sound commercial footing. Norfolk was littered with examples of gentry families who had failed to grasp the nettle, and others who had capitalised on their misfortunes.

If Sir Hamon had failed, the likelihood is that his uncle, Sir Henry Hobart would have added Hunstanton to the portfolio of estates he had acquired from other less provident members of his extended family.[27] With sustained effort and much thought, Sir Hamon and his wife Alice avoided this outcome, tripling their income by 1630 and placing the estate on a sound commercial footing. Work on their estate records is still in progress but from what we already know, it was an extraordinary achievement which owed much to the management and accountancy skills of Lady Alice.[28]

In the early seventeenth century the Hunstanton estate offered much scope for improvement on its marshes and heathlands, but these areas were not easy to manage or administer. This partly derived from the complex system of rights and customs which governed the agriculture of this area, but also from the need to maintain viable communities to effect and sustain radical improvements in this remote part of Norfolk. The Le Stranges had to achieve a balance between their own interests and those of the people who

25   Overton, *Agricultural Revolution*, p. 156.
26   C. Oestmann, *Lordship and Community: The Lestrange Family and the Village of Hunstanton, Norfolk, in the First Half of the Sixteenth Century* (Woodbridge, 1994), pp. 12–26.
27   Griffiths, 'Sir Henry Hobart', 33–4.
28   Elizabeth Griffiths, ed., 'The Farming Records of Lady Alice Le Strange', *Norfolk Record Society* (forthcoming).

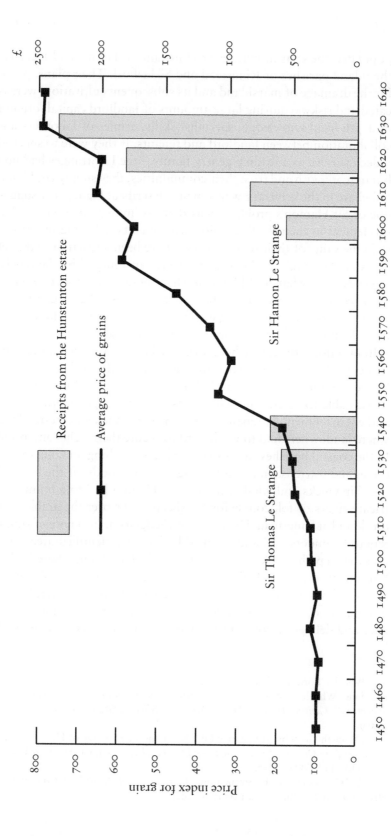

Figure 10.1: The decline in rental value on the Hunstanton estate, 1540–1600

populated the coastal villages at Hunstanton, Holme and Heacham, and the inland parishes of Ringstead and Sedgeford. Their plans, particularly for the drainage of marshland and its subsequent cultivation, were complicated and risky, requiring large amounts of landlord capital, organisation, in-depth local knowledge, specialist skills, armies of labourers and close collaboration between landlord and tenants. If they were to succeed – and indeed survive as a leading gentry family – the Le Stranges had no option but to work with and trust their communities; they simply could not afford to behave in the arbitrary way Tawney described. Figure 10.1 suggests that one of Sir Hamon's problems was that his immediate forebears had been too lenient in their dealings with their tenants, allowing inflation to outstrip the value of their rents; this may have been a reaction to the rebellion of 1549. Although the Le Stranges were not touched by the rebels it was a reminder of what could happen when these delicate social relationships in the countryside were disturbed.[29] Nevertheless, they urgently needed to tackle the issue of a declining income which, apart from diminishing their lifestyle, impinged on their ability to improve their estate.[30]

In his efforts to restore his estate, Sir Hamon pursued a multi-pronged strategy.[31] First, he researched his rights and titles to his property, which he recorded in two memoranda books from 1605.[32] With this knowledge he was able to defend himself against the challenge of other landowners and encroachment by tenants. This was very much a contested landscape, where landowners had to work hard to secure their rights and privileges.[33] In the coastal parishes rights extended to sea fishing, grazing the marshes, dunes and warrens, and to collecting valuable goods off the beach, including shipwrecks and whales. Inland, Sir Hamon had to administer the intricate rights of foldcourse for his sheep flocks over the arable and sandy breckland at Ringstead, Heacham and Sedgeford. In 'a note of sundry matters to be understood and rectified by law', he identified areas of dispute and the steps he took to resolve them. At Heacham, where he had been 'misinformed and misled' on the stocking rates of Caly Foldcourse when 'his own knowledge was raw and imperfect', he insisted that 'it should be inquired into, altered and reformed in such a manner (upon full conference and deliberate consultation with the inhabitants) as may be thought

29   Whittle, 'Lords and Tenants', 16, 26, 30.

30   Jane Whittle and Elizabeth Griffiths, *Consumption and Gender in the Early Seventeenth-Century Household: The World of Alice Le Strange* (Oxford, 2012), pp. 34–6, 203–9.

31   Elizabeth Griffiths, 'A Country Life: Sir Hamon Le Strange of Hunstanton, Norfolk, 1583–1654', in *Custom, Improvement and the Landscape*, ed. Hoyle, pp. 203–34.

32   NRO, LEST/Q36; Q37.

33   A. Winchester and E. Straughton, *Brancaster and Thornham Commons, Norfolk: Historical Briefing Paper* (draft February 2010).

reasonable'.[34] At Holme, where the sea bailiff abused his position, he was less amenable, as his great grandson, Sir Nicholas noted: 'in late years, the water bailiff had appropriated wrecks to themselves allowing the lord only half the value. As the lord became more sensible of the abuse they denied the right of copyholders to hold the office and appointed their own water bailiff.'[35] In 1606 he successfully won a case against Sir Nathanial Bacon for the sole privilege of taking rabbits from Holme Meeles or dunes.[36] These examples illustrate the value of common grazing and the sea shore to those who lived in these coastal communities and the need for Sir Hamon to be wary. Sir Nicholas explained how Sir Hamon hung up a 'Past Bord Table' in 'his evidence house' listing the court rolls and books for the different parishes. In 1698, using this evidence, he was able to refute the claims of a purchaser of a small estate in Ringstead to rights of warren on the meeles.[37]

From 1605, Sir Hamon also surveyed his estate and drew up new rentals and fieldbooks, providing the family with further tools for managing their estate. The maps start with Holme and Ringstead and progress to Hunstanton (1615), Heacham (1623), and Sedgeford (1631).[38] They reflect a point in time, whereas the field books, rentals and firmals, redrafted at intervals by Lady Alice, record changes in the size and occupation of holdings.[39] Those for Hunstanton survive for 1623, 1648, 1671 and 1689 and show little alteration in the layout of field patterns before the 1670s and 1680s.[40] At that time, as corn prices declined, small landholders increasingly sold their lands to Sir Nicholas, allowing him to consolidate strips and enclose holdings. But in the first half of the seventeenth century, Sir Hamon and his eldest son worked alongside the open-field system and concentrated their efforts on neglected pasture, breckland and marsh which lay within their immediate control. In fact, it was difficult for them not to take this course; ownership in the open fields, particularly in West Field, which surrounded the village of Hunstanton, was far too fragmented for strategies of engrossment or enclosure. It was much better to focus

34 NRO, LEST/Q37.
35 NRO, LEST/Q37.
36 NRO, LEST/Q37.
37 NRO, LEST/Q36.
38 Holme has not survived – it is referred to in Sir Hamon's memoranda book NRO, LEST/Q37 as being carried out in 1605; Ringstead NRO, LEST/OB5 and OB6; Hunstanton, NRO, LEST/AO1; Heacham NRO, LEST/OC2 and OB2; Sedgeford NRO, LEST/OC1.
39 Lady Alice managed her own estate at Sedgeford from 1621; from 1632 she took on the records for the rest of the estate, streamlining accounts, rentals and firmals. Firmals, listing rents for leasehold farms, were kept separately from the rentals, which listed rents, bond and free, for manorial holdings.
40 NRO, LEST/BH1; BH2; BH3; BH9.

on those areas with the greatest scope for improvement and to utilise the plentiful supply of local labour which the open fields supported.

As new holdings were created on the marshes and brecks, the Le Stranges worked closely with their farm tenants to help them get established; this assistance included the provision of working capital. Sir Hamon sometimes concluded sharefarming agreements providing the seed corn and halving the crop. Thus in 1613, with his servant, Thomas Ketwood, he 'sowed of barley to halves in the upper close, 10 c, in the lower close 5c', and with Will Cobb he 'sowed of gray pease and fetches to halfes with me in Poole Close'.[41] In Ringstead, he went to great lengths to support the three foldcourses, leasing the flocks to syndicates of farmers and sowing the arable to halves.[42] He provided incentives for shepherds, allowing them to place one hundred sheep in each flock of eight hundred sheep, and built houses for them to be near the flocks. Similarly, with the tenants on newly drained marshland, Sir Nicholas farmed 'to Halfes'. In 1637, for The Bogge at Hunstanton he halved the cost of ploughing, sowing and harrowing with Woodrow and Murton, and for the Whin Pasture he halved the cost of barrowing and levelling with Richard Giles. In 1646 he agreed to 'beare halfe the charge of cutting and bunching' at Holme Marsh for the osier grounds, an agreement which continued until 1653.[43] In these ways, the Le Stranges supported their tenants and shared the risk of farming on newly improved land.

These initiatives by father and son do not look like the activities of landowners from hell bent on dispossessing their tenants or wringing the last farthing from them. The rise in estate income achieved by the 1630s, evident in figure 10.1, derived almost entirely from the sale of corn, sheep and wool and improved rents on demesne lands. In 1653, at the end of her account for Hunstanton, Lady Alice included 'A note of what lands are in the Lords hands and how rated'. The park and closes (402 acres) she valued at 6s 8d per acre, a meadow at 10s, a few acres of brecks for 5s and forty-four acres of the Marsh, Bogge and Meeles at 3s per acre. This compared to rents for open-field arable (520 acres), mostly in West Field of 3s per acre, with sixty acres in the more consolidated East Field at 4s; these figures remained static for the entire period of the account from 1632 to 1653.[44] Earlier rentals and firmals show that Sir Hamon's approach to 'increases' had been moderate from the outset. In 1611, when he re-let leasehold farms on seven-year terms, he raised the rent for open-field arable in West Field from 2s to 2s 8d per acre, and then to 3s in 1618; in the

41   NRO, LEST/BK3.
42   NRO, LEST/Q38.
43   NRO, LEST/KA6; KA9, KA10; KA24.
44   NRO, LEST/BK15.

East Field, rents rose from 3s 4d to 4s with no increase in 1618. Going back further, in 1587 some closes in the park were let for 2s 2d and 2s per acre, which indicates only a threefold increase by 1653; the increase for open-field arable was no more than twofold over an even longer period from 1575.[45] These figures are significantly less than Thomas Windham achieved at Felbrigg over the same period, suggesting that other factors were at play in Hunstanton.

Manorial tenants remain highly visible in all these documents: there is no sense of them being written off as at Felbrigg and elsewhere. In West Field, nearly half the strips were owned by thirty-three freeholders and eighteen copyholders, who rented intermixed demesne strips from Sir Hamon, effectively locking him into their economy.[46] In 1612 he drew up a rental reflecting this reality. Each tenant was listed with their portfolio of leasehold lands in West Field and East Field, the rent per acre and their ma-norial rents and payments. This was the format adopted by Lady Alice in 1632 and retained until the 1640s. In 1648, of the forty-two farm tenants (a number which had barely altered since 1611) thirty rented holdings of less than 10 acres, eight of 10–50 acres, two of 50–100 acres, and one of 121 acres.[47] We can see that the Le Stranges, like the Windhams and Hobarts, were more or less forced to work within existing constraints and modify their strategy accordingly.

Despite this seemingly impeccable behaviour, Sir Hamon, like his cousin Sir John Hobart, found himself embroiled in an acrimonious dispute with a copyhold tenant.[48] In 1638 he brought a case against Robert Creamer, who had accused him of falsely obtaining his copy of the manor court rolls of Heacham Calys and altering the nature of his tenure, thus enabling Sir Hamon to augment the rent and to plough at will. Creamer had already brought a suit in Star Chamber and the hundred court against Sir Hamon's steward, Roger Warner, and his son, Sir Nicholas Le Strange, for making the alterations. He refused to accept Sir Hamon's assurances that this had been done without his knowledge. Robert Creamer acted with the sup-port of his uncle, Robert Stileman of Snettisham, and they proceeded with a petition to the assizes accusing Sir Hamon of authorising the changes, calling him a 'riotour and peacebreaker'. One of the judges, Sir George Croke warned Stileman that 'it was a foule business' and 'he should take heed that he proved it' to which Stileman replied that if he could not do so, let him 'be whipped out of towne'. His defence was that he had no

45   NRO, LEST/BK1; BK2; BK3; BK4; BK6/1; BK6/2.
46   Oestmann, *Lordship and Community*, pp. 30–44.
47   NRO, BH2. Field Book of 1648.
48   R. P. Cust and A. J. Hopper, *Cases in the High Court of Chivalry, 1634–1640* (Harleian Society, new series, 18, London, 2006); for the full court record, see www.court-of-chivalry. bham.ac.uk/index.htm.

intention of defaming Sir Hamon and that it was not in his character to 'scandalize' a gentleman; he was simply pursuing his nephew's rights in the matter of land tenure. Yet, as the witness depositions attest, some months later he was boasting to his friends of his confrontation with Sir Hamon and his determination 'to bring him to book'. These tenants, like those of Aylsham Lancaster, were not intimidated by the prospect of taking their landlord to court, in fact, they clearly relished it.

In the event, Sir Hamon won the case in 1640, receiving damages and costs amounting to over £500 and the apologies of the defendants for their scandalous petition; they promised thereafter to behave themselves 'with all due observance and respect towards Sir Hamon Le Strange and other gentry of the kingdome'. At the same time, Sir Hamon was at pains to demonstrate that he was 'a worthy man and a stud [pillar] of the cuntrie and a good commonwealth's man' and 'a good landlord to his tenants', a claim, it must be said, not entirely borne out by the testimony. A witness noted his partiality, 'he doth let to some of his tenants good pennyworths, but to others he let hard pennyworths', but the same witness continued 'he never heard that he hath wronged any of his tenants'. Creamer, a landlord in his own right, was similarly criticised for renting his land 'at so deare a rate as fearmours cannot live by them'. Significantly, the land in question was a piece of marsh desired by Sir Nicholas for embanking and linking the sea banks of Heacham and Snettisham, the latter in the possession of Robert Stileman. Read by Tawney, this would be a classic example of dispossession of the peasantry. However, from a different perspective, we can see a smaller landowner seizing an opportunity to grab some land, witnesses complaining about rents and a larger landowner determined to defend his reputation and property. It may have been, as Warner stated, that he was simply correcting an error made by the previous steward, Edward Spratt. A glance at the complexity of these documents suggests that this was a reasonable explanation. It may also have been the case that tenants were reticent in making more incriminating complaints, particularly as Lady Alice may have been involved.[49] But either way, Sir Hamon had every right to defend his position and would have been considered negligent if he had failed to do so. Despite the risks of litigation, it is clear that he wanted to be regarded as a benevolent landlord to his tenants and a pillar of the wider community. Interpretations of this case differ, but it confirms the delicate and indeed fractious nature of relationships in the countryside; disputes were fiercely contested, and landowners, large and small, needed to be vigilant and hard-headed in defence of their rights and property if they were to survive in an increasingly competitive environment.

49   In 1632, Alice started work on Heacham, NRO, LEST/DI 19; DI 22.

IV

So what can we conclude from the activities of these three Norfolk families? How do we rate them: improving landlords or villains of the piece? All were renowned for reforming their estates, but all became involved in disputes with their tenants, as Tawney would quickly point out. On this issue the timing appears significant. While Roger Windham pursued his tenants relentlessly in the 1570s and 1580s, his family and successors in the 1590s were appalled by this behaviour and strove to remedy the situation by rescinding decisions. In the first decade of the seventeenth century, his nephew Sir John Wyndham and his son Thomas offered no challenge to the hundreds of tenants that held their land on fixed copyhold rents; in this way thousands of acres were effectively written off and the issue firmly resolved. Sir Henry Hobart as a matter of policy avoided buying properties with complicated landholding structures. His one weakness, the purchase of Blickling for his family seat, which led to his petition to buy the neighbouring manor of Aylsham Lancaster, proved disastrous, involving the family in a long and costly legal dispute with the copyhold tenants. Sir Hamon's brush with Robert Creamer seems mild by comparison. In fact, the issue at the heart of the case was not resolved, only the narrow question of the libel against Sir Hamon. All of these cases were notorious in their day, offering a warning to landowners not to meddle with their tenants, who were not remotely intimidated by the prospect of a session at court. As Overton says, it seems fair to conclude that by the early seventeenth century the law increasingly favoured the tenant and landowners needed to be wary. Careful landowners, like the Le Stranges, who had no alternative but to work with their manorial tenants, made sure they had the knowledge to counter any challenge.

Judged from a modern perspective, the behaviour of these Norfolk landowners in the early seventeenth century appears reasonably fair and perfectly sensible. They understood the delicate nature of relationships in the countryside and strove to avoid confrontation as far as possible; they could not afford to alienate the rural communities on which they depended. Tawney would not have seen it this way. We need to remember that when he was writing in 1912 nearly ninety per cent of the land of England was leased to tenants by wealthy landowners; as an active politician Tawney campaigned to end their privileged position. Today, the majority of farms are owner-occupied and tenants enjoy significant legal protection.[50] In a period far removed from the anti-landlordism of the early twentieth century we can see that landowners managing their estates in the early seventeenth

---

50   Elizabeth Griffiths and Mark Overton, *Farming to Halves: The Hidden History of Sharefarming in England from Medieval to Modern Times* (2009), pp. 183–8.

century provided vital leadership during a difficult and transitory phase. With their investment, knowledge and commitment, they helped to modernise farming practices, expand opportunities and develop resources.

11

The Agrarian Problem in Revolutionary England

CHRISTOPHER BROOKS

R. H. Tawney thought that the causes of the rural impoverishment, collapse of community, and domination of great landowners characteristic of his own lifetime lay in the English civil wars of the mid-seventeenth century and the decades that followed the Restoration of the monarchy in 1660. A key conclusion of *The Agrarian Problem of the Sixteenth Century* is that, despite the challenges they faced, the smallholders who made up the 'intelligence of toiling England' survived reasonably well into the seventeenth century largely because they could rely on the relief offered them by the royal prerogative courts.[1] Indeed, in anticipation of the famous articles on the 'rise of the gentry' that Tawney wrote a quarter of a century later, *The Agrarian Problem* identifies the English 'revolution' as a triumph of the landowning class that demolished the institutional restraints, such as Chancery and Star Chamber, that had traditionally kept their rapacity at bay.[2] Since the 'good side of Absolute Monarchy was swept aside with the bad',[3] there was no longer any obstacle to 'enclosure, evictions [and] rackrenting' other than a not very sympathetic common law.[4] 'For a century and a half after the Revolution [the gentry] had what power a Government can have to make and ruin England as they please.'[5] If economic conditions made the new agrarian regime profitable, 'legal causes decided by whom the profits should be enjoyed'.[6]

Tawney's consideration of the interplay of social, economic, political and legal issues makes his thesis richly thought-provoking, but neither he nor subsequent generations of historians have done much to investigate

---

1 Tawney, *Agrarian Problem*, pp. 320–1,
2 R. H. Tawney, 'The Rise of the Gentry 1558–1640', *Economic History Review*, 11:1 (1941), 1–38. For the subsequent 'storm over the gentry' see: Lawrence Stone, *Social Change and Revolution in England, 1540–1640* (London, 1965).
3 Tawney, *Agrarian Problem*, pp. 399–400.
4 Ibid., p. 400. Tawney did not explain exactly why he found the common law unsympathetic.
5 Ibid., p. 404.
6 Ibid., p. 407.

what he identified as the critical moment of change.[7] There are few detailed modern studies of agrarian society in the later seventeenth century.[8]
While Tawney's own grasp of the legal history of the post-1640 era was
rudimentary, even today the subject remains profoundly understudied.
Hence, this chapter aims at a preliminary examination of the legal issues
surrounding landlord–tenant relations during the civil war years and just
afterwards, while also addressing some of the broader social and economic
questions that Tawney encouraged us to ask.

I

Taking the 1630s as a point of departure, there is much that rings true
in Tawney's characterisation of the pre-civil war years, but he underesti-
mated the degree to which the common law courts, alongside the courts of
equity, had already created a body of law relating to smaller landholders
and, critically, to the class of 'tenants' known as copyholders. Elizabethan
legislation against the erection of cottages on wastes was driven largely by
the interests of smallholders rather than their landlords, and the decision
reported by Sir Edward Coke in *Gateward's Case* (1607)[9] confirmed that
rights to common were proprietary rights that could be most effectively
claimed by those with tenurial interests exercised through manorial courts
(i.e. copyholders). At the same time, while enclosure by agreement amongst
smallholders could be accomplished through the Court of Chancery, and
sometimes Acts of Parliament, the common lawyers thought that their
jurisdictions had contributed to the transformation of English society by
greatly increasing the security of smaller holders with customary tenures.
By the end of the 1620s, the analogy between the rights of customary tenants as against their landlords, and the rights of the subject as against the
king, had become a leading metaphor in national political life.[10] Yet, to an
extent that Tawney seems not to have appreciated fully, during the Personal
Rule of Charles I, the 'fiscal feudalism' of the Crown was accompanied by
a not altogether successful reassertion of seigniorialism by ordinary landlords. While the Crown engaged in the rhetoric of hostility to depopulating enclosure, it licensed 'improvement' in the East Anglian fens and in the

7   See, also: Brenner, 'Agrarian Class Structure', and the work it has inspired.
8   An exception that proves the rule can be found in French and Hoyle, *Character of
English Rural Society*.
9   *La size part des reports Sir Edward Coke Chiualer, chiefe Iustice del Common banke
des diuers resolutions & iudgements* . . . (London, 1607), p. 59 .
10 Christopher W. Brooks, *Law, Politics and Society in Early Modern England*
(Cambridge, 2008), chapters 8, 11.

Derbyshire peaks which undermined customary holdings.[11] In reasserting its long-forgotten rights in the royal forests, it took action that could have come straight from the business plan of an aggressive landowner dealing with his customary tenants. Although a lesser country squire such as the Hertfordshire diarist William Drake was aware of speeches by Lord Keeper Thomas Coventry which encouraged judges to be on the look-out for de-populating enclosures, he sought advice on how to get the most out of his tenants, observed the practices of the most successful magnate landlords, and collected notes on the history of manorial jurisdictions which in-cluded consideration of the question of whether copyholders had existed before the Norman Conquest, or been created afterwards as a result of a process of feudalisation.[12] The Caroline approach to rural society hap-pily endorsed a return to pre-lapsarian seigniorial communalism, but the Crown, like other landowners, was also interested in doing as much as possible to ensure the exploitation of 'economic rents'.

It is difficult to go beyond these impressions into any more meaning-ful general statistical analysis of agrarian life in the decade prior to the civil wars, but it is essential to take some measure of the scope of the landlord–tenant relationship at the time. In 1671, Heneage Finch, a future Lord Chancellor, remarked in Parliament that every house, and nearly every farm, in England had at least two titles (and often many more), the present tenant's and the landlord's, which might itself be a tenancy, or subtenancy, freighted with various encumbrances.[13] An implicit argu-ment in this chapter is that this state of affairs had something to do with developments in the thirty years between the outbreak of the civil wars and the time of Finch's speech, but various forms of subleasing had for so long been an integral part of rural and urban life that it is dangerous to underestimate its extent well before 1640.[14] According to a survey of the Earl of Huntingdon's copyholds in Loughborough in 1651, for instance, many of over 150 houses and holdings were subleased by copyholders to third parties at annual rents that were worth considerably more than what they paid the earl.[15] A better understanding of landlord–tenant relation-ships in the seventeenth century must take into account leases as well as

11   Andy Wood, *Politics of Social Conflict: The Peak Country 1520–1770* (Cambridge, 1999).

12   Henry E. Huntington Library, San Marino, Calif. (hereafter HEHL), Huntington Manuscript 55,603, William Drake's Journal, fols 15v–16v; 21v–22, 28, 21(reversing). Drake is the 'reader' in Kevin Sharpe's *Reading Revolutions: The Politics of Reading in Early Modern England* (New Haven, 2000).

13   D. E. C. Yale, ed., *Lord Nottingham's Chancery Cases*, 2 (2 vols, Selden Society, 1961), p. 972.

14   French and Hoyle, *Earls Colne*, chapter 8.

15   HEHL, Hastings Manuscripts Box 26/19.

common law and customary tenures. Nearly everyone had some experience of being a tenant, and surprisingly large numbers were landlords of one kind or another as well. Parcels of land completely free of some kind of encumbrance, or complication, in terms of rights and tenures seem to have been few and far between.

II

Turning to the civil wars and Interregnum, it is difficult to see how they can be characterised as the best of times for gentry landlords.[16] Even if political delinquency did not result in sequestration and the loss of rent,[17] there were losses due to the depredations of war.[18] Litigants in Chancery claimed that they were unable to pay off mortgages because of high taxes and other costs of the conflict.[19] By the mid-1650s, there are signs from towns that post-war reconstruction presented opportunities for property development.[20] It is unclear how far this might have been the case in rural areas, but the break-up of Crown lands, as well as those of the Church, contributed to what appears to have been a very active property market that often involved lawyers or other agents based in London.[21] After peace had been restored in the late 1640s, levels of court business, including that in Chancery, increased to, and probably surpassed pre-civil war levels – a situation that persisted into the Restoration.[22] According to Bulstrode Whitelocke, who was a commissioner in Chancery, one reason for the deluge of litigation was that English people could dispose of their property by will. Another was 'the freedom of our Nation where everyone hath equal right and title to his estate', and where there 'is as full a propriety, to the meanest as to the greatest person, which causeth our countrymen to insist upon their right'.[23]

16   This is not to gainsay Joan Thirsk's conclusions about the overall impact of the wars on gentry estates, which downplayed the long-term damage: 'The Restoration Land Settlement', *Journal of Modern History* 35 (1945), 315–28; 'The Sale of Royalist Land during the Interregnum', *Economic History Review*, second series, 5 (1952), 188–207.
17   HEHL, Hastings Personal Papers Box 19 (11). Leicestershire committee of sequestration to Huntingdon, April 1653.
18   BL, MS Additional 37,343, fols 259–60.
19   TNA C33/139 (Orders and Decrees), fols 73v, 122v.
20   Bristol City Record Office, Common Council Minutes, fols 94–101 (1654). Rebuilding after the demolition of Bristol Castle.
21   See below, p. 197.
22   Christopher W. Brooks, *Lawyers, Litigation and English Society since 1450* (London, 1998), pp. 30–1. Henry Horwitz, *Chancery Equity Records and Proceedings 1600–1800: A Guide to Documents in the Public Record Office* (London, 1995), chapter 2.
23   BL, MS Additional 37,345, fol. 24v.

There was so much continuity in the personnel and operation of the legal system before and after the execution of Charles I in 1649 that radical change within jurisdictions, or between them, was limited. In Chancery, Whitelocke, the best known of the parliamentary commissioners of the great seal, was the son of an early Stuart judge. Although a regicide, John Lisle, the longest-serving commissioner was a barrister who compiled an analytical abridgment of the case work of the court that moves seamlessly from pre-civil war *dicta* to decisions on cases heard just before his dismissal by the recalled Rump Parliament in 1659.[24]

Nevertheless, there was a significant law reform 'movement' during the civil war period, and Chancery was more frequently targeted than the common law jurisdictions. Calls for change came from a variety of interest groups, including parliamentary soldiers, but country squires and lawyers were not conspicuously amongst them. The (religiously) radical Barebones Parliament went so far as to draw up a motion to abolish the court that collapsed when Cromwell dissolved the assembly.[25] Other proposals for root and branch reform called for the return to a back-to-basics equitable jurisdiction where the strict letter of the law would be more easily relieved by conscience and natural justice.[26] But abolition was also endorsed by those who objected in principle to 'prerogative courts', where decisions about men's property were left to individual judges empowered with personal discretion exercised behind closed doors, as opposed to the common law, where trials took place before juries and the watchful eye of the public.[27] There are also hints at corruption amongst officials such as the Six Clerks and the Masters in Chancery,[28] and the political preoccupations of commissioners of the great seal such as Whitelocke, Lisle and Sir Thomas Widdrington may have distracted their attention from the business of the court. But there is little evidence of this.

The system of commissioners in fact tripled the number of judges available to hear cases, and in their view the real problem with Chancery was that it was being swamped by business, new as well as old. The atrophy of the ecclesiastical jurisdiction, which accompanied the abolition of episcopacy in the 1640s, led to increases in the number of cases relating to wills

24   'Lisle, John (1609/10–1664)', *ODNB* online. Spencer Research Library, University of Kansas, Lawrence, KS, MS D87, 'Abridgement of Chancery Causes'.
25   S. E. Prall, 'Chancery Reform and the Puritan Revolution', *American Journal of Legal History* 6:1 (1962), 35ff.
26   [Anon], *Observations concerning the Chancery* (1655). See also, D. Veall, *The Popular Movement for Law Reform 1640–1660* (Oxford, 1970), chapter 8.
27   TNA C41/14 (Chancery affidavits), reports a litigant saying that it was a pity Chancery was not put down because it was an unjust court.
28   Philostratus Philodemius, *Seasonable Observations on a late book intitled A System of the Law* . . . (1653), p. 16.

and legacies. In May 1654, Widdrington and Lisle went to see Protector Cromwell in order to beg him, unsuccessfully, to do something about the court's newly acquired jurisdiction with regard to marriage breakdown and alimony.[29] Instead, in August 1654 the Protector and Council issued a highly detailed ordinance for the reform of Chancery, which they pursued with some determination before it lapsed in 1658. The main aim was to reduce the numbers of clerks and underclerks who acted as attorneys in the court, but there were also a number of substantive rules laid down, not least with regard to important subjects such as mortgages and debts on bonds. The ordinances re-emphasised traditional *dicta* that litigants should not use Chancery to frustrate actions at common law. In addition, there was a novel provision for the creation of panels of justices of the peace in the shires, who would be sworn to act as commissioners for taking evidence in the form of depositions to interrogatories. Undoubtedly designed to answer the demand for a return of justice to the localities, this proposal would have reduced the capacity of litigants to name their own commissioners while at the same time (perhaps inadvertently) institutionalising the role of the gentry in the court's procedures.[30]

The Cromwellian ordinance was vehemently opposed by most of the lawyers. Whitelocke, Widdrington and the master of the rolls, William Lenthall, all resigned in protest. Whitelocke was infuriated that the commissioners had not been consulted in drawing up the measures, which were presented to them as a *fait accompli.*[31] He objected in Parliament to many of the specific provisions before concluding that the implementation of the ordinance would harm men's rights.[32] Furthermore, given the weight of business, the plan to cut the number of court officials – and attorneys – was also seen as misguided by outside observers such as Sir Mathew Hale, who had been charged with heading a committee on law reform established by the Rump Parliament.[33]

Indeed, the most common theme amongst moderate proposals for Chancery reform – including those coming from sections of the legal profession – was the idea that the only way to prevent equity courts from becoming over clogged with business was to expand the scope of the common law and jury trials while at the same time denying equitable relief

29   Spencer Research Library, MS D87, fol. 103.
30   C. H. Firth and S. R. Rait, *Acts and Ordinances of the Interregnum*, 2 (London, 1911), pp. 946–67.
31   *The Diary of Bulstrode Whitelocke, 1605–1675*, ed. R. Spalding (British Academy, Records of Social and Economic History, new series, 13, 1990), pp. 402, 407–9.
32   B. Whitelocke, *Memorials of the English Affairs* (1682), pp. 602–3.
33   William Andrews Clark Memorial Library, Los Angeles, Calif. 'Sir Mathew Hale's Cases and Opinions' (3 vols), ii, fol. 87; Philodemius, *Seasonable Observations*, p. 12.

where cases could be heard in the common law courts.[34] But this was already a familiar refrain in the pre-civil war period, and in the case of landlord–tenant relations and customary tenures, one of the most striking features of the Interregnum is precisely that this movement from Chancery to the common law courts was already well underway. Lisle's manuscript compilation on Chancery contains sections relevant to customary tenants, but they are embedded in hundreds of folios of other kinds of business. Furthermore, many of the cases he refers to in this connection date back to before the civil wars. Equity might still be called upon in certain circumstances (especially in connection with, for example, the disruptions of war or the loss of documents and the repayment of mortgages), but such cases were apparently not frequent.[35] By contrast, there are a number of references to customary tenants in the various common law cases noted or commented upon by lawyers and judges in the 1650s.

The enormous collection of 'opinions' that Mathew Hale accumulated as part of his private practice in the 1650s, and the printed and manuscript law reports, indicate that the questions at stake for those who consulted lawyers about customary tenures usually involved the alienability and inheritability of small parcels of land. In nearly all instances, moreover, the lawyers and the courts were making it increasingly easy for the holders of copyhold land to do what they pleased with it so long as there was some recognition of the interest of the lord of the manor in the fate of his copyhold tenements. Thus copyhold estates could be created and disposed of by will, usually but not always in conjunction with a surrender and re-grant by the lord.[36] Copyhold land in Shropshire could even be held by properly admitted heirs who were born in Holland to English parents. Copyhold land could be involved with uses and trusts, and it could be mortgaged.[37] Copyhold land was very frequently sublet with or without the knowledge of the lord of the manor, and often for extended periods of years. Last but hardly least, there were cases about the consequences

---

34　*The Continuance of the High Court of Chancery vindicated, to be absolute necessary (the abuses and corruptions being removed) and the removal thereof, and the perfect Reformation of the proceedings in that Court . . .* (1654), p. 3. *Certaine Assayes Propounded to the consideration of the Honourable [Hale] Committee for regulating the proceedings at Law, Whereby it is made evident that most cases now determined in Chancery and other Courts of Equity may be reduced to Tryall at Law to the great ease and benefit of the Commonwealth* (1652).

35　Spencer Research Library, MS D87, fols 178 (enclosure by agreement), 279 (moderating uncertain fines), 284 (injunctions against ploughing of meadows), 420 (suits brought by customary tenants against lords).

36　HEHL, Huntington MS 103: George Wither's commonplace and reports, Case 19. Hale's Cases . . ., i, fol. 697.

37　Ibid., i, fols 453, 459; iii, fol. 74.

for services and the survival of the manor when there was a contractual conversion of copyhold to freehold.[38]

Cases and queries frequently turned on hair-splitting technicalities such as whether a will or a conveyance to uses effectively created the estate by properly naming the heirs. Then, again, there were questions about allegedly fraudulent activities including attempts by mortgagors to deceive mortgagees by subletting the mortgaged property. On occasion, however, the post-medieval legal history of copyholds was discussed, and some of the details appear to have struck younger lawyers as interesting, perhaps because needing to know about them came as something of a surprise. In the case of *Harrington v. Smith* (1658), for instance, which involved the descent of a piece of copyhold land that had been devised by will in the reign of Elizabeth to the wife and children of a marriage, there was some discussion of the application of statute law to copyholds which referred to their early history as 'unfree tenures' not recognised at common law. Thus it was argued that the statute 11 Henry VII, c.20, which limited the power of wives to alienate lands of their deceased husbands, did not apply to copyhold because

> at that time & longe after it was conceived that a Copyhold estate could not be intayeled [and] that the estates of copyholders are of little account in Law and not within the remit of other general statutes, as to be impanelled as jurors, chosen knights to parliament, etc.

In this particular case, the reluctance to apply the statute to copyholders' estates in fact worked in favour of greater powers to alienate, but at the same time it was clearly held that more recent legislation, such as Elizabethan statutes against fraudulent conveyances, did apply to them. According to Sir John Glynn, Chief Justice of the Upper Bench, it had long been a rule that where a statute would create a change in tenure prejudicial to the lords, tenants, or customs of a manor, it would not be deemed to include copyholders unless they were explicitly mentioned. Following this logic, he maintained that the Jacobean statute of limitations, which made claims to land void after a period of twenty years from the point at which an 'entry' could have been justified, applied to copyholds because the aim of the statute had been to fix and settle estates, not make a transformation of them. At the same time, he was worried about descents of copyhold which took place without proper surrenders in the manorial court, because these threatened to deprive lords of manors of their fines and to render them unaware of who was actually a tenant.[39]

---

38 Ibid., i, fol. 189.
39 Folger Shakespeare Library, Washington, DC, MS V.b.6, 'Jones's Reports', fols 121–2.

While this evidence points decisively to the ongoing recognition of copy-hold estates at common law, the customary character of copyhold tenure remained an essential consideration. In one of his opinions, Hale repeated the mantra, familiar from at least Elizabethan times, that the 'custom of the manor was the law of copyholders'.[40] Yet few of these cases involved straightforward questions about the direct relationship between landlords and tenants, such as the payment of fines and rents, or rights to common.[41] Hale referred to the supremacy of the custom of the manor in a case that involved questions about reversionary interest to copyhold. In another, he was asked to consider whether a lord might be able to distrain an under-tenant for rent due from the direct tenant. This case involved a series of long-forgotten subleases and revealed how ancient customs might be over-taken by more recent practices which the lawyers described as prescription. Hale's opinion was that the lord could only distrain the subtenant temporarily while he sought relief against his copyhold tenant who had granted the lease.[42]

In the early 1650s the most highly respected of the Interregnum judges, Sir Henry Rolle, stressed the traditional distinction between customs, which were attached to places (such as manors), and had existed beyond the memory of man, and practices that had arisen by prescription within known historical times, and which applied to individuals only.[43] There is not the least evidence that other lawyers would have dissented from this, but some of Hale's opinions suggest that he was aware of the difficulties that could arise in connection with such distinctions. He observed at one point that any claim to a grant or custom that was alleged to have begun before 1189 had to be accompanied by a history of subsequent usage be-fore it could be accepted, and that without such a record it was void. In an odd case where copyholders and freeholders claimed that the lord of their manor was largely excluded from pasturing beasts and taking wood from common land, he warned that the mere fact that it had been a long time since any lord had asserted his right to common could not in itself be taken as proof of the tenants' claim. What was needed was evidence from court rolls showing the lord had been distrained for commoning his beasts, or from surveys or custumals which mentioned the restriction.

There is an incomplete version in *The English Reports* (London, 1900–32) 2 Siderfin, 42.

40 Hale's Cases . . ., ii, fol. 10.

41 One of the few notable cases about entry fines was that of the Countess of Pembroke in connection with a manor at Appleby in Yorkshire. However, the question here was not about the value of the fine but about whether due notice had been given to an heir that he needed to pay it. HEHL, Wither's Commonplace, Case 42.

42 Hale's Cases . . ., i, fol. 468.

43 HEHL, Wither's Commonplace, Case 5. *Baker v. Andrews*. Prescription in copyhold for repair of hedges.

Most strikingly of all, however, he went on to insist that the question of whether or not a custom existed was a question of fact that should be left to a jury to decide. Even though the evidence from court rolls might be strong, it was impossible for him to give a definitive opinion until both sides had been heard in open court.[44]

The idea that the determination of customs and other obligations in relation to the titles of copyholders should be left to jurors fit with the thinking of those who wanted to limit the use of Chancery in such cases, and to the extent that it was practised it would have had the effect of moving the tricky business of verifying customs out of the hands of the prerogative court judges and lawyers and into the hands of neighbours, or at least other residents of the county in which a case arose. This was in line with the thrust of the persistent Interregnum calls for a return of justice into the localities. Yet, while these nearly always included praise for the jury as an instrument of justice, so little is reliably known about early-modern jury trials that it is difficult to determine conclusively who was most likely to gain from them, landlords or tenants. Since it is known that some country squires such as Sir Richard Temple of Stowe paid out large sums of money to jurors for travel and 'hospitality', there are inevitably questions about how far gentry wealth could be used to corrupt juries – a point that had already been raised in the early seventeenth century by those who maintained that the gentry hated the prerogative courts and the Romano-canonical procedures they used, largely because they could not determine the outcomes in such courts by intimidating jurors.[45] On the other hand, litigants could challenge jurors for taking illicit payments or, for example, proclaiming that they knew the outcome of a trial before it had taken place.[46] Furthermore, most legal discussions about customary tenures in fact took place after juries had given their verdicts, either in arrest of judgements that had already been given, or in connection with 'special verdicts', where juries had decided the matter of fact in question but where its legal implications for a judgement remained in doubt.

Despite all this, however, there were also calls in the civil-war period for the complete abolition of manors and the root and branch reformation of copyhold tenure. Some writers plausibly argued that both reflected the Norman Yoke and the feudal subjection of the English countryside that followed the Conquest.[47] Others suggested that the best way to re-

---

44   Hale's Cases . . ., i, fol. 85. The manor is not named.

45   HEHL, MS Stowe Temple, MS 51; E. F. Gay, 'Sir Richard Temple, Debt Settlement and Estate Litigation', *Huntington Library Quarterly* 6 (1942–3); Brooks, *Law, Politics and Society*, p. 117.

46   Folger MS V.b.6, 'Jones's Reports', fol. 58v, 83 (*Viscount Bolingglass v. Sir Richard Temple*).

47   Brooks, *Law, Politics and Society*, p. 350.

solve controversies between copyholders and their landlords would be to convert all copyholds into freeholds, but this was never seriously put forward as a plan without taking into consideration the need to compensate lords of the manor for their losses.[48] For instance, an author who offered fairly well-balanced advice to the commission on law reform chaired by Sir Mathew Hale went so far as to suggest that commissioners assigned to each county should be armed with a set of 'rules' or guidelines, about how much should be paid to lords in return for converting copyholds into freeholds that would henceforward be completely devisable at common law.[49] Yet, by the mid-seventeenth century, the economic and social relationships surrounding copyhold land were so multifaceted that rational revolutionary schemes such as this one must have been considered bureaucratically unthinkable. Nor is there reason to suspect that copyholders as a class would have been any keener on the changes than manorial lords. The whole process could be identified as the kind of attack by the state on the property of citizens that Henry Ireton made so much of in his opposition to Leveller proposals for the extension of the franchise at the Putney Debates. At best, too much would depend on how the authorities from London assessed the value of copyholds, and that could only be unpredictable and potentially costly. In practice, many smaller to medium holders, as well as the great landlords, measured their landed wealth in terms of customary tenures, and many enjoyed their holdings on terms that were probably more advantageous than those likely to be offered in return for reform. Customary tenures were associated with rights, such as rights to common, as well as obligations, which had been negotiated over the centuries.[50] As discussed earlier, there was in any case an unmistakable trend in the direction of making copyhold a common law tenure that was as flexible and user-friendly in the world of devices by wills, uses, subleases and mortgages as any other. In the end the recommendation of the Hale commission on one of the most contentious issues surrounding copyholds – the level of fines due for descents and alienations where these were unfixed and left to the arbitrary will of the lord – is probably a good indication of the most that might have been achieved. According to the proposal offered to Parliament and rejected by it, fines in such cases should be set at one full year's rent of the copyhold (according to the true yearly value). This was probably fair, and from a reforming lawyer's point of view, it had

48 Veall, *Popular Movement for Law Reform*, chapter 10.
49 *Certaine Assayes Propounded . . .*
50 There are Restoration cases where freeholders claimed the rights of copyholders for this reason. *English Reports*, 2 Keeble 517 (*Potter v. North*, 1670); 3 Modern 250 (*Fisher v. Wren*, 1688).

the advantage of removing a contentious and uncertain class of litigation from the courts.[51]

From the perspective of the central common law courts, therefore, the civil-war period appears to have accelerated, though it did not create, the process whereby 'customary' tenures were being ever more fully integrated into the common law, including jury trials. What landholders of all sorts wanted from the lawyers was 'assurance' that they could use and enjoy, demise or alienate their lands with as much room for manoeuvre as possible. How this played out in terms of social relations within individual manorial jurisdictions around the country is difficult to tell, at least partly because we know so little about what smaller farms actually looked like in terms of the portfolios of land they contained. One measure is that by 1689, manorial institutions seem to have survived most successfully in those places where courts baron became reliable registries for copyhold transactions. Although manorial lords did not stop counting rents, there is little evidence of heavy-handed seigniorialism of the pre-civil war variety, and where customary manorial institutions survived, it was usually because they were useful to the communities they encompassed.[52]

Furthermore, if we expand the focus to the broader issue of agrarian landlord–tenant relationships, we need to move away from the tenurial straightjacket that Tawney's 'agrarian problem' tends to lock us into. In this regard, an action of slander brought in the common law courts by 'a farmer' in 1654 is particularly revealing. Describing himself as a tenant who leased land out of a demesne on a yearly basis, he demanded damages against an adversary who had declared that he was nothing but a 'beggarly and bankrupt fellow, and if every man had his own, you are not worth a groat'. Although the jury in the country had been certain that the words carried an action of slander, and awarded damages accordingly, the lawyers were doubtful about the case when it was considered in arrest of judgement after the trial. The principal argument against the decision was that the words were spoken about a farmer rather than a tradesman who got his living by buying and selling of wares, the economic group explicitly covered by the bankruptcy legislation. Yet the original judgement was ultimately upheld because the farmer claimed that he had been 'warned' by his landlord to quit his holding as a direct result of the slanderous words. The slur on his reputation, according to the court, had damaged his tenant-worthiness, and was therefore a potential cause of material loss.[53] In

---

51 *A Collection of Scarce and Valuable Tracts . . . of the late Lord Somers*, ed. Walter Scott (2nd edn, 13 vols, 1809–15), 6:177. 'The Draught of an Act for ascertaining of Arbitrary Fines upon Descent and Alienation of Copyholds of Inheritance'.

52 Brooks, *Law, Politics and Society*, chapter 9.

53 Folger MS V.b.6, 'Jones's Reports', fol. 65, *Youngs v. Woodyard*.

this case at least, it would seem that agrarian life, and land, had become part and parcel of Craig Muldrew's 'economy of obligation'.[54]

Even so, the world of smallholders continued to be one where sharp terms and conditions associated with tenures always needed to be taken into account or defended. Doubtless for this reason, there does not seem to have been much common cause between customary tenants with rights to wood or common ground, and the landless poor who either built dwellings on common and waste, or else depended on it for their livelihoods. The only evidence Tawney could adduce in connection with this dimension of the 'agrarian problem' during the 1640s and 1650s was a Leveller petition from Londoners against depopulation and enclosure, and of course the writings of Gerrard Winstanley, who led a group of refugees out of London to set up camp and plant the common at Cobham in Surrey in 1649.[55] Yet Winstanley's religiously inspired assertion that the earth was a 'common' available for the equal enjoyment of everyone was not expressed in the largely legal language that made up everyday discourse about common right.[56] While doles to the poor were evidently seen as proper ways to dispose of some of the profit of enclosures, lawyers in the Interregnum courts continued to refer to *Gateward's Case* (1607), the decision that firmly declared that rights to common were proprietary rights attached to other kinds of landholding, most often copyholds.[57] There is little evidence that the Digger movement was widespread; the critical fact is that its most vigorous enemies were copyholders.[58]

Indeed, Tawney compared Winstanley's gentle calls for dig-ins unfavourably with the more belligerent unrest he uncovered in the sixteenth century.[59] Yet he did not have much to say about ongoing conflicts in the East Anglian fens, where drainage projects in effect licensed by the Crown before the civil wars allegedly caused hundreds of families to lose access to common marshland on which they depended for their livelihoods.[60] The technical issues were complicated; the legal battles were drawn-out and accompanied by disturbances described by the authorities as riots. Some of the commoners, such as those at Epworth in the Isle of Axholm, were in fact freeholders who claimed rights to common based on usages established by a charter kept in a strongbox under a stained-glass window in the parish church at Haxey that depicted the document being signed by

54　C. Muldrew, *The Economy of Obligation: The Culture of Credit and Social Relations in Early Modern England* (Basingstoke, 1998).

55　Tawney, *Agrarian Problem*, 320–1.

56　Brooks, *Law, Politics and Society*, pp. 349–51.

57　Birtles, 'Common Law, Poor Relief and Enclosure'.

58　Tawney, *Agrarian Problem*, p. 396.

59　Ibid., pp. 320–1, 340.

60　Keith Lindley, *Fenland Riots and the English Revolution* (London, 1982), p. 1.

Sir John Mowbray in the fourteenth century.[61] The commoners maintained that their opponents, 'the undertakers', at various points enjoyed the support of Parliament and Cromwell, and that they used underhand methods to frustrate legal decisions that went against them. By the later 1650s, the lawyers were particularly agitated by the fact that claims to common were often being made in connection with messuages, or houses, rather than agricultural land. [62] But on the general issues, the fenmen drew on support from the Levellers John Lilburne and John Wildman as well as that of the heavyweight parliamentarian lawyer, Sir John Maynard, who vigorously supported their cause. Maynard argued that neither the Crown nor Parliament could make grants that infringed property rights. He depicted the undertakers as particularly egregious examples of the excesses of prerogative power that could flow from Crown, Parliament, or protector, and he compared their modern commissions unfavourably with the traditional commissions of sewers, through which the nobility, gentry and commoners had maintained the finely balanced ecology of the fens. Just as the Earl of Strafford had used blank general warrants to justify his illegal acts in Ireland, the 'undertakers' produced 'the Kings Letters upon all occasions, especially to destroy Juries, and to take away our real estates, without consulting the Owners'.[63]

III

As Tawney suggested, the civil wars helped to consolidate the incorporation of customary tenures into the common law. Furthermore, although it is worth noting that the influential post-Restoration judge Sir Mathew Hale was reluctant to commit whole-heartedly to the proposition that the ownership of land was a natural right,[64] this process ultimately advanced the concept to the extent that Locke could plausibly make it the basis of political obligation in the *Two Treatises of Government*.[65]

But Tawney misjudged many of the related details. The importance of fairness and equity in landlord–tenant relationships was reinforced in the 1660s and 1670s by the successes of the judges who acted in the statutory

---

61   Ibid., p. 26. *To the Parliament of the Commonwealth of England and every individual member thereof, the declaration of Daniel Noddel, solicitor for the freeholders and commoners within the manor of Epworth* . . . (1653), pp. 9ff.

62   Folger MS V.b.6, 'Jones's Reports', fol. 132.

63   *The Picklock of the Old Fen Project: or, Heads of Sir John Maynard his several speeches* (1650), p. 5.

64   BL, MS Hargrave 485, 'Treatise of the Nature of Lawes in Generall and touching the Law of nature' by Sir Mathew Hale, fols 35v–37.

65   Tawney, *Agrarian Problem*, p. 309.

court set up after the Great Fire of 1666 to arbitrate settlements in connection with the rebuilding of London.[66] The increased ability to alienate, sublease or mortgage copyhold land was merely a corollary of the greater security under which it was held. These developments had likely been accompanied in the century prior to 1640 by greater social differentiation in rural society, but it must also be associated with that still insufficiently studied phenomenon, the rise of the yeomanry, as much as with the 'rise of the gentry'.[67] Post-Restoration squires may well have been as concerned with raising money through mortgages as finding ways of maximising rents from customary tenants. It is true that the famous Restoration statute abolishing feudal tenures touched only those services, such as knights' service, and wardship, which mainly affected the gentry, but this hardly left the customary tenant at the mercy of his landlord.[68] As long as the demand for agricultural products remained high, small farmers were well placed to profit.

At the same time, the way Tawney articulated the 'agrarian problem' loses sight of the accelerated growth of a market in land from the 1650s through to the 1670s, a tendency for this to have been increasingly, though not exclusively, centred on London, and the simultaneous growth of banking and the greater integration of land into the overall financial system that was typified by the growing popularity of mortgages. The monumental fortune of the sometime Lord Mayor of London, Sir Robert Clayton, which included real estate interests in thirty-nine counties, was founded in the money-lending business of his uncle, the scrivener Robert Abbot, whose banking activities were already thriving in the 1650s.[69] Similarly, the papers of William Harvey of Taunton in Somerset indicate that he was engaged in similar activities in a provincial setting, and with a clientele that was distinctly middling rather than gentry in social composition.[70] Although, there is an enormous amount of change from the intervening period that needs to be taken into account, the emergence of something that can be described as banking in the second half of the seventeenth

66   BL, MSS Additional 5063–5103. Records of the London Fire Court, 27 Feb 1666–18 Feb 1675. The portraits of all the judges were painted by Michael Wright to express the gratitude of the City for their work.
67   A. Shepard and J. Spicksley, 'Worth, Age and Social Status in Early Modern England', *Economic History Review* 64:2 (2011), 517; Allen, *Enclosure and the Yeoman*.
68   2 Charles II, c.24. An act for taking away the court of wards and liveries, and tenures *in capite*, and by knights' service, and purveyance.
69   C. W. Brooks, R. H. Helmholz, and P. G. Stein, *Notaries Public in England since the Reformation* (Society of Public Notaries of London, 1991), pp. 73–5.
70   Somerset Record Office, Taunton, DD/SP: Letters and other materials relating to William Harvey.

century certainly looks significantly different from the 'dispersed' rural credit described by Chris Briggs as characteristic of the fourteenth.[71]

For prominent Restoration lawyers such as Hale and Sir Francis North, the potential for fraud rather than the respective rights of lords and tenants was the most pressing problem. English landholding practices involved a myriad of different interests and a large capacity of individual holders and subtenants to lease or otherwise encumber land that was frequently held for twenty years or more. Hale favoured the trial of titles at common law as the most effective means of determining 'ownership', and both he and North endorsed the establishment of registries that would help solve the problem of secret conveyances which prevented buyers of land from being certain what they were getting for their money.[72] This was not a problem associated exclusively with customary tenures, but they were certainly part of it. According to an anonymous tract published in 1677, the growing tendency of copyholders for life to grant 99-year leases meant that once the grantor died or moved away, there was no person willing or available to make the ancient transfers through the manorial court. This cheated the lord out of his fine, and ultimately made it impossible to know who his tenants actually were. The consequence was eventually that there was no one who owed suit of court, or available to hold office, and hence the manor itself died as a community institution. It was lawful for a copy-holder to make leases, but not such secret long leases 'as shall destroy the Reputation of the Tenure by Copy'.[73]

In conclusion, so many qualifications are needed for Tawney's character-isation of the mid- and later seventeenth century that it is probably best to throw out the baby with the bath water and start again. Although the pro-cess doubtless had a deleterious impact on the landless poor, the common law had already become deeply involved with customary tenures by 1640. The lawyers themselves associated this with a strengthening of the security of smaller holders which contributed to something like a social revolution in which patriarchal and seigniorial landlord–tenant relationships had been replaced by 'economic ones', and where a class of smaller holders existed alongside the gentry, and vigorously exercised their 'rights'. The enormous success of the common law as a business in the early modern period was built as much on serving the interests of middling agricultural

71   C. Briggs, *Credit and Village Society in Fourteenth-Century England* (Oxford, 2009), pp. 214ff.
72   Lambeth Palace Library, London, MS Fairhurst 3475, fols 150–3, 172–81, 186, 240 (Hale); BL MS Additional 32,518 (North), 'Notes on the establishment of registration', fols 51ff. Registration had also been proposed in the 1650s by the Hale Commission.
73   [Anon], *Reasons Humbly Submitted to the Consideration of Both Houses of Parliament for Passing an Act for Preservation of Manors and of Copyhold Estates and Tenures* (1677), pp. 1–4.

society as those of the gentry. There was change in the civil-war years, but this seems to have been a continuation of a process already in train which put greater emphasis on the role of common law juries in the determination of titles, and customs, and increased the flexibility of copyholders in dealing with their land to such an extent that there was further atrophy of the manorial system in many localities. By the 1680s all land, including copyhold, had become caught up in a broader market for both property and credit.

12

Agrarian Capitalism and Merchant Capitalism

Tawney, Dobb, Brenner and Beyond

DAVID ORMROD

This chapter examines the place of R. H. Tawney's *Agrarian Problem* and other writings in debates about the rise of capitalism. It tracks two broad strands in ideas about capitalist development: the neo-Smithian approach which stresses the rise of market relations and trade, and the productionist or physiocratic approach which stresses changes in the agrarian economy, particularly the dispossession of small landowners, and the rise the tripartite capitalist organisation of landlords, leaseholding farmers and wage labourers. In the second part of the chapter the implementation of the Corn Laws and information on levels of rent for agricultural land between 1550 and 1900 are used to pinpoint the era when capitalist agriculture became dominant in England.

I

The 1970s saw a major revival of interest in the debate over the transition from feudalism to capitalism within which the agrarian origins of capitalist development became a strongly contested issue. Its starting point was Maurice Dobb's *Studies in the Development of Capitalism* (1946) and a series of commentaries led by the American Marxist Paul Sweezy.[1] Central to this revival of interest – which we can regard as forming the second of three phases of an intermittent and long-running debate – was a provocative article by Robert Brenner on 'Agrarian Class Structure and Economic Development in Pre-industrial Europe' (1976).[2] Essentially, this revived an old argument in Marxism about production versus exchange as the driving

---

1 Dobb, *Studies*. Discussion of this book appeared in *Science and Society*, in a debate initiated by Paul Sweezy; these were reprinted with further material in Hilton, ed., *Transition from Feudalism to Capitalism* (1976). See also Samuel, 'British Marxist Historians', 81–3.
2 Brenner, 'Agrarian Class Structure', reprinted with the ensuing debate in Aston and Philpin, eds, *The Brenner Debate*.

Figure 12.1: The transition from feudalism to capitalism: the first two phases of a debate

		Phase I
R. H. Tawney	1912	*The Agrarian Problem*
	1926	Religion and the Rise of Capitalism (1922)
	1941	'The Rise of the Gentry', Econ. Hist. Rev.
J. E. C. Hill	1940	*The English Revolution, 1640*
M. H. Dobb	1946	*Studies in the Development of Capitalism* (1926)
	1950	Debate on the above, led by P. Sweezy, *Science & Society*, repr. 1976, ed. R. Hilton, *The Transition from Feudalism to Capitalism*
	1964	'The Transition from Feudalism to Capitalism', *Science & Society*
		Phase II
E. J. Hobsbawm	1954	'The Crisis of the Seventeenth Century', *Past & Present*
	1959	Debate on the above, led by H. Trevor-Roper, in *Past & Present, 1965*
	1964	*Pre-Capitalist Economic Formations* (taken from Marx's *Grundrisse*, 1857–8)
P. Anderson	1974	*Passages from Antiquity to Feudalism*
	1974	*Lineages of the Absolutist State*
I. Wallerstein	1974	*The Modern World-System* (to 1600)
B. Hindess and P. Hirst	1975	*Pre-Capitalist Modes of Production*
R. H. Hilton	1976	Reprint of the Dobb-Sweezy debate (see above)
R. Brenner	1976	'Agrarian Class Structure and Economic Development in Preindustrial Europe', *Past & Present*, debated 1976–85; ten contributions ed. Aston and Philpin, The Brenner Debate, 1985
	1977	'The Origins of Capitalist Development. A Critique of Neo-Smithian Marxism', *New Left Review, 1977*
I. Wallerstein	1980	*The Modern World-System* II (1600–1750)
	1983	*Historical Capitalism*
	1989	*The Modern World-System* III (1730–1840s)

Figure 12.2: Capitalism, world systems and global history

Incorporating Phase III of the Transition Debate		
F. Braudel	1979	*Civilisation and Capitalism: Fifteenth–Eighteenth centuries*, I: *The Structures of Everyday Life* (trans. 1981); II: *The Wheels of Commerce* (trans. 1982); III: *The Perspective of the World* (trans. 1984)
K. Chaudhuri	1985	*Trade and Civilisation in the Indian Ocean: An Economic History from the Rise of Islam to 1750*
——	1990	*Asia before Europe: Economy and Civilisation of the Indian Ocean from the Rise of Islam to 1750*
J. Abu-Lughod	1989	*Before European Hegemony: The World System AD 1250–1350*
G. Arrighi	1994	*The Long Twentieth Century: Money, Power and the Origin of Our Times*
——	1999	*Chaos and Governance in the Modern World System* (with B. Silver)
G. Frank	1998	*ReOrient: Global Economy in the Asian Age*
K. Pomeranz	2000	*The Great Divergence: China, Europe and the Making of the Modern World Economy*
I. Wallerstein	2004	*World Systems Analysis. An Introduction*
G. Arrighi	2007	*Adam Smith in Beijing: Lineages of the Twenty-First Century*

force behind economic development. The division was present in Marx's own thinking about the accumulation of capital in pre-capitalist societies, which in the first volume of *Capital* is shown to originate in agrarian expropriation. The third volume proposes an alternative answer cast in terms of money supply, markets and exchange, involving the build-up of merchant's capital. In fact the argument predates Marx, and can be traced back to the different emphasis placed on agriculture and trade in British and French economic thought between Adam Smith and the physiocrats, especially Quesnay.[3] Brenner took up the traditional Marxist–Leninist position which regarded merchant capitalism as involving a gradualist, non-revolutionary, and therefore unacceptable reading of history. In its place, Brenner proposed a model of agrarian capitalism in which rural class conflict was central, driven principally by landlords against a largely defenceless and undifferentiated peasantry.[4]

3   See especially Cooper, 'In Search of Agrarian Capitalism'.
4   See Hoyle, 'Tenure and the Land Market', 2–3, which highlights the issues of differen-

Not only did Brenner emphasise the centrality of the rural class struggle against the claims of what he described as a prevalent 'neo-Malthusian' school of thought which emphasised demographical change, he also followed this up with a lengthy and sharper critique of 'neo-Smithian' Marxism, that is, commercially induced growth, aimed against Gundar Frank, Immanuel Wallerstein and other proponents of the emerging world-systems school.[5] Many regarded the Brenner thesis as useful in provoking debate but at the end of the day historically untenable. By the 1990s, however, Brenner's Marxist paradigm had shifted to accommodate his earlier detailed work on commercial history and import-led growth, with the publication in 1993 of his *Merchants and Revolution*, which brought merchant capitalism and the politics of mercantile interests into a centre-stage position. The postscript to *Merchants and Revolution* attempted a synthesis between an impressive body of empirical research on the trans-formative impact of new merchant capitalists on the Cromwellian state and the 'further consolidation' of agrarian capitalism after 1660. Brenner wrote that in the post-Restoration decades:

> Larger landlords won out over smaller landlords and owner-occupiers, who were caught in a squeeze between falling prices and rising taxes ... At the same time, the commercial revolution in overseas trade, already in full flower by 1650, had matured much further, profoundly strengthening, in both absolute and relative terms, those social groups of merchants based in the newer areas of commercial penetration.[6]

With hindsight it is clear that during the 1970s Brenner exaggerated the supposed contradiction between productionist and market-based explanations of economic development in classical Marxism to a degree which was not actually present in the earlier debates between Dobb and Sweezy. Although Dobb discussed the decline of feudalism in terms of a crisis in agricultural production, his analysis of the origins of capitalism rested on the transformative impact of merchant capital in manufacturing and commerce, through the agency of an urban middle class. These chapters formed the core of Dobb's book, and owed much to the work of Tawney's historical mentor and close friend, George Unwin, especially his *Studies in Industrial Organisation in the Sixteenth and Seventeenth Centuries*, based mainly on the history of the London craft guilds.[7]

---

tiation and legal protection available to copyholders.

5   R. Brenner, 'The Origins of Capitalist Development: A Critique of Neo-Smithian Marxism', *New Left Review* 104 (1977), 25–92.

6   R. Brenner, *Merchants and Revolution: Commercial Change, Political Conflict, and London's Overseas Traders, 1550–1653* (Cambridge, 1993), p. 711.

7   Dobb, *Studies*, chapters 4–7; G. Unwin, *Industrial Organisation in the Sixteenth and*

In spite of his limited interest in Marxist analysis, Tawney shared much common ground with Dobb, at least in terms of historical substance, and each read and commented on the other's work. Dobb began writing the *Studies* in 1926, the year which saw publication of Tawney's *Religion and the Rise of Capitalism*, and in his first chapter credited Tawney with providing capitalism with 'authoritative recognition as a historical category'. Tawney in turn admired Dobb's combination of history with theory, and its analytical strength as an example deserving imitation. Both agreed that commercial and financial capitalism were already well developed in the sixteenth century, but Tawney felt that Dobb placed too great an emphasis on the prevalence of the wage contract at a time when permanent wage workers formed a minority of the labour force. Piece rates, commissions, intermittent fees, various hybrids and 'other more eccentric methods of re-muneration' were the norm in pre-industrial England. 'Wages, like rents', Tawney mused, 'remain for long an elusive category.'[8]

Leaving aside this significant difference of emphasis, both Tawney and Dobb recognised early modern English capitalism as the product of market growth, and the agrarian capitalism discussed by Tawney in *The Agrarian Problem* was identified closely with the *commercialisation* of agriculture, especially of landholding. Shorn of its military significance, the basis of landownership now became the command of money rather than the command of men.[9] Seen from a wider perspective, Tawney maintained that the 'New Rural Economy' of the sixteenth century should be regarded as the foundation for the commercialisation of English life, via the expansion of pasture farming and woollen cloth exports which 'first brought England conspicuously into world commerce' and encouraged the search for new export markets. In an important review of *The Agrarian Problem*, Michael Havinden argued that its main assertion was not that customary tenants were evicted in large numbers, as some of Tawney's critics claimed, but that they were obliged to pay higher entry fines; and that 'it was the commercialisation of agriculture, by which the profits were transferred to landlords rather than retained by peasants, which constituted the most revolutionary agrarian change in the sixteenth century'.[10] To this assess-

---

Seventeenth Centuries (Oxford, 1904), based on the then unpublished records of the smaller London companies. Tawney discussed its importance in his Introductory Memoir to *Studies in Economic History: The Collected Papers of George Unwin*, ed. R. H. Tawney (London 1927), pp. xxxviii–xxxix. It was largely on the basis of Unwin's pioneering work that Dobb argued that there were 'two decisive moments in the history of capitalism in England, the first in the early seventeenth century centring on the struggle within the char-tered corporations and the parliamentary struggle against monopoly, and the second, the industrial revolution' (Dobb, *Studies*, pp. 18–19).

8   Winter, ed., *History and Society*, p. 207.

9   Tawney, *Agrarian Problem* (1912 edn), p. 187; Dobb, *Studies*, p. 2.

10 M. A. Havinden, 'Review of E. Kerridge, ed., *Agrarian Problems in the Sixteenth*

ment, we should add Jane Whittle's findings for Norfolk that lords were reluctant to transfer customary tenancies to leaseholds in the sixteenth century, and that expropriation, where it occurred, was often instigated by richer peasants through the land market.[11]

If we turn from *The Agrarian Problem* to *Religion and the Rise of Capitalism*, it is clear that Tawney saw the religious changes of the sixteenth century as involving an adaptation of Christianity to an increasingly individualistic society, and the new element in public life was not the agrarian problem, which was already present long before the Reformation, but the achievement of unrestricted liberty in business matters: 'The triumph of Puritanism swept away all traces of any restriction or guidance in the employment of money.'[12] In his unpublished writings and lectures too we find the same recognition of early capitalism as the product of commercial growth. In drafts for his Ford Lectures and Chicago lectures given in the late 1930s, he emphasised that in pre-industrial Europe, industry remained less important than trade as long as men found it cheap to plunder nature and old civilisations. He repeatedly emphasised that 'trade is the dynamic which sets everything in motion', whilst at the same time expressed undisguised contempt for the 'mundane ambitions and vulgar cupidities of uninspired business men'.[13]

The first phase of the transition debate laid down the foundations for post-war discussion of the history of capitalism, and the Brenner thesis carried these same fundamental issues forward into the 1970s for the scrutiny of agrarian historians. The distinctiveness of the second phase of debate, however, lay in a broadening of regional boundaries along with an increased emphasis on state power, state structures and autonomous political change. It was Eric Hobsbawm's interpretation of the English revolution as part of a European-wide 'general crisis' which provided this new point of departure. The uniqueness of the English revolution was called into question, and several of Hobsbawm's critics agreed that the mid-seventeenth-century crisis was actually a crisis in relations between society and the state rather than a crisis of production. Some years later, Perry Anderson's *Lineages of the Absolutist State* echoed this conclusion in viewing the English revolution less as the 'classic case of a bourgeois revolution' than a symptom of a crisis of the absolutist state in the West.[14]

Century and After', in *Agricultural .History. Review*, 19 (1971), 181.

11   Whittle, *Development of Agrarian Capitalism*, pp. 308–9; Hoyle, 'Tenure and the Land Market', 1–20.

12   R. H. Tawney, *Religion and the Rise of Capitalism* (London, 1926), p. 213.

13   LSE Archives, Tawney Papers, 5/1, p. 2; Ormrod, 'R. H. Tawney and the Origins of Capitalism', 141, 146–9.

14   E. J. Hobsbawm, 'The Crisis of the Seventeenth Century', *Past & Present* 6 (1954), reprinted together with many of the contributions to the ensuing symposium and debate

As orthodox Marxist paradigms grew weaker with the rise of the New Left, the contribution of Brenner's critics combined to undermine the traditional emphasis on rural class relations. In their place there arose an increasing preoccupation with market growth in the context of an expanding world economy, notably in the early writings of Immanuel Wallerstein on the origins of the modern world system.[15] Significantly, the 'agrarian capitalism' which formed the subtitle of the first volume of the *Modern World System* was defined by Wallerstein as 'agricultural production for profit in a market'. As we have already noticed, Brenner dealt with this challenge head-on, in his critique of what he termed 'Neo-Smithian' Marxism. The Smithian model, he felt, was unsuited to pre-capitalist societies based predominantly on coercive labour relations. The 'either/or' logic underlying Brenner's position was combined with an unwillingness to acknowledge the freedoms and legal protection sometimes enjoyed by small owner-occupiers in England, and their capacity for innovation and improvement in an increasingly commercialised society, as his critics continually emphasised. It was several years later, in 1992, that Robert Allen added further weight to the view that large-scale capital-intensive farming was not a pre-requisite for major improvements in agricultural productivity in his study of yeoman farmers in the South Midlands.[16]

During the 1980s and 1990s, the transition debate was opened up and transformed by a new drive to move beyond Eurocentric preoccupations, and by the diversification of neo-Marxist and post-Marxist approaches to economic development. Braudel's incorporation of Wallerstein's world-systems perspectives into the third volume of his magisterial *Civilisation and Capitalism* (1979), alongside central place theory, provided another new point of departure for the transition debate.[17] We can regard it as marking the third phase of that debate, albeit one which now formed part of an even larger project to explore the history of capitalism in a global

in *Past & Present*, led by H. R. Trevor-Roper in T. Aston, ed., *Crisis in Europe, 1560–1660: Essays from Past & Present* (London, 1965); P. Anderson, *Passages from Antiquity to Feudalism* (London, 1996) and *Lineages of the Absolutist State* (London, 1974).

15   I. Wallerstein, *The Modern World System, 1: Capitalist Agriculture and the Origins of the European World-Economy in the Sixteenth Century* (New York, 1974); *The Modern World System, 2: Mercantilism and the Consolidation of the European World-Economy, 1600–1750* (New York, 1980); *The Modern World System, 3: The Second Era of Great Expansion of the Capitalist World-Economy* (New York, 1989); *The Capitalist World-Economy: Essays* (Cambridge, 1979); *Historical Capitalism* (London, 1983); *World Systems Analysis: An Introduction* (Durham, NC, and London, 2004).

16   Allen, *Enclosure and the Yeoman*.

17   F. Braudel, *Capitalism and Civilisation, 15th to 18th Century, 1: The Structures of Everyday Life* (London, 1981); *Capitalism and Civilisation, 15th to 18th Century, 2: The Wheels of Commerce* (London, 1982); *Capitalism and Civilisation, 15th to 18th Century, 3: The Perspective of the World* (London, 1984).

historical context. In the post-communist world of the 1990s, debates about the decline of feudalism which prioritised north-west European patterns of development began to take on an arcane significance, eclipsed by renewed interest in the history of capitalist globalisation and the need to discover its 'territorial logic'.[18]

It would be out of place to summarise this burgeoning literature here, but it is important to recognise that the underlying thrust moved in a strongly neo-Smithian direction – *neo*-Smithan in the sense that it rejected those parts of traditional modernisation theory which failed to explain growing disparities in levels of wealth and income in the late twentieth century. The line of argument from Wallerstein, Braudel and Chaudhuri through to Arrighi in tracing the evolving structure of the global economy stresses the *flexibility* of capital rather than its permanent embodiment in specific production strategies, along with the preference of capitalist agencies for liquidity and capital circulation – the familiar formula M–C–M in Marx's notion of merchant capital.[19] Arrighi's volumes have brought Smith and Marx much closer together, not least in Arrighi's project to rescue Adam Smith from neo-liberal distortion. *Adam Smith in Beijing* is the authentic Adam Smith who, far from trusting the self-regulating power of markets, actually saw the market as an instrument of government, believing that 'a strong state . . . would create and reproduce the conditions for the existence of the market'.[20] Trade and merchant elites provide the dynamic, as Brenner came to recognise in *Merchants and Revolution*, while Arrighi in turn agreed with Brenner that market growth alone is an insufficient condition for capitalist development: pre-existing social conditions help shape developmental outcomes.[21]

II

If we strip away the polemics which inevitably surround the history of capitalism, it is not difficult to identify the continuities between agrarian and commercial capitalisms, but less easy to define the difference between agrarian capitalism and a merely commercialised agricultural sector. As Eric Hobsbawm put it, 'even the most capitalist agriculture is not a rural

---

18   G. Arrighi, *Adam Smith in Beijing: Lineages of the Twenty-First Century* (London, 2007), chapter 8, *passim*.

19   G. Arrighi, *The Long Twentieth Century: Money, Power, and the Origin of Our Times* (London, 1994), p. 5. The circuit M–C–M, where M= money and C=commodities, represented the process of buying in order to sell at a higher price.

20   Arrighi, *Adam Smith in Beijing*, pp. 42–3.

21   Brenner, *Merchants and Revolution*, Postscript, *passim*; Arrighi, *Adam Smith in Beijing*, p. 24.

opposite number of the factory', but is distinguished by capital-intensive methods of production and division of labour.[22] Capitalist agriculture is not easily defined in simple productionist terms, partly because productivity-raising methods were much more difficult to achieve than in industry, involving organic rather than mechanical techniques; and partly because foodstuffs in early modern Europe formed part of a moral economy of provision. Animals were seen as domestic companions, plants were valued for their healing properties, and the fair pricing and distribution of cereals was subject to popular consensus operating within regulated internal markets.[23] Changes in land tenure, the movement towards larger farms, and the pull of urban markets, especially London, facilitated the commercialisation of farming in sixteenth- and seventeenth-century England, but historians have been slow to recognise that food production is historically much more resistant to commodification than is the case with manufactured goods.

Some years ago, as the Brenner debate was drawing to a close, I touched on this issue in a study of the eighteenth-century English grain export trade. Its central argument was that changes in the institutional environment of English farming from the outbreak of the Civil War in 1642 to the 1670s provided a firm basis for the emergence of capitalist agriculture, culminating in the experimental Corn Law of 1672. The new outlook was first expressed in 1663 and 1670 when grain export was encouraged rather than discouraged, with imports permitted only in years of abnormally high prices. It was in 1672 that an experimental 'bounty' or subsidy of 5s per quarter on exported wheat was approved, along with smaller bounties on other grains.[24] The Corn Laws were made permanent in 1689, and placed foodstuffs fully within the sphere of commodity production and exchange, following the slow demise of customary controls on prices. The 1630s saw the last application of a 'dearth policy' by central government to counteract food shortages. Thereafter, as Outhwaite explained,

22   E. J. Hobsbawm, 'Perry Anderson's History', author's transcript of a tape-recorded lecture given at the University of Kent, Canterbury, May 1976, p. 14.
23   K. Thomas, *Man and the Natural World: Changing Attitudes in England, 1500–1800* (London, 1983), p. 94; J. Thirsk, *Alternative Agriculture: A History from the Black Death to the Present Day* (Oxford, 1997), conclusion; R. B. Outhwaite, *Dearth, Public Policy and Social Disturbance in England, 1550–1800* (London, 1991), chapters 3 and 4; E. P. Thompson, 'The Moral Economy of the English Crowd in the Eighteenth Century', *Past & Present* 50 (1971), reprinted in Thompson, *Customs in Common*, which also includes 'The Moral Economy Reviewed', pp. 259–351.
24   David Ormrod, *English Grain Exports and the Structure of Agrarian Capitalism, 1700–1760* (Hull, 1985), chapter 1, *passim*; David Ormrod, *The Rise of Commercial Empires: England and the Netherlands in the Age of Mercantilism, 1650–1770* (Cambridge, 2003), chapter 7; D. G. Barnes, *A History of the English Corn Laws from 1660–1846* (London, 1930), chapter 2.

'food crises produce more belated and less comprehensive responses. Anti-dearth measures are increasingly left to local communities, without urgent prompting from the centre.'[25] The background to this change of policy was abundance and a consequent stagnation of grain prices, but subsidised export and the dismantling of the moral economy marked a permanent shift in policy which remained in place until the repeal of the Corn Laws in 1846. The approach was one which, on balance, favoured producers at the expense of consumers by artificially raising prices and maintaining the arable acreage.[26]

Other institutional changes included the demise of anti-enclosure legislation following the abolition of the prerogative courts; widespread revision of rentals following royalist land sales and repossessions; concentration of land ownership into fewer hands, a process which accelerated up to c.1740, and its correlate, a reduction in the number of small landowners which was particularly severe during the years of heavy war taxation from 1689–1714. Their combined effect was to accelerate the expansion of the tripartite system of farming, involving increased reliance on rural wage labour. Significantly, changing rural property relations were reflected in late seventeenth-century economic discourse, and some indeed have regarded Locke as an early theorist of agrarian capitalism.[27]

These institutional changes are well known. But it is worth emphasising that England's ability to compete successfully in continental food markets from the 1670s to c.1750 was facilitated by the protectionist policies of a strong fiscal-military state. It was because the state placed 'defence above opulence' that Adam Smith approved of the Navigation Code as 'the wisest

25   R. B. Outhwaite, 'Dearth and Government Intervention in English Grain Markets, *Economic History Review*, second series, 34 (1981), 396, and *Dearth, Public Policy and Social Disturbance*, p. 42; J. Chartres, 'The Marketing of Agricultural Produce', in *The Agrarian History of England and Wales, 5: 1640–1750*, ed. Joan Thirsk (Cambridge, 1985), pp. 501–2, which concludes that increasing market freedom and better commercial information resulted in more efficient networks of supply, at the expense of oligopolistic tendencies in some markets and commodity trades.

26   The impact of export bounties was keenly debated in the 1750s, and the issue is still unsettled: Chartres, 'Marketing of Agricultural Produce', pp. 497–8, and Ormrod, *English Grain Exports*, pp. 17–18. More recently, Chartres suggests that 'in Britain . . . after the middle of the seventeenth century, the market was permitted to attain sovereignty, and its market integration liberated producers and offered greater security to consumers than traditional regulation' (J. Chartres, 'Producers, Crops and Markets, 1600–1800', in *A Common Agricultural Heritage? Revising French and British Rural Divergence*, ed. J. Broad (Agricultural History Review Supplement, series 5, Exeter, 2009), p. 143.

27   Ormrod, *English Grain Exports*, pp. 12–14; N. Wood, *John Locke and Agrarian Capitalism* (London, 1984), *passim*. See also K. Tribe, *Land, Labour and Economic Discourse* (London, 1978), chapter 3, and *Genealogies of Capitalism* (London, 1981), chapter 2.

of all the commercial regulations of England'.[28] The Corn Laws also had a strategic aspect in maintaining self-sufficiency in cereal growing but drew Smith's criticism on the grounds that export bounties raised prices above their natural level and increased the tax burden. He nevertheless conceded that they were advantageous to merchants and carriers, and that high duties on grain imports were beneficial to farmers 'in times of moderate plenty'.[29] The intensity and variegated character of Smith's engagement with almost every aspect of mercantilist regulation underlines Arrighi's reading of *The Wealth of Nations*, with an emphasis on its perception of the market as an instrument of government.

The rise of a subsidised overseas market for English grain from c.1672 to 1765 represented a convergence of landed and mercantile interests, although some contemporaries saw the 1689 act as a reward to Tory landowners for placing William III on the throne.[30] Certainly, its immediate purpose was to raise revenue to underwrite the long wars against France. It eased the burden of a steep increase in the Land Tax through a policy of price supports designed to enhance rents and maintain land under arable cultivation. Commercialised agriculture and merchant capital thus combined to form the basis of a new rural economy, a system of capitalist agriculture underpinned with centralised state support. Tawney recognised that the bounty on grain exports was exceptional in that it was never prefigured in any of the demands for changes in agrarian policy pressed in Parliament before the Civil War, and commented:

> The seamy side of the new order was of course the cessation of the attempt to protect the poorer classes against exploitation. The social policy of the Tudors and early Stuarts had been fitful and intermittent: but they had, at least, recognised the need for a policy, and had done more to provide one than is usually recognised. With the rapid advance after 1660 of capitalism in agriculture and industry, the need for a counterforce to the downward pressure on the weak was steadily increasing, but the old protective measures cease to be enforced, and no new measures take their place.[31]

Protection of the consumer was now subordinated to the interests of landowners in maintaining rent levels, at precisely the time when a series of institutional changes were facilitating the rapid expansion of the modern tripartite system of farming – which in turn depended on the clear separa-

28   A. Smith, *An Inquiry into the Nature and Causes of the Wealth of Nations* (1776), ed. J. R. McCulloch (Edinburgh, 1864), p. 204.
29   Smith, *Wealth of Nations*, p. 198.
30   Barnes, *History of the English Corn Laws*, p. 11.
31   LSE Archives, Tawney Papers, 1/8, p. 21; 4/1, p. 36.

tion of rents, profits and wages. Nonetheless Turner, Beckett and Afton have shown that traditional forms of land tenure and labour contracts, such as beneficial rents and leases and service in husbandry, persisted well into the nineteenth century.[32] The emergence of a system of full market rents was a gradual process until the middle of the eighteenth century, when it began to accelerate on the eve of the parliamentary enclosure movement (figure 12.3). As Avner Offer explains, like Adam Smith before him, the distinctiveness of English land tenure lay in the ease with which landowners were able to shift risk onto the farmer. Rack-renting essentially involved the conversion of rent from a residual surplus into a fixed overhead, leaving the farmer to bear the burden of risk and market fluctuations. The English tenurial system, in other words, can be seen as 'an arrangement for converting agriculture, an inherently risky enterprise, into landownership, a secure and stable one'.[33] Its logic and resilience worked against the survival of small-scale family farming of the kind found in many parts of Europe.

Reconstructing the emergence of modern market rents is a complex process, both conceptually and technically, and careful analysis of long-run rent movements was virtually impossible until the publication of Turner, Beckett and Afton's work in 1997 (TBA), covering the period 1690–1914.[34] Recently completed research on the estates of the Rochester Bridge Trust (RBT) in Kent, Essex and the City of London for the period 1580–1914 confirms the robustness of the TBA index.[35] Rents per acre on the RBT Kent estates rose about ten-fold between 1690 and 1870, compared with an eleven-fold increase in the TBA national rents index. On the Essex estates however, an already high level of rent (more than twice the level for Kent farms) registered a five-fold increase during the same period. The TBA index suggests that productivity rose most dramatically between c.1800 and

32 M. E. Turner, J. Beckett and B. Afton, *Agricultural Rent in England, 1690–1914* (Cambridge, 1997), pp. 24–32; A. Kussmaul, *Servants in Husbandry in Early Modern England* (Cambridge, 1981), chapter 3; D. Woodward, 'Early Modern Servants in Husbandry Revisited', *Agricultural .History. Review* 48:2 (2000), 141–50.

33 A. Offer, 'Farm Tenure and Land Values in England, c.1750–1950', *Economic History Review* 44:1 (1991), 8–9; Smith, *Wealth of Nations*, pp. 66–80.

34 Turner, Beckett and Afton, *Agricultural Rent*. The problems are discussed in Bowden, 'Agricultural Prices, Wages, Farm Profits and Rents', pp. 62–83 and C. Clay, 'Landlords and Estate Management in England', pp. 198–251, both in Thirsk, ed., *Agrarian History of England and Wales 5*.

35 University of Kent, City and Region project: phase I funded by ESRC (RES-000–22–2185); phase II funded by the Rochester Bridge Trust. Rental data, together with supporting estate maps, building plans, details of leases and tenancies are available on www.cityandregion.org; see also D. Ormrod, J. Gibson and O. Lyne, 'City and Countryside Revisited: Comparative Rent Movements in London and the South-East, 1580–1914', *University of Kent, School of Economics Discussion Paper*, KPDE 1117, October 2011 and RePEC (online Research Papers in Economics).

Figure 12.3: Kent and Essex farm rents compared with TBA, Kerridge, and Clark, 1577–1914 (assessed rents per acre, £s)

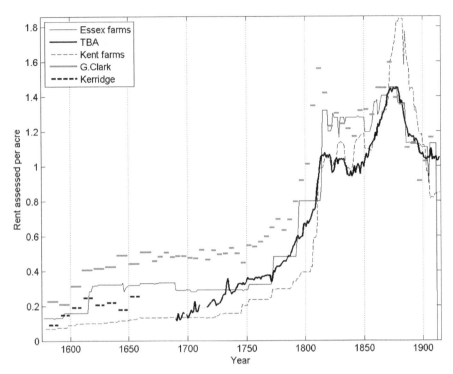

1820, with something like a fifteen-year lag of rents behind food prices. Greg Clark describes this in terms of an 'agricultural revolution accompanying the industrial revolution'.[36] Clark's own results however, derived as they are from the early nineteenth-century Charity Commissioners' reports, cannot be regarded as providing a reliable measure of authentic agricultural rents, as numerous urban fringe properties are included in the sample, together with housing. This explains the generally high level of Clark's index until the early years of the nineteenth century.

If we place the TBA index against the RBT farm rents and those of the charitable lands (figure 12.3), it is evident that a convergence has emerged by 1800 following a period of parallel movement during the preceding half-century when agricultural rents began their steady upward climb. The years from c.1620 to 1750, it appears, represent a period of relative

36   G. Clark, 'Renting the Revolution', *Journal of Economic History* 58 (1998), 206. Clark's own results, are presented in Clark, 'Land Rental Values and the Agrarian Economy: England and Wales, 1500–1914', *European Review of Economic History* 6:3 (2002), 281–308; see also Clark's 'The Charity Commission as a Source in Economic History', *Research in Economic History* 18 (1998).

stagnation when rents were set across a broad range of different market levels, including some assessed on beneficial terms. It would be misleading to assume a hard and fast distinction between, on the one hand, fines and beneficial rents, and on the other, full rack rents. As late as 1741, the Senior Warden at Rochester Bridge explained that their rents were 'very unequal', some being let at 'near their full, some at two-thirds, some at half, and others at one-third or less of their improved value'. Measures were soon put in place to reassess rents through the implementation of a series of 'Orders concerning Leases'.[37] The charity rents and the RBT farm rents represent upper and lower limits during a period of slow adjustment from beneficial to rack rents in the period 1620–1750 when, by late eighteenth-century standards, 'under-renting' was evidently a normal state of affairs. Institutional landlords such as the Rochester Bridge Trust and the charitable trusts comprising Clark's sample exercised a paternalistic generosity towards their tenants before the mid-eighteenth century which was evidently not matched by private landlords who form the bulk of the TBA sample. The TBA series shows something resembling an early burst of growth from the 1690s to the 1730s, as Clark notes, although Turner, Beckett and Afton themselves emphasise the limitations of their index for the years before 1730 when they are reliant on a small handful of estates in Yorkshire and Staffordshire.[38] Local studies have pointed to the 1650s as a critical period when private landlords, especially aristocratic owners, began to convert remaining copyholds to leasehold tenures, abolishing fines and replacing them with rack rents – though the speed of that process should not be exaggerated.[39]

III

Tawney's *Agrarian Problem* marked the beginnings of detailed historical research into the transition from feudalism to capitalism in north-western Europe, and opened up debates which have continued to the present day. It was during the gentry controversy of the early 1940s that Tawney came closest to Dobb and Hill's view of the mid-seventeenth-century crisis in

37 N. Yates and J. Gibson, ed., *Traffic and Politics: The Construction and Management of Rochester Bridge* (Woodbridge, 1994), p. 175. A statute of 1576 made them free of fines, but the estates held at that time were valued on terms favourable to tenants.

38 M. E. Turner, J. V. Beckett and B. Afton, 'Renting the Revolution: A Reply to Clark', *Journal of Economic History* 58 (1998).

39 Clay, 'Landlords and Estate Management', pp. 162–98; I. Ward, 'Rental Policy on the Estates of the English Peerage, 1649–1660', *Agricultural History Review* 40:1 (1992), 23–37; R. W. Hoyle, 'Some Reservations on Dr Ward on the 'Rental Policy of the English Peerage, 1649–1660', *Agricultural History Review* 40:2 (1992), 156–9.

England, although it was his reading of Sir John Harrington (d. 1612) rather than Marx which led him to identify the English gentry as a rising and 'tenacious' *class*, 'agricultural capitalists . . . who were making the pace and to whom the future belonged'.[40] By 1950, he felt that the language of class and the term *bourgeoisie* were 'too blunt an instrument to dissect the . . . complexities of social organisation . . . The truth is that much water has flowed under historical bridges since the expression "a bourgeois revolution" was coined.'[41] It seems clear that Tawney's considered view of the history of capitalism involved a strong emphasis on slow commercialisation during the sixteenth and early seventeenth centuries. A change in tempo, he felt, even a new order of things had developed after the upheavals of the Civil War, from which point the advance of capitalism in agriculture and industry became irresistible in 'the concentration of energy on economic interests'. A 'disorderly multitude of peasants and small masters' was giving way to 'men wielding substantial resources', unsophisticated individualists putting into practice a philosophy which would be expounded two generations later in the *Wealth of Nations*.[42]

The neo-Smithian emphasis of Tawney's history of capitalism is unmistakable, and provides a connecting thread running through twentieth-century debates surrounding the topic. The rise of large-scale tenant farms worked with wage labour obviously plays a large part in the story, but taken by itself obscures the extent of productivity gains which could be achieved by small owner-occupiers before the more famous 'landlord's revolution' of the later eighteenth century. This has been illustrated by Eric Kerridge and Bob Allen, providing a useful corrective to the physiocratic line of argument pursued by Brenner, in what Allen describes as 'the yeoman alternative', and a recent audit by Michael Turner confirms that the disappearance of the yeoman was surprisingly protracted process.[43] Market growth, however, benefited both small owners and larger tenant farmers. The commodification of food supplies and the demise of the moral economy after 1650 widened access to overseas and internal markets, and must be considered as a major step on the road to capitalist agriculture by increasing the separation of consumption from production in agriculture.[44]

The history of rent movements and the separation of farm rents, prof-

---

40 Tawney, 'The Rise of the Gentry' (repr. in Winter, ed., *History and Society*), p. 87.

41 R. H. Tawney, 'A History of Capitalism', *Economic History Review*, second series, 2 (1950) repr. in Winter, ed. *History and Society*, p. 211.

42 LSE Archives, Tawney Papers, 1/4, pp. 3–4.

43 M. E. Turner, 'The Demise of the Yeoman, c.1750–1940', in *Common Agricultural Heritage?*, ed. Broad, pp. 83–103.

44 Chartres, 'Marketing of Agricultural Produce', pp. 406–502; J. Chartres, 'Cities and Towns, Farmers and Economic Change in the Eighteenth Century', *Historical Research* 64 (1991), 138–55.

its and wages have sometimes been considered the hallmark of agrarian capitalism. Full market rents and long leases encouraged the division of landlord's capital from tenant's capital, and helped preserve the latter while encouraging improved farming practice and higher rent levels. With the consolidation of larger private and aristocratic estates in the later seventeenth and early eighteenth centuries, revision of leases proceeded apace, and the upward movement of rents after 1690 certainly appears to have been more pronounced on private estates than was the case for institutional landowners. But in fact rents were not generally determined by competition for farmland for much of the eighteenth century. Beneficial leases persisted and rent was commonly negotiated on an individual basis, as Turner, Beckett and Afton have shown. 'Whatever Adam Smith and the classical economists may have argued', they maintain, 'bargains were struck according to perceived economic conditions and almost in defiance of any clear notions of accountancy.'[45]

English agrarian capitalism came to maturity during the middle decades of the nineteenth century, often viewed as a golden age of prosperity for the farming community. By the end of the century, aristocratic landowners had 'exchanged broad acres for larger, non-agricultural revenues', especially in towns and cities.[46] On the Rochester Bridge estates, it was from the 1830s onwards that rents for London property soared ahead, with the promise of much larger increases to come through the granting of long building leases and/or investment in rebuilding. At the same time, development on the rural–urban fringe areas of Kent increased the flow of non-agricultural sources of income, carrying the wardens into a new era of land ownership as urban rentiers. Although the industrial development of the Medway valley contributed greatly to their increased revenues, commercial, residential, retail and office development form a more significant part of the story. Of all the processes involved in the formation of agrarian capitalism, it is the growing separation and re-integration of town and countryside that best expresses the totality of smaller changes which comprised the slow shift from a peasant society to a commercial-industrial state. This was well understood by Smith and Marx, and by Smith's predecessors including Steuart, Ferguson and Millar, the earliest writers to investigate the origins of 'commercial society' based on first-hand observation of the Scottish path to capitalist agriculture.[47]

45   Turner, Beckett and Afton, *Agricultural Rent*, pp. 2–3; Turner, 'Demise of the Yeoman', p. 84–5.
46   D. Cannadine, *Lords and Landlords: The Aristocracy and the Towns, 1774–1967* (Leicester, 1980), p. 425.
47   J. Merrington, 'Town and Country in the Transition to Capitalism', in Hilton, ed., *Transition from Feudalism to Capitalism* (1976), p. 170; Ormrod, *English Grain Exports*, pp. 9–11; Davidson, 'The Scottish Path to Capitalist Agriculture 1'.

Conclusions

JANE WHITTLE

The key social and economic relationship in agrarian England between the early medieval period and nineteenth century has always been seen as that between lord and tenant, where the lord is typically a member of the gentry or aristocracy, and the tenant a working farmer engaged in agriculture. While Marxists, and socialists such as Tawney, have seen this relationship as inherently one of conflict – the lord seeking to maximise revenue from rent and the tenant seeking retain as much of the profits of their labour as possible; neo-Smithians have characterised it as a contractual relationship, and one in which landlords' demands for higher rent and tighter controls over tenants could encourage greater efficiency in agricultural production and thus economic development. This volume suggests the debate has moved on. In early modern Britain the social and economic relationships regarding rights to land were more complicated than either of these models suggests. From the late fifteenth century onwards, particularly in areas of copyhold of inheritance, gentlemen purchased customary landholdings. In the sixteenth and seventeenth centuries, customary tenants increasingly sublet their land, creating another layer of tenancy below that of the manor. These trends blurred the boundaries between lords and tenants. Tenants of customary land often included gentlemen who were manorial lords elsewhere. Customary tenants often became landlords who had their own tenants paying commercial rack rents.

The consequences of these blurred boundaries are evident in many of the chapters in this volume. The enclosure disputes and the disputes over forms of tenure of the type described by McDonagh, Falvey, Morrin and Holt, were not necessarily between powerful gentry landlords and powerless tenants: tenants often included amongst their ranks and allies men of considerable wealth and legal training. Garrett-Goodyear shows that the legal impetus to allow disputes about customary tenures to be heard in the central legal courts came not from an altruistic government, but from manorial lords who found they could not impose the verdicts of their own manorial courts on increasingly powerful tenants. While some tenants certainly suffered eviction or raised payments as a result of their lords' actions, the overall picture is one of decreasing lordly power within the manorial system of landholding. Holt shows the extent to which lords lost the benefits of rising land values when customary tenures remained

in place. Morrin shows how difficult it was for lords, even with government backing, to dislodge customary tenures. Griffiths demonstrates that
many manorial lords, even those with the most sophisticated legal training
and experience, such as Sir Henry Hobart, had to leave their customary
tenants' rights to land unchanged. Instead, lords sought to exploit other
elements of their manorial rights, leasing their manorial demesnes and
bringing areas of waste into more intensive cultivation. Shannon shows
the profits that lords could gain from this course of action, actions that
benefited some tenants, but not others.

As Tawney perceptively pointed out, the agrarian relationships of
1440–1660 were poised between a world where customary rights dominated, and a new capitalist regime of contractual relationships.[1] By the
sixteenth century both lords and customary tenants were familiar with
contractual relationships of land tenure: lords bought and sold land, and
leased demesne land; tenants bought and sold freeholds, and customary
tenures where copyhold of inheritance dominated; and everywhere manorial tenants sublet land and houses on commercial terms. But customary
rights also remained important. For tenants this meant not only the rights
that made customary tenure secure and beneficial (especially fixed rents,
rights of inheritance, reasonable fines), but also common rights of grazing
and collecting fuel and other resources. Lords also valued their customary
rights to grazing and other resources from the land very highly. Enclosure
disrupted these customary rights, and here again we find that in different
circumstances lords might encourage or oppose enclosure, as McDonagh's
example of Sir Robert Constable shows, and the same was true of tenants.
Manorial custom, rather than being an undifferentiated expression of ordinary people's rights and benefits, became a form of privilege. Attempts
to exclude 'the landless', in fact largely the subtenants of customary tenants, from rights to common land show customary tenants acting in collu-
sion with manorial lords to reinforce custom as privilege for their mutual
benefit. Wood shows how this battle was fought out in an urban context.
Urban commons, which had once been used for the benefit of all the
town's inhabitants in Malmesbury, were redefined as for the exclusive use
of the town's governing class, the urban equivalent of customary tenants.
The bitterness of the dispossessed poor inhabitants of Malmesbury can
be taken as an indication of the feeling of many smallholders across rural
England when they found themselves excluded from valuable resources by
their more wealthy neighbours.

The value of customary tenures to those who held them is demonstrated
by Brooks. Proposals during the Interregnum to transform the muddled
variety of customary tenures into a standard freehold tenure were roundly

1   Tawney, *Agrarian Problem*, p.350.

opposed, despite the fact freehold had traditionally been the more valuable and privileged tenure. The added benefits of customary tenures, along
with their more newly established security, made them a desirable way
of holding land. By the late seventeenth century acquiring a customary
tenure had become a way of investing in land: such holdings were very
often mortgaged or sublet. Goodare's comparison between England and
Scotland is informative. Both countries needed clearly defined land tenures which could operate effectively in an increasingly commercial agrarian economy. England took the route of increased security for customary
tenures, Scotland turned decisively against this strategy in the early seventeenth century, removing rights of inheritance from customary tenures and
handing power to the landlords. It is possible the reason for this contrast
lay in the social composition of customary tenants in the two countries:
if fewer gentlemen and townsmen had acquired customary landholdings
in Scotland, it would have been easier for the government, representing
landlords' interests, to turn against customary tenants as a group.

Viewed from a wider western European perspective, the harmonious
combination of commercial agriculture with the tenacious retention of the
remnants of the manorial system was an English peculiarity. In the Low
Countries, the most advanced agrarian economy of Europe in the sixteenth
and seventeenth centuries, the manorial system had either never existed or
had largely withered away before 1500: contractual leasehold tenures with
market rents were the norm.[2] France presents a great deal more variety,
with leases and sharecropping superseding manorial structures in some
regions, but the manorial system remaining strong elsewhere up until the
revolution.[3] As Ormrod shows, the development of important elements
of capitalist agriculture in England, such as market rents, was a long and
slow process. Even English leases often bore the hall marks of customary tenure. 'Beneficial' leases were common across much of the country in
the seventeenth and eighteenth centuries: these were generally for longer
periods of time, with low fixed rents but a high fine paid on entry, in fact
very similar to the customary tenure of copyhold for lives. Such leases were

2   Peter Hoppenbrouwers and Jan Luiten van Zanden, eds, *Peasants into Farmers? The
Transformation of Rural Economy and Society in the Low Countries in the Light of
the Brenner Debate* (Turnout, 2001); Bas van Bavel, 'Land, Lease and Agriculture: The
Transition of the Rural Economy in the Dutch River Area from the Fourteenth to the
Sixteenth Century', *Past and Present* 172 (2001), 3–43.

3   There are many good regional studies of France, those available in English include
Jonathan Dewald, *Pont-St-Pierre 1398–1789: Lordship, Community and Capitalism in
Early Modern France* (Berkeley and Los Angeles, Calif., 1987); Philip T. Hoffman, *Growth
in a Traditional Society: The French Countryside 1450–1815* (Princeton, NJ, 1996); Hilton
L. Root, *Peasants and King in Burgundy: Agrarian Foundations of French Absolutism*
(Berkeley and Los Angeles, California, 1987); John W. Shaffer, *Family and Farm: Agrarian
Change and Household Organisation in the Loire Valley 1500–1900* (Albany, NY, 1982).

only gradually phased out in the eighteenth and early nineteenth century in favour of genuinely commercial leases at market rates.

The other crucial element of capitalist agriculture was a labour force. Tawney and Marx envisaged a large class of small farmers being evicted from the land and forced to become a rural proletariat of landless wage labourers. As Dyer notes, we now see the agricultural wage-labour force of sixteenth-century England less as a proletariat, and more as a combination of servants and smallholders. Servants lived with their employers providing a reliable year-round workforce in return for payment which was largely paid in kind (as food, drink and lodgings) rather than cash. Most servants were young people aged between fourteen and twenty-four and not yet married. Recent research by Muldrew suggests that even in 1750 servants outnumbered day labourers in agriculture. Smallholders had their own house and access to land: for these people waged work was just one element in a multi-stranded strategy of survival. Again, Muldrew's work suggests that smallholders only gradually and partially lost their access to land and became more dependent on wages between 1550 and 1750.[4] Just as landlords and tenants cannot be seen as two sharply divided opposing groups in this period, nor can a sharp line be drawn between landholding tenants and landless wage labourers: the two groups shaded into one another. Servants, on the other hand, were in a life-cycle phase that had always been characterised by landlessness. There was a great deal of continuity in these patterns. Servants and labourers were already plentiful constituents of English rural society in the late fourteenth century; they were also present in large numbers in the 1520s.[5] The development of a class of landless wage workers was remarkably gradual throughout the whole period up to 1750.

The exploration of agrarian change in early modern Britain continues with much work remaining to be done. The publication of Hoyle's research mapping the types of customary tenure found across England using tenurial disputes in Chancery is keenly anticipated.[6] It will need to be complemented by a similar mapping of types of leasehold tenure, and a more concerted effort to gage the extent of subtenure, if we are to create an adequate understanding of the variety of terms by which tenants held their land across the period from the late fifteenth to mid-eighteenth century. Subtenancy also has a bearing on another crucial issue, the size of farms. Manorial documents tell us about units of tenure, but the varying incidence of subletting means this information does not necessarily relate

4   Craig Muldrew, *Food, Energy and the Creation of Industriousness: Work and Material Culture in Agrarian England, 1550–1780* (Cambridge, 2011), pp. 222 and 246–57.
5   Whittle, *Development of Agrarian Capitalism*, pp. 301–4.
6   R.W. Hoyle, *Landlords and Tenants in Tawney's Century: Tenurial Change in England 1540–1640* (forthcoming).

to the size of working farms. Here Barker's recent work on farm size using parish rates and tithe returns shows one possible route to a clearer picture.[7] We need to know much more about the agricultural workforce and their circumstances. Muldrew's research is an important step in the right direction.[8] Scattered research on women's contribution to agriculture needs to be expanded into something a great deal more systematic.[9] Yet there are reasons to be hopeful. Tawney's concerns live on through the approaches to local history and interdisciplinary landscape studies inspired by W. G. Hoskins and Maurice Beresford,[10] and in the concern for ordinary people and importance of custom inspired by E. P. Thompson.[11] The work of Hindle and Wood has pulled political history down to the level of the village and everyday interactions.[12] This is a fruitful mix, and one that allows a much richer understanding of how ordinary people experienced change in rural England.

The emphasis on the blurred boundaries between different social groups and the slow rate of change over time might lead us to ask, as Tawney suggested, ' "What is the upshot of it all? What are the main landmarks that stand out from the bewildering variety of scenery?" '[13] Tawney attempted to argue simultaneously that change was gradual, but that an 'agrarian revolution' took place in the sixteenth century.[14] Having ditched any notion of a sixteenth-century agrarian revolution, what is left? The new history of rural Britain that is being written is perhaps less concerned with explaining the rise of capitalism or the causes of industrialisation. Instead it focuses more on explaining how people negotiated the changes, economic,

7   Joseph Barker, 'The Emergence of Agrarian Capitalism in Early Modern England: A Reconsideration of Farm Sizes' (unpublished PhD thesis, 2012). See also, Leigh Shaw-Taylor, 'The Rise of Agrarian Capitalism and the Decline of Family Farming in England', *Economic History Review* 65:1 (2012), 26–60.

8   Muldrew, *Food, Energy and the Creation of Industriousness*. See also, G. Clark, 'The Long March of History: Farm Wages, Population and Economic Growth, England 1209–1869', *Economic History Review* 60:1 (2007), 97–135, for the most comprehensive agricultural wage series.

9   Work on the period before 1650 includes A. Hassell Smith, 'Labourers in Late Sixteenth-century England: A Case Study from North Norfolk [Part 1]', *Continuity and Change* 4:1 (1989), 11–52; Jane Whittle, 'Housewives and Servants in Rural England 1440–1650: Evidence of Women's Work from Probate Documents', *TRHS* 15 (2005), 51–74.

10   W. G. Hoskins' influence comes via the establishment of the Centre for English Local History at Leicester University as well as his classic books, *The Making of the English Landscape* (London, 1955) and *The Midland Peasant: The Economic and Social History of a Leicestershire Village* (London, 1965); Beresford, *Lost Villages of England*, 4th edn (Stroud, 1998).

11   Thompson, *Customs in Common*.

12   Hindle, *State and Social Change*; Hindle, *On the Parish?*; Wood, *Politics of Social Conflict*; Wood, *The 1549 Rebellions*.

13   Tawney, *Agrarian Problem*, p.401.

14   Ibid., p.402.

legal and political, that did take place. These changes both offered opportunities and threatened livelihoods: they were not just economic trends, but the lived experience of millions of people. And it is in this sense that we have returned to Tawney's *Agrarian Problem* and found inspiration.

Select Bibliography

Albright Knittl, Margaret, 'The Design for the Initial Drainage of the Great Level of the Fens: An Historical Whodunit in Two Parts', *Agricultural History Review* 55:1 (2007), 23–50

Allen, Robert C., *Enclosure and the Yeoman: The Agricultural Development of the South Midlands 1450–1850* (Oxford, 1992)

Allison, K. J., 'The Sheep-corn Husbandry of Norfolk in the Sixteenth and Seventeenth Centuries', *Agricultural History Review* 5:1 (1957), 12–30

Arrighi, G., *Adam Smith in Beijing: Lineages of the Twenty-First Century* (London, 2007)

Ashton, T. S., 'Richard Henry Tawney', *Proceedings of the British Academy* 48 (1962), 460–82

Aston, T., and C. H. E. Philpin, eds, *The Brenner Debate: Agrarian Class Structure and Economic Development in Pre-industrial Europe* (Cambridge, 1985)

Baker, John, *The Oxford History of the Laws of England, VI: 1483–1558* (Oxford, 2003)

Barnes, D. G., *A History of the English Corn Laws from 1660–1846* (London, 1930)

Bender, B. ed., *Landscape: Politics and Perspectives* (Oxford, 1993)

Bender, B., and M. Winer, eds, *Contested Landscapes: Movement, Exile and Place* (Oxford, 2001)

Beresford, Maurice W., 'The Lost Villages of Yorkshire', *Yorkshire Archaeological Journal* 38 (1954), 344–70

Beresford, Maurice W., *The Lost Villages of England* (London, 1954; 4th edn repr. Stroud, 1998)

Birtles, Sara, 'Common Law, Poor Relief and Enclosure: The Use of Manorial Resources in Fulfilling Parish Obligations 1601–1834', *Past & Present* 165 (1999), 74–106

Blomley, N., 'Making Private Property: Enclosure, Common Right and the Work of Hedges', *Rural History* 18:1 (2007), 1–21

Bowden, P., 'Agricultural Prices, Farm Profits and Rents', in *The Agrarian History of England and Wales, 4: 1500–1640*, ed. Joan Thirsk (Cambridge, 1967)pp. 593–695, 814–70

Bowden, P., 'Agricultural Prices, Wages, Farm Profits and Rents', in *The Agrarian History of England and Wales, 5: 1640–1750*, part 2, ed. Joan Thirsk (Cambridge, 1985), pp. 1–118

Braddick, Michael J., *State Formation in Early Modern England, c.1550–1700* (Cambridge, 2000)

Braddick, Michael J., and John Walter, eds, *Negotiating Power in Early Modern Society: Order, Hierarchy and Subordination in Britain and Ireland* (Cambridge, 2001)

Braudel, F., *Capitalism and Civilisation, 15th to 18th Century, 1: The Structures of Everyday Life* (London, 1981)

Braudel, F., *Capitalism and Civilisation, 15th to 18th Century, 2: The Wheels of Commerce* (London, 1982)

Braudel, F., *Capitalism and Civilisation, 15th to 18th Century, 3: The Perspective of the World* (London, 1984)

Brenner, R., 'Agrarian Class Structure and Economic Development in Pre-industrial Europe', *Past & Present* 70 (1976), 30–75

Brenner, R., *Merchants and Revolution: Commercial Change, Political Conflict, and London's Overseas Traders, 1550–1653* (Cambridge, 1993)

Broad, John, *Transforming English Rural Society: The Verneys and the Claydons, 1600–1820* (Cambridge, 2004)

Broad, John ed., *A Common Agricultural Heritage? Revising French and British Rural Divergence* (Agricultural History Review Supplement series 5, Exeter, 2009)

Brooks, Christopher W., *Law, Politics and Society in Early Modern England* (Cambridge, 2008)

Brooks, Christopher W., *Lawyers, Litigation and English Society since 1450* (London, 1998)

Brumhead, D., and R. Weston, 'Seventeenth-Century Enclosures of the Commons and Wastes of Bowden Middlecale in the Royal Forest of Peak', *Derbyshire Archaeological Journal* 121 (2001), 244–86

Bush, M. L., *The Pilgrimage of Grace: A Study of the Rebel Armies of October 1536* (Manchester, 1996)

Campbell, Bruce, 'England: Land and People', in *A Companion to Britain in the Later Middle Ages*, ed. S. H. Rigby (Oxford, 2003), pp. 3–25

Campbell, M., *The English Yeoman in the Tudor and Early Stuart Age* (Yale, 1942)

Chambers, J. D., 'The Tawney Tradition', *Economic History Review* 24:3 (1971), 355–69

Chartres, J., 'The Marketing of Agricultural Produce', in *The Agrarian History of England and Wales, 5: 1640–1750*, ed. Joan Thirsk (Cambridge, 1985), pp. 406–502

Clark, G., 'Land Rental Values and the Agrarian Economy: England and Wales, 1500–1914', *European Review of Economic History* 6:3 (2002), 281–308

Clark, G., 'The Long March of History: Farm Wages, Population and Economic Growth, England 1209–1869', *Economic History Review* 60:1 (2007), 97–135

Clark, M., 'The Gentry, the Commons and the Politics of Common Right in Enfield, c.1558–c.1603', *Historical Journal* 54:3 (2011), 609–629

Clay, Christopher G. A., 'Landlords and Estate Management in England', in *The Agrarian History of England and Wales, 4: 1500–1640*, ed. Joan Thirsk (Cambridge, 1967), pp. 119–251

Clay, Christopher G. A., 'Lifeleasehold in the Western Counties of England 1650–1750', *Agricultural History Review* 29:1 (1981), 83–96

Clay, Christopher G. A., *Economic Expansion and Social Change: England 1500–1700, 1: People, Land and Towns* (Cambridge, 1984)

Coleman, D. C., *History and the Economic Past: An Account of the Rise and Decline of Economic History in Britain* (Oxford, 1987)

Connerton, P., *How Societies Remember* (Cambridge, 1989)

Cooper, J. P., 'In Search of Agrarian Capitalism', *Past & Present* 80 (1978), 27–9, and reprinted in *The Brenner Debate: Agrarian Class Structure and Economic Development in Preindustrial Europe*, ed. T. H. Aston and C. H. E. Philpin (Cambridge, 1985), pp. 138–191

Cox, J. C., 'The Forest of the High Peak', *Victoria History of the Counties of England: Derbyshire 1*, ed. W. Page (London, 1905–07), pp. 397–413

Davidson, Neil, 'The Scottish Path to Capitalist Agriculture, 1: From the Crisis of Feudalism to the Origins of Agrarian Transformation (1688–1746)', *Journal of Agrarian Change* 4:3 (2004), 227–68

Dennis, Norman, and A. H. Halsey, *English Ethical Socialism: Thomas More to R. H. Tawney* (Oxford, 1988)

Dobb, Maurice, *Studies in the Development of Capitalism* (London, 1946)

Dodgshon, Robert A., *Land and Society in Early Scotland* (Oxford, 1981)

Dodgshon, Robert A., *From Chiefs to Landlords: Social and Economic Change in the Western Highlands and Islands, c.1493–1820* (Edinburgh, 1998)

Dyer, Christopher, *Lords and Peasants in a Changing Society: The Estates of the Bishopric of Worcester 680–1540* (Cambridge, 1980)

Dyer, Christopher, 'Deserted Medieval Villages in the West Midlands', in *Everyday Life in Medieval England*, ed. Christopher Dyer (London, 1994), pp. 27–46

Dyer, Christopher, *Making a Living in the Middle Ages* (New Haven, 2002)

Dyer, Christopher, *An Age of Transition? Economy and Society in England in the Later Middle Ages* (Oxford, 2005)

Dyer, Christopher, 'Conflict in the Landscape: The Enclosure Movement in England, 1220–1349', *Landscape History* 29 (2007), 21–33

Dyer, Christopher, *A Country Merchant: Trading and Farming at the End of the Middle Ages, 1495–1520* (Oxford, 2012)

Falvey, H., 'Crown Policy and Local Economic Context in the Berkhamsted Common Enclosure Dispute, 1618–42', *Rural History* 12:2 (2001), 123–58

Fentress, J., and C. Wickham, *Social Memory* (Oxford, 1992)

Fox, Adam, *Oral and Literate Culture in England, 1500–1700* (Oxford, 2000)

Fox, H. S. A., 'The Chronology of Enclosure and Economic Development in Medieval Devon', *Economic History Review* 28:2 (1975), 181–202

French, H. R., and J. Barry, eds, *Identity and Agency in England, 1500–1800* (Basingstoke, 2004)

French, H. R., and R. W. Hoyle, *The Character of English Rural Society: Earls Colne, 1550–1750* (Manchester, 2007)

Gibson, A. J. S., and T. C. Smout, *Prices, Food and Wages in Scotland, 1550–1780* (Cambridge, 1995)

Goldie, M., 'The Unacknowledged Republic: Office-holding in Early Modern England', in *The Politics of the Excluded, c.1500–1850*, ed. T. Harris (Basingstoke, 2001)

Goodare, Julian, *State and Society in Early Modern Scotland* (Oxford, 1999)

Goodare, Julian, *The Government of Scotland, 1560–1625* (Oxford, 2004)

Griffiths, Elizabeth, 'Sir Henry Hobart: A New Hero of Norfolk

Agriculture?', *Agricultural History Review* 46:1 (1998), 15–34

Griffiths, Elizabeth, and Mark Overton, *Farming to Halves: The Hidden History of Sharefarming in England from Medieval to Modern Times* (2009)

Gritt, Andrew John, 'The Operation of Lifeleasehold in South-West Lancashire 1649–97', *Agricultural History Review* 53:1 (2005), 1–23

Gritt, Andrew John, 'Making Good Land from Bad: The Drainage of West Lancashire c.1650–1850', *Rural History* 19:1 (2008), 1–27

Hannay, R. K., 'On the Church Lands at the Reformation', *Scottish Historical Review* 16:61 (1918), 52–72

Harris, Jose, *William Beveridge: A Biography* (Oxford, 1977)

Harrison, C. J., 'Elizabethan Village Surveys: A Comment', *Agricultural History Review* 27:2 (1979), 82–9

Harrison, C. J., 'Manor Courts and the Governance of Tudor England', in *Communities & Courts in Britain, 1150–1900*, ed. Christopher Brooks and Michael Lobban (London, 1997), pp. 43–60

Hatcher, John, *Plague, Population and the English Economy: 1348–1530* (London, 1977)

Heal, Felicity, and Clive Holmes, *The Gentry in England and Wales, 1500–1700* (Basingstoke, 1994; repr. Basingstoke and New York, 2002)

Hilton, R. H., ed., *The Transition from Feudalism to Capitalism* (London, 1976)

Hindle, Steve, 'Persuasion and Protest in the Caddington Common Enclosure Dispute 1635–1639', *Past & Present* 158:1 (1998), pp. 37–78

Hindle, Steve, *The State and Social Change in Early Modern England* (Basingstoke, 2000)

Hindle, Steve, *On the Parish? The Micro-Politics of Poor Relief in Rural England, c.1550–1750* (Oxford, 2004)

Hindle, Steve, 'Imagining Insurrection in Seventeenth-Century England: Representations of the Midland Rising of 1607', *History Workshop Journal* 66:1 (2008), 21–61

Hipkin, S., ' "Sitting on His Penny Rent': Conflict and Right of Common in Faversham Blean, 1595–1610', *Rural History* 11:1 (2000), 1–35

Holt, Jennifer S., 'Hornby Town and the Textiles of Melling Parish in the Early-Modern Period', *Transactions of the Lancashire and Cheshire Antiquarian Society* 101 (2005), 39–70

Hoskins, W. G., *The Making of the English Landscape* (London, 1955)

Houston, Rab, 'Custom in Context: Medieval and Early Modern Scotland and England', *Past & Present*, 211 (May 2011), 35–76

Hoyle, R.W., 'Lords, Tenants and Tenant Right in the 16th Century: Four Studies', *Northern History* 20 (1984), 38–63

Hoyle, R.W., 'Tenure and the Land Market in Early Modern England: Or a Late Contribution to the Brenner Debate', *Economic History Review* 43:1 (1990), 1–20

Hoyle, R.W. ed., *The Estates of the English Crown, 1558–1640* (Cambridge, 1992)

Hoyle, R.W., *The Pilgrimage of Grace and the Politics of the 1530s* (Oxford, 2001)

Hoyle, R.W., 'The Management of the Estates of the Earls of Derby 1575–1640: Some New Sources', *Northern History* 39:1 (2002), 25–36

Hoyle, R.W. ed., *Custom, Improvement and the Landscape in Early Modern Britain* (Farnham, 2011)

Kerridge, Eric, *The Agricultural Revolution* (London, 1967)

Kerridge, Eric, *Agrarian Problems in the Sixteenth Century and After* (London, 1969)

Kesselring, K., *The Northern Rebellion of 1569: Faith, Politics and Protest in Elizabethan England* (Basingstoke, 2007)

Ketton-Cremer, R. W., *Felbrigg: The Story of a House* (Woodbridge, 1962)

Kiralfy, A., 'Custom in Medieval English Law', *Journal of Legal History* 9:1 (1988), 26–39

Lamont, William, 'R. H. Tawney: "Who Did Not Write a Single Work Which Can be Trusted"?' in *Historical Controversies and Historians*, ed. William Lamont (London, 1998), pp. 107–17

Langton, J., and G. Jones, eds, *Forests and Chases of England and Wales c.1500–c.1850* (Oxford, 2005)

Leadam, I. S., 'The Inquisition of 1517: Inclosures and Evictions' (in two parts), *Transactions of the Royal Historical Society* second series 6 (1892), 167–314, and 7 (1893), 127–292

Lennard, Reginald, 'Agrarian History: Some Vistas and Pitfalls', *Agricultural History Review* 12.2 (1964), 83–98

Lindley, Keith, *Fenland Riots and the English Revolution* (London, 1982)

Luce, R. H., *The History of the Abbey and Town of Malmesbury* (Minety, 1979)

Manning, R. B., *Village Revolts: Social Protest and Popular Disturbances in England, 1509–1640* (Oxford, 1988)

Marcombe, D. ed., *The Last Principality: Politics, Religion and Society in the Bishopric of Durham, 1494–1660* (Nottingham, 1987)

Martin, J. E., 'Sheep and Enclosure in Sixteenth-Century Northampton-shire', *Agricultural History Review* 36:1 (1988), 39–54

McDonagh, B., 'Subverting the Ground: Private Property and Public Protest in the Sixteenth-Century Yorkshire Wolds', *Agricultural History Review* 57:2 (2009), 191–206

Miller, Edward ed., *The Agrarian History of England and Wales, 3: 1348–1500* (Cambridge, 1991)

Muldrew, C., *The Economy of Obligation: The Culture of Credit and Social Relations in Early Modern England* (Basingstoke, 1998)

Muldrew, C., *Food, Energy and the Creation of Industriousness: Work and Material Culture in Agrarian England, 1550–1780* (Cambridge, 2011)

Oestmann, C., *Lordship and Community: The Lestrange Family and the Village of Hunstanton, Norfolk, in the First Half of the Sixteenth Century* (Woodbridge, 1994)

Offer, A., 'Farm Tenure and Land Values in England, c.1750–1950', *Economic History Review* 44:1 (1991), 1–20

Ormrod, David, 'R. H. Tawney and the Origins of Capitalism', *History Workshop* 18 (1984), 138–159

Ormrod, David, *English Grain Exports and the Structure of Agrarian Capitalism, 1700–1760* (Hull, 1985)

Outhwaite, R. B., *Dearth, Public Policy and Social Disturbance in England, 1550–1800* (London, 1991)

Overton, Mark, *Agricultural Revolution in England: The Transformation of the Agrarian Economy, 1500–1850* (Cambridge, 1996)

Poos, L. R., and Lloyd Bonfield, *Select Cases in Manorial Courts 1250–1550: Property and Family Law* (Selden Society 114 for 1997, London, 1998)

Poos, L. R., *A Rural Society after the Black Death: Essex 1350–1525* (Cambridge, 1991)

Razi, Z., and R M. Smith, eds, *Medieval Society and the Manor Court* (Oxford, 1996)

Reed, M., 'Enclosure in North Buckinghamshire, 1500–1750', *Agricultural History Review* 32:2 (1984), 133–44

Samuel, Raphael, 'British Marxist Historians, 1880–1980: Part One', *New Left Review* 120 (1980), 21–96

Sandall, S., 'Custom, Memory and the Operations of Power in Seventeenth-Century Forest of Dean', in *Locating Agency: Space, Power and Popular Politics*, ed. F. Williamson (Newcastle, 2010)

Sanderson, Margaret H. B., *Scottish Rural Society in the Sixteenth Century* (Edinburgh, 1982)

Sanderson, Margaret H. B., *A Kindly Place? Living in Sixteenth-Century Scotland* (East Linton, 2002)

Shannon, William D., 'On the Left Hand above the Staire: Accessing, Understanding and Using the Archives of the Early-Modern Court of Duchy Chamber', *Archives* 35:123 (2010), 19–36

Shannon, William D., 'Approvement and Improvement in the Lowland Wastes of Early Modern Lancashire', in *Custom, Improvement and the Landscape in Early Modern Britain*, ed. R. W. Hoyle (Farnham, 2011), pp. 175–202

Sharp, C., ed., *Memorials of the Rebellion of the Earls of Northumberland and Westmoreland* (London, 1840; repr. Durham, 1975)

Shaw-Taylor, Leigh, 'Labourers, Cows, Common Rights and Parliamentary Enclosure: The Evidence of Contemporary Comment, c.1760–1810', *Past & Present* 171 (2001), 95–126

Shepard, A., and J. Spicksley, 'Worth, Age and Social Status in Early Modern England', *Economic History Review* 64:2 (2011), 493–530

Stone, Lawrence, 'Introduction to the Torchbook edition', in Tawney, *The Agrarian Problem in the Sixteenth Century* (London, 1967), pp.vii–xviii

Stride, K. B., 'Engrossing in Sheep-Corn-Chalk Areas: Evidence in Norfolk 1501–1633', *Norfolk Archaeology* 40:3 (1989), 308–18

Tawney, R. H., *The Agrarian Problem in the Sixteenth Century* (London, 1912; repr. New York, 1967)

Tawney, R. H., 'The Rise of the Gentry 1558–1640', *Economic History Review* 11:1 (1941), 1–38 and repr. in Winter, ed. *History and Society*

Terrill, Ross, *R. H. Tawney and His Times: Socialism as Fellowship* (Cambridge Mass., 1973)

Thirsk, Joan, ed., *The Agrarian History of England and Wales, 4: 1500–1640* (Cambridge, 1967)

Thirsk, Joan, 'Enclosing and Engrossing', in *The Agrarian History of England and Wales, 4: 1500–1640*, ed. Joan Thirsk (Cambridge, 1967), pp. 200–55

Thirsk, Joan, ed., *The Agrarian History of England and Wales, 5: 1640–1750* (Cambridge, 1985)

Thirsk, Joan, *England's Agricultural Regions and Agrarian History, 1500–1750* (Basingstoke, 1987)

Thomas, D., 'Leases of Crown Lands in the Reign of Elizabeth I', in *Estates of the English Crown, 1558–1640*, ed. R.W. Hoyle (Cambridge, 1992), pp. 169–90

Thomas, K., *Religion and the Decline of Magic* (London, 1971)

Thomas, K., *Man and the Natural World: Changing Attitudes in England, 1500–1800* (London, 1983)

Thompson, E. P., *Customs in Common* (London, 1991).

Thornton, T., *Prophecy, Politics and the People in Early Modern England* (Woodbridge, 2006)

Tilley, C., *A Phenomenology of Landscape: Places, Paths and Monuments* (Oxford, 1994)

Tupling, G. H., *The Economic History of Rossendale* (Manchester, 1927)

Turner, M. E., J. Beckett and B. Afton, *Agricultural Rent in England, 1690–1914* (Cambridge, 1997)

Turner, M. E., 'The Demise of the Yeoman, c.1750–1940', in *Common Agricultural Heritage? Revising French and British Rural Divergence*, ed. J. Broad (Exeter, 2009), pp. 83–103

Veall, D., *The Popular Movement for Law Reform 1640–1660* (Oxford, 1970)

Wallerstein, I., *The Modern World System, 1: Capitalist Agriculture and the Origins of the European World-Economy in the Sixteenth Century* (New York, 1974)

Wallerstein, I., *The Modern World System, 2: Mercantilism and the Consolidation of the European World-Economy, 1600–1750* (New York, 1980)

Walter, John, 'A "Rising of the People"? The Oxfordshire Rising of 1596', *Past & Present* 107 (1985), 90–143

Walter, John, *Understanding Popular Violence in the English Revolution: The Colchester Plunderers* (Cambridge, 1999)

Ward, I., 'Rental Policy on the Estates of the English Peerage, 1649–1660', *Agricultural History Review* 40:1 (1992), 23–37

Watts, S. J., 'Tenant Right in Early Seventeenth-Century Northumberland', *Northern History* 6 (1971), 64–87

Whittle, Jane, 'Individualism and the Family-land Bond: A Reassessment of Land Transfer Patterns among the English Peasantry, *c.*1270–1580', *Past & Present* 160 (1998), 25–63

Whittle, Jane, *The Development of Agrarian Capitalism: Land and Labour in Norfolk, 1440–1580* (Oxford, 2000)

Whittle, Jane, 'Leasehold Tenure in England c.1300–c.1600: Its Form and Incidence', in *The Development of Leasehold in North-Western Europe, c.1200–1600*, ed. B. J. P. van Bavel and P. R. Schofield (Turnhout, 2008), pp. 139–54

Whittle, Jane, 'Lords and Tenants in Kett's Rebellion, 1549', *Past & Present* 207 (2010), 3–52

Whyte, Ian D., *Agriculture and Society in Seventeenth-Century Scotland* (Edinburgh, 1979)

Whyte, Ian D., 'Poverty or Prosperity? Rural Society in Lowland Scotland in the Late Sixteenth and Early Seventeenth Centuries', *Scottish Economic and Social History* 18:1 (1998), 19–32

Whyte, N., *Inhabiting the Landscape: Place, Custom and Memory, 1500–1800* (Oxford, 2009)

Winter, J. M. ed., *History and Society: Essays by R.H. Tawney* (London, 1978)

Wood, Andy, 'The Place of Custom in Plebeian Political Culture: England, 1550–1800', *Social History* 22:1 (1997), 46–60

Wood, Andy, 'Custom and the Social Organisation of Writing in Early Modern England', *TRHS*, sixth series, 9 (1999), 257–69

Wood, Andy, *Politics of Social Conflict: The Peak Country 1520–1770* (Cambridge, 1999)

Wood, Andy, *Riot, Rebellion and Popular Politics in Early Modern England* (Basingstoke, 2002)

Wood, Andy, 'Subordination, Solidarity and the Limits of Popular Agency in a Yorkshire Valley c.1596–1615', *Past & Present* 193:1 (2006), 41–72

Wood, Andy, *The 1549 Rebellions and the Making of Early Modern England* (Cambridge, 2007)

Woodward, D., 'Early Modern Servants in Husbandry Revisited', *Agricultural History Review* 48:2 (2000), 141–150

Wright, Anthony, *R. H. Tawney* (Manchester, 1987)

Wrightson, Keith, 'The Politics of the Parish in Early Modern England', in *The Experience of Authority in Early Modern England*, ed. Paul

Griffiths, Adam Fox and Steve Hindle (Basingstoke, 1995), pp. 10–46

Wrightson, Keith, *Earthly Necessities: Economic Lives in Early Modern Britain* (New Haven, Conn., 2000)

Wrigley, E. A., and R. S. Schofield, *The Population History of England 1541–1871: A Reconstruction* (Cambridge, 1981)

Yates, M., *Town and Countryside in Western Berkshire, c.1327–c.1600: Social and Economic Change* (Woodbridge, 2007)

Yelling, J. A., *Common Field and Enclosure in England, 1450–1850* (London, 1977)

Index

Printed and bound by CPI Group (UK) Ltd, Croydon, CR0 4YY

05/11/2024

14586506-0001